I0834495

Hardeman County, Tennessee

Marriages

1823 – 1861

Byron and Barbara Sistler

JANAWAY PUBLISHING, INC.
2013

Hardeman County, Tennessee, Marriages 1823-1861

Originally printed, Nashville, 1986

Reprinted
by

Janaway Publishing, Inc.
732 Kelsey Ct.
Santa Maria, California 93454
(805) 925-1038
www.JanawayPublishing.com

2007, 2013

ISBN: 978-1-59641-050-3

Made in the United States of America

HARDEMAN COUNTY, TN MARRIAGES

1823-1861

Where two dates appear on an entry, the first one is the date license was issued, the second (in parentheses) the date marriage was solemnized. If only one date, it usually means that the date of execution was the same as the date of license issuance.

Sometimes the execution of the marriage was not reported to the courthouse, and occasionally the clerk failed to note in the marriage book that the license was returned. We would usually make a notation in the entry to indicate the non-execution of a marriage if the book so revealed.

When we prepare a county marriage record book we purchase a copy of the microfilm of the original book from the Tennessee State Library, thus having a primary source as our guide. Unfortunately, in the case of Hardeman Co. marriages, this microfilm was a copy of marriage books prepared in the 1960s by Mr. Quinnie Armour, the only exception being the marriages for 1860 and 1861.

If the bride and groom were black, a B is placed at the end of the entry.

It should be remembered that essentially this and other marriage books we have prepared are indexes, not including all the information to be found in the original marriage book. Such data as names of bondsmen, ministers, justices of the peace, churches etc. is omitted. Often such information is helpful to the researcher. Consequently the serious researcher, to obtain this additional information as well as to check on the accuracy of the transcriber, should examine the original marriage record if at all possible, or at least another marriage record book which may contain this data.

Byron Sistler
Barbara Sistler

Nashville, TN
December, 1986

Ables, Luther to Amanda P. German 4-10-1858 (4-13-1858)
Abraham, Saml. N. to Ann E. Darnall 2-27-1860 (3-15-1860)
Adams, Charles to Dephy Smith 1-1-1838 (1-6?-1838)
Adams, Ephraim B. to Mary Ann Bray 10-30-1841 (10-31?-1841)
Adams, H. G. to Sarah C. Rainy 3-1-1858
Adams, Jno. to Elizabeth Wells 1-4-1838 (1-5-1838)
Adams, John D. to Martha Hodges 3-4-1847
Adams, John to Mary Nunnally 12-24-1833
Adams, Logan B. to Martha Bright 10-14-1851
Adams, Lonis? to Elizabeth V. Carroll 4-13-1833 (4-16-1833)
Adams, Martin G. to Lucy Ann Gambriel 8-1-1840
Adams, Washington to Mary Walden 2-18-1832
Adams, Win to Matilda Cornelius 7-2-1827 (7-4-1827)
Adams, Wm. C. to Eliza W. Newland 5-4-1846 (5-5-1846)
Adkins, Thomas to Ellen Rose 5-13-1846 (5-14-1846)
Adkins, William H. to Frances A. Stuart 2-12-1842 (2-17-1842)
Akin, James E. to Mary F. Portice 12-25-1847 (12-30-1847)
Alestock, James S. to Elizabeth Thurman 7-26-1837 *
Alexander, Elias to Clarentine M. Boyle 2-9-1847 (2-11-1847)
Alexander, Ezekiel Z. to Mary E. Robinson 7-20-1846 (7-24-1846)
Alexander, James H. to Martha E. Pryor 9-14-1837
Alexander, Robert P. to Emily E. Anderson 7-31-1837
Alexander, William R. to Elizabeth German 11-3-1829 (11-4-1829)
Alexander, William R. to Susan Needham 4-30-1830
Alford, James to Mariah Sellers? 3-31-1847 (4-1-1847)
Allbright, Jacob to Sarah L. Nelson 10-1-1827
Allen, Charles J. to Mary E. Townsend 6-23-1835
Allen, Jas. W. to Eliza J. James 12-28-1857
Allen, John G. to Angelina Hughes 8-9-1837 (8-24-1837)
Allen, John to Susanah R. Johnson 8-23-1852 (8-24-1852)
Allen, William A. to Jane Montgomery 9-1-1826) (9-7-1826)
Allison, David to Margaret Cox 5-16-1828 (5-22-1828)
Allison, Elihu C. to Margaret Neely 9-11-1829 (9-17-1829)
Allison, James to Delilah Howard 8?-31-1829 (8-6-1829)
Alloway, A. to C. Garrett? 9-7-1846
Alsup, Benjamin to Dorothy Crain 1-20-1830
Alsup, Benjamin to Nancy Thomas 12-25-1833
Alsup, James to Polly Slaughter 10-24-1829
Ammon, Hiram to Susan? Terry 11-1-1832
Ammons(Powell?), Wm. H. to Alice Powell 7-28-1847 (7-29-1847)
Ammons, Doctor to Sarah Crawford 12-13-1854 (12-14-1854)
Ammons, Jesse T. to Mary E. Rogers 10-28-1848 (10-29-1848)
Ammons, Josiah to Clarissa A. Toller 3-8-1842 (3-16-1842)
Ammons, William H. to Mary H. Boyte 1-6-1844 (1-11-1844)
Ammons, Wm. H. to Elizabeth Ann Ammons 2-21-1837 (2-26-1837)
Anderson, Chamberlin H. to E. W. Perry 2-7-1845 (2-9-1845)
Anderson, Garland to Julia Vernon 10-17-1854
Anderson, H. M. to Elizabeth V. Hundley 12-16-1858 (12-18-1858)
Anderson, Jno. C. to Lucy J. Richardson 10-3-1859
Anderson, M. D. L. to Louisa Cross 7-25-1856 (8-5-1856)
Anderson, Redman to Elizabeth Vincent 7-30-1832 (8-3-1832)
Anderson, Richard to Nancy Fleet 3-20-1856
Anderson, Thos. F. to Jane H. Gates 12-5-1834 (12-9-1834)
Anderson, W. P. to Frances M. Moon(Moore) 12-26-1849
Anderson, William to Mary McMillan 1-6-1837 (1-12-1837)
Anderson, Wm. R. to Permelia Reed 9-21-1839
Andlerson, Hiram to Harnett N. Isaacs 3-14-1842
Andrews, Eli M. to Chrisriana Clark 6-28-1843
Andrews, Ott to Elizabeth H. Cain 11-25-1850
Andrews, Robt. E. to Sarah Campbell 6-13-1846 (6-14-1846)
Antwine, James to Susan Brown 3-17-1849
Arbuckle, D. C. to Marion Lake 12-18-1852 (1-4-1853)
Arms, William to Martha Huddleston 11-14-1839
Armstead, Geo. E. to Mary C. Caldwell 10-12-1860 (10-17-1860)
Armstrong, J. C. to Eliza Jane Anderson 12-20-1847
Armstrong, Jehu H. to Jane Pankey 1-13-1844 (1-17-1844)
Armstrong, John C. to Jane Nunnelly 10-18-1837 (?-19-?)
Arnett, J. M. to Sarah Smart 12-18-1858 (12-22-1858)
Arnold, Asa to Racheal Hill 9-22-1828
Arnold, James W. to Margaret Benson 9-21-1850 (9-25-1850)
Ary, Gabriel to Rebecca Brown 10-20-1842 (10-21-1842)
Asburry, L. L. to Bettie T. Gray 11-4-1858
Ash, John L. to Ebby Jackson 8-4-1835
Aston, James to Sarah R. Hardin 2-14-1837
Atkinson, Ira to Catharine(Elisabeth) White 7-11-1859
Atkinson, Nathaniel to Ann E. Hunt 10-27-1837 (10-29-1837)
Atwood, William W. to Mary C. Neely 6-9-1829 (6-10-1829)
Augustus, S. W. to Mollie Bradley 3-3-1860 (3-5-1860)
Avant, Peter A. to Margaret A. Traylor 2-19-1855 (2-21-1855)
Avant, Saml. T. to Ella M. Alexander 1-13-1860
Avent, Drewry to Susan Gates 3-29-1845 (4-3-1845)
Avent, Wash D. to Nanney McKinnie 11-17-1855 (11-19-1855)
Ayers, T. J. to Lucy Jane Lowery 9-28-1859 (10-2-1859)
Ayers, W. F. to Ann Huddleston 7-27-1848
Ayres, Allen to Mary Rosson 8-21-1830 (8-22-1830)
Ayres, Eli to Caroline Wilson 10-13-1829 (10-15-1829)
Babb, David W. to Rachael Murphy 1-27-1852 (1-29-1852)
Babb, Mathew G. to Jane Catharine Lambert 2-5-1852 (2-8-1852)
Babb, Stevin Oliver to Malinda E. Mayfield 5-3-1858 (5-4-1858)
Babb, Wm. F. to Mary M. Cooper 3-26-1860 (4-3-1860)
Bagby, James P. to J. F. Owen 12-8-1855 (12-12-1855)
Bagg, Mathew G. to Juliann Paterson 10-7-1854 (10-9-1854)
Bagley, James to Mary A. High 4-12-1836 (4-14-1836)
Bailey, Alpha to Elizabeth A. Sain 1-9-1855 (1-11-1855)
Bailey, Burton to Mahina E. Carter 6-1-1843
Bailey, Elijah to Hannah Norris 1-12-1837
Bailey, James T. to Elizabeth Forbess 8-5-1856 (8-6-1856)
Bailey, Joseph E. to Martha Huckaby 1-6-1844 (1-8-1844)
Bailey, Silvester to Julia C. Tyler 3-28-1833
Bailey, Tho. J. to Eliza Anderson 3-18-1835 (3-24-1835)
Bailey, W. L. to Mary Wilkinson 1-4-1832 (1-5-1831?)
Baily, John C. to Rosa Ann Binkly 4-11-1853 (4-12-1853)
Bain, John to Matilda Bass 8-4-1837
Baker, Abijah to Arlamesa Holiday 5-18-1830
Baker, Abraham to Cholley Crawford 11-16-1858 (11-18-1858)
Baker, Isaac to Mary F. King 8-1-1853 (8-2-1853)
Baker, John A. to Martha A. Hudson 8-20-1857 (8-26-1857)
Baker, John A. to Martha Jane Shinn 5-31-1848 (6-8-1848)
Baker, John to Rebecca Burleson 12-15-1831
Baker, John to Sarah C. Henson 3-1-1850 (3-7-1850)
Baker, Jonas to Sary Hodge 10-30-1828
Baker, Joseph to Nancy Green 7-25-1837
Baker, Lorenso D. to Sarah Burleson 7-10-1834 (7-15-1834)
Baker, William to Cynthia Reagan 5-8-1828 (5-11-1828)
Baldwin, G. W. to Emily P. Washington 4-30-1849 (5-2-1849)
Bangues, B. A. to Lydia Ann Minter 3-8-1844 (3-12-1844)
Bansfield(Bunsfield), N. T. to Rhoda M. Rhodes 12-7-1858 (12-9-1858)
Barber, Joseph to Mary Ann Luttrell 7-28-1847 (7-29-1847)
Barham, Edwin J. to Susan E. Cooper 11-8-1849
Barham, James A. to Mary Murdaugh 11-2-1853 (11-3-1853)
Barham, Richard A. to Terissa S.? Cooper 3-28-1848 (3-30-1848)
Barnes, John B. to Eliza V. Jones 1-22-1848 (1-23-1848)
Barnes, T. A. to Mary Ann McKerly 3-23-1833
Barnett(Bennett), John C. to Mary E. Morrow 2-21-1832 (2-23-1832)
Barnett, Hyram to Sarah Webb 2-10-1832 (2-14-1832)
Barnett, James J. to Elizabeth Willie 3-22-1834 (3-27-1834)
Barnett, James S. to Narcissa Box 10-22-1855 (10-24-1855)
Barnett, John M. to Lavanda Ferguson 3-20-1860
Barnett, John W. to Mary Jacobs 6-7-1834 (6-12-1834)
Barnett, Robert W. to Mary M. Alexander 12-4-1827 (12-6-1827)
Barret, T. J. to Rachael Jackson 1-2-1860 (1-5-1860)
Barrett, A. G. to Sarah G. Seaton 4-13-1832 (4-16-1832)
Barrett, Cornelius to Matilda Baker 10-13-1830 (10-14-1830)
Barrett, J. M. C. to M. A. Jackson 12-16-1857 (12-17-1857)
Barter?, Neel to Crotia Ann Robson 6-4-1829
Bartlett, John to Ann M. Morrison 8-19-1833 (8-20-1833)
Barton, Roger to Eudora Barry 5-2-1832
Bass, Edward to Elmina Jacobs 7-15-1828 (not executed)
Bass, John to Sarah Sullenger 4-15-1826 (4-20-1826)
Bass, Reuben to Mary Matthews 12-18-1837
Bass, Thomas A. to S. J. Dunn 4-12-1861
Bass, Wm. H. to Lucy Henson 9-20-1859
Bates, David C. to Martha B. Carruthers 10-9-1854 (10-10-1854)
Bates, James to Harriet New 3-7-1836
Bates, James to Mary W. North 5-8-1848 (5-9-1848)
Baty, William to Rebecca Aulton 4-8-1843 (4-9-1843)
Bayliss, Thomas H. to Mary Mask 4-8-1848 (4-13-1848)
Bazel, Bird to Mary Spurling 6-22-1827 (6-24-1827)
Beachum, C. H. to Martha Ann Burnett 7-6-1854

Beachum, William to Jane Burleson 1-14-1833 (1-15-1833)
Beany(Beny), Berry to Susannah Garner 10-23-1841 (10-24-1841)
Beard, B. B. to Elizabeth D. McCommun? 12-16-1847 (12-23-1847)
Beard, Thomas to Sally Warren 7-10-1830
Beard, William W. to Maria Jane Lowrance 11-3-1855 (11-4-1855)
Beard, Wm. E. to Ann C. McAlexander 4-20-1846 (4-26-1846)
Beasley, Geo. W. to Jane Pulliam 9-29-1859
Beaton, William S. to Mahala Cheshier 1-1-1850
Beaty, Cicero to Lucretia Turner 2-25-1861
Beauchamp, Louis to Mary Ann Holliday 12-18-1827
Beavers, W. J. to Sophia F. Beabers(Biebers) 11-9-1858
Beck, George to Easter Kelley 7-27-1833
Beck, George to Elizabeth Barker 8-19-1834
Beck, James to Lucy Lennard 9-27-1836
Belieu, Wm. C. to Sarah A. J. Neely? 4-15-1846 (4-16-1846)
Beliles, Ira to Lucinda Smith 6-6-1835
Bell, Benjamin to Elizabeth Sneed 12-29-1860 (12-31-1860)
Bell, Benjamin to Olivia Ervin 4-24-1857
Bell, Benjamin to Polly Fox 12-5-1834
Bell, David to Elisza Ornsby 8-21-1826 (8-23-1826)
Bell, Davis N. to Melvina Fariss 11-21-1832
Bell, James G. to Adelia Neely 4-26-1831
Bell, John to Racheal Box 5-17-1832 (5-24?-1832)
Bell, Mayfield to Jane Morris 11-28-1855 (12-3-1855)
Bell, Van S. to Elinder Rook 7-2-1833 (7-10-1833)
Bell, W. S. to Martha J. Smith 2-22-1859
Belote, Benj. R. to Mary J. Wooden 12-28-1856
Belote, George W. to Rachel S. Glass 6-2-1838
Belotte, Clement to Rebecca Standback 7-23-1855 (8-16-1855)
Belotte, John S. to Amanda Moore 2-11-1853
Belotte, William N. to Rebecca J. Williams 10-31-1854 (11-2-1854)
Bennett, John to Elizabeth Wilson 9-13-1848
Bennett, Josiah to Marinda M. Brown 9-2-1850 (9-17-1850)
Bennett, William A. to Susan O. Land 11-12-1861
Benson, Cullen to Margaret Parmer 2-7-1839
Benson, Cullin to Edny Pate 7-1-1835
Benson, James R. to Elizabeth Pate 11-30-1836
Benson, James to Nancy J. Newman 10-2-1858 (10-7-1858)
Benson, Robt. W. to Frances D. Moore 5-4-1859 (5-5-1859)
Benson, Uzzell to Cely Johnson 6-16?-1833
Benson, William to Sarah E. Lawhorn 10-19-1858 (10-26-1858)
Benton, James to Nancy Fields 7-11-1837
Berry, Daniel D. to D. M. Guin? 4-12-1831
Bevils, Henry R. to Elizabeth G. Taylor 12-22-1832
Bibb, Benjamin F. to Mary Wilson 2-21-1851
Bickers, H. E. to Jane R. Mason 7-25-1853
Bickers, Jefferson R. to Elizabeth Pace 12-22-1853
Bickers, John W. to D. Jane Mallay 8-7-1851
Biggs, Reuben W. to Miss Martha M. Hullum 12-24-1845
Billingsly, David to Elizabeth Leeton 12-31-1856
Billingsly, Thomas J. to Amanda A. McKaugn 2-6-1849 (2-7-1849)
Bills, A. S. to Nancy Dodson 12-22-1853 (12-25-1853)
Bills, Leonidas to Mary Miller 5-18-1857
Bills, Wilson T. to Lucy C. Wood 12-2-1857
Binkly, John G. to Levanda Carley 3-2-1850 (3-3-1850)
Bird, John to Nancy Williams 8-16-1859
Birdin, Spencer to Polly Conner 8-23-1830
Birdsong, H. B. to M. J. Newland 12-27-1845 (12-31-1845)
Birdsong, Patrick H. to Martha Ann Moss 12-20-1852 (12-21-1852)
Birdsong, William L. to Ann Mariah Jones 12-17-1849 (12-20-1849)
Birkhead, D. S. to E. A. Sparks 8-17-1861 (8-19-1861)
Bishop, Alvin to Mary Jane Cox 10-15-1841 (10-21-1841)
Bishop, Asa to Elizabeth Stephens 5-23-1850
Bishop, David to Louisa Grantham 10-1-1856 (10-2-1856)
Bishop, Hardeman to Elizabeth Prewitt 11-20-1855 (11-22-1855)
Bishop, Harmon to Mary Williams 10-9-1834
Bizzel, Raiford to Mary Bennett 1-23-1835 (1-29-1835)
Bizzell, Henry to Nancy C. Tilmon 4-20-1857
Bizzle, Martin to Mary Margaret McKee 1-26-1850 (1-27-1850)
Bizzle, Wm. to Nancy A. Daniel 12-22-1856 (12-23-1856)
Black, C. A. to Emma J. M. E. Lewis 7-2-1858
Black, Cyrus to Emily H. S. Bailey 11-20-1843
Black, Hamilton to Ann Eliza Russell 3-29-1854 (3-30-1854)
Black, James R. to Mary Gibson 10-1-1857
Black, James W. to Isabella Adams 9-3-1847
Black, Joseph A. to Sarah Catharine Gibson 3-17-1859
Black, Matthew to Margaret Reed 1-30-1828 (2-3-1828)
Black, Robert R. to Eliza A. Toons 5-10-1855
Black, W. H. to Sarah A. Ferguson 12-11-1852 (12-22-1852)
Black, William to Catharine Barker 11-3-1835 (11-5-1835)
Black, William to Mary Ann Pirtle 2-6-1854 (2-12-1854)
Black, Wm. F. to P. C. Murray 1-26-1858
Blackard, Radford F. to Sarah Ann Clift 7-30-1836
Blackburn, William to Mathena C. Hampton 2-14-1831
Blackwell, John C. to Arimencia Hale 8-23-1830 (9-3-1830)
Blackwell, John to Mary Philpott 11-2-1829
Blackwood, William to Rebecca Kesterson? 1-11-1826
Blair, George W. to Ann H. Lewis 7-3-1848 (7-6-1848)
Blair, William J. to Nancy Suggs 2-6-1856 (2-7-1856)
Blalock, Jesse to Rosana Lea 4-13-1833 (4-14-1833)
Bland, James R. to Mary C. Ragan 10-26-1860 (10-27-1860)
Blasingame, William S. to Amanda Duncan 12-21-1857 (2-12-1858)
Blount, Jesse to Christiana Hight 9-7-1840
Blunt, Jno. W. to Serbnny? Hooper 12-25-1844 (12-26-1844)
Boatman, Charles to Aussale? N.? Murray? 2-16-1834
Bogard, James to Annis Harris 7-14-1837 (7-27-1837)
Bogards, Alexander to Frances A. A. Hudspeth 2-13-1861 (2-14-1861)
Boguss, Joseph J. to Frances Hamlet 9-24-1845 (9-27-1845)
Bohanan, Jackson to Mary Ann Vails 7-23-1848
Bohanon, Jackson to Permelia Jane Sweeton 8-4-1841
Bohanon, John to Amanda Savage 11-18-1852
Bolen, John to Rebecca Hudspeth 5-27-1837 (5-30-1837)
Bolin, John to Mary Ann Sanders 8-31-1840
Boling, James to Jane Hanson 7-13-1830 (7-15-1830)
Bolling, Clayton L. to Genevia Monom 7-1-1829 (7-2?-1829)
Bomer, Elijah H. to Hulda Ann Garrett 8-28-1856
Bond(Vaughan), Benjamin to Elizabeth Mathis 6-26-1834
Bonds, Jas. W. to Martha A. Rogers 9-5-1857
Boney, James S. to Susannah E. Hunt 6-7-1838 (6-10-1838)
Boney, John W. to Nancy Thrailkill 2-12-1842 (2-13-1842)
Booe, George A. to Sarah Ann Hainline 7-4-1839
Booe, Isaac to Julia Ann Anderson 1-13-1842
Boon, James to Sousin Bradly 3-14-1848
Booth, Joel to Martha Gregory 10-2-1851
Boothe, Abijah H. to Melinda McCarley 2-2-1842 (2-3-1842)
Borroughs, Aaron to Eliza S. Bradshaw 6-22-1835 (6-23-1835)
Bosberne, John to Polly Hay(May) 9-9-1829
Bostian, J. C. to Louisa Price 10-5-1859 (10-6-1859)
Boswell, J. M. to Mary H. Route 2-7-1857 (2-8-1857)
Bottoms, William to Elizabeth McBride 6-26-1848 (7-6-1848)
Boucher, Gilbert B. to Philadelphia Ann Hankley 12-1-1858
Bowden, Thomas to Elizabeth Z. McKinnie 3-6-1843 (3-8-1843)
Bowers, Algernon S. to Sarah Ann Rebecca Bowers 9-22-1840
Bowers, John A. to Amanda Whitaker 1-24-1831
Bowers, John H. to Mary A. Allen 2-16-1848 (2-17-1848)
Bowles, Calvin to Nancy A. Sheets 5-30-1854 (6-1-1854)
Bowling, Bernard to Olivia Bowers 2-13-1861 (2-14-1861)
Box, James M. to Frances S. Hudson 10-7-1846
Box, Robert to Edny Ron? 7-31-1830 (8-10-1830)
Box, Robert to Temperance Gray 1-4-1841 (1-7-1841)
Box, Stephen to Elizabeth Harper 1-28-1835
Box, Steven to Adaline Moore 11-25-1854 (11-30-1854)
Boxley, D. S. to Agness W. Smith 11-23-1835
Boyce, Leonidas H. to Margaret A. Bass 12-31-1861 (1-5-1861)
Boyd, Alfred to Frances Leea? 6-5-1833 (6-6-1833)
Boyd, Amos to Mary Williams 2-6-1861 (2-8-1861)
Boyd, Hal to Catharine Williams 1-13-1859 (1-17-1859)
Boyd, John C. to Sarah J. Myrick 11-30-1859
Boyd, Robt. A. to Emily G. Bagley 11-8-1858 (11-11-1858)
Boydston, Benjamin J. to Elizabeth Jacobs 11-12-1825 (11-15-1825)
Boyle, Thomas to Margaret Owen 11-23-1847 (11-25-1847)
Boyle, Thomas to Mary Browning 11-3-1846
Boyle, Thomas to Mary Jane Love 10-19-1841 (10-21-1841)
Boyte, John A. to Ann A. Butler 1-11-1854 (1-12-1854)
Boyte, John B. to Nancy M. McKaughan 7-6-1842 (7-7-1842)
Boyte, Ollen to Mary A. Turner 12-12-1848 (12-21-1848)
Boyte, Patrick to Nancy McVay 8-3-1853 (8-4-1853)
Bozzle, John to Clara Jackson 4-29-1851 (5-4-1851)
Bradford, James M. to Narcissa C. Nuckolls 2-25-1860 (2-26-1860)
Bradford, Jno. S. to Caroline N. Browning 12-17-1855

Bradford, John to Emily Nuckolls 7-19-1849
Bradford, L. H. to Susan Foot 2-11-1856 (2-12-1856)
Bradford, W. G. to Elisa Oates 8-6-1848
Bradford, William G. to Matildy Wilie 1-24-1829
Bradshaw, Robert K. to Martha M. Wisdom 11-5-1850
Brady, Hugh to Sarah L. Anthony 9-7-1857 (9-30-1857)
Branch, Boling to Sarah E. T. Ingram 7-22-1840 (7-23-1840)
Brantley, Joseph J. to Susannah Clayton 7-19-1835
Brantly, Johns to Frances Poyner 6-20-1840 (6-27-1840)
Brantly, Philip to Jemima Cox 7-9-1833 (7-11-1833)
Brantly, William J. to Nancy A. Glass 12-31-1844 (1-2-1845)
Bray, H. L. to Sarah Phillips 10-13-1859
Bray, T. to Sarah Sheets 1-15-1857
Brazeal, Jackson to Susannah Price 4-10-1836 (4-12-1836)
Brazell, James M. to Merseny House 9-8-1838
Breeding, Archibald to Lucinda Moore 11-15-1832
Breeding, Lott to Jemima Ragan 11-21-1833
Brewer, Henry to Elizabeth Price 10-31-1839 (11-1-1839)
Brewer, Isaac to Charlotte Harriss 3-13-1843 (3-14-1843)
Brewer, Jesse J. to Mary E. McDonald 7-19-1838 (7-20-1838)
Brewton, Chas. P. to Josephine Davis 4-2-1857
Bridges, Geo. R. to Mariah V. Howard 11-6-1844 (11-8-1844)
Bright, Greenberry to Elizabeth Crisp 1-28-1830
Bright, Simeon to Keziah Box 4-24-1828 (4-29-1828)
Brim, James to Mary Ann Elizabeth Cup 7-27-183 (7-28-1833)
Brim, William to Mary Ann Hobbs 4-8-1834
Brimm, William to Elizabeth Millsap 6-8-1836
Brinkley, George A. to Nikolas Ann Perkins 3-26-1844
Brint, James B. to Alsy Boyte 9-13-1828
Brint, James H. to Leusi Powell 3-16-1850 (3-19-1850)
Britt, Lamuel to Mary Rose 7-22-1839 (7-25-1839)
Brogden, George M. to Elizabeth Neill 10-18-1850 (10-20-1850)
Brook, Josiah to Jane Stabough 5-20-1830 (5-25-1830)
Brook, Silas to Rebecca H. Hays 1-6-1832 (1-5?-1832)
Brook, Stephen L. to Jane Davis 8-6-1829
Brooks, B. F. C. to Mary V. Steel 3-8-1858
Brooks, Benjamin to Rhoda Merick 2-3-1835
Brooks, Henry H. to Freedonia Duncan 1-17-1855
Brooks, Jno. to Eliza Joyes 1-10-1845 (1-12-1845)
Brooks, John to Elizabeth Dollar 3-16-1853 (3-17-1853)
Brooks, Joseph to Agnes Neilson Dandridge 2-22-1847 (2-25-1847)
Brooks, Martin V. to Elizabeth Brown 7-29-1856
Brooks, Samuel R. to Frances Turner 10-13-1852
Brooks, Thompson to Rachel Blackwood 8-10-1832 (8-14-1832)
Brooks, William to Berthena Bass 7-2-1832 (7-15-1832)
Brotherton, George L. to Jane Alexander 1-2-1830
Brotherton, John S. to Eliza Morris 6-13-1843 (6-15-1843)
Brotherton, Logan D. to Henrietta Jobe 7-8-1835
Brough, John H. to Eliza Woodard 1-16-1836
Brown, Anson to Polly Sellers 12-30-1835 (12-31-1835)
Brown, Anson to Rachel Grantham 2-12-1831 (2-14-1831)
Brown, Benjamin to Peggy Lowdermilk 10-6-1829
Brown, Daniel to Lucinda Jones 12-29-1843 (12-31-1843)
Brown, Danl. W. to Nancy Pirtle 7-30-1859
Brown, David F. to Jane F. McNeal 10-14-1829 (10-15-1829)
Brown, Elijah V. to Elvira Hudson 6-12-1843 (6-13-1843)
Brown, Elijah to Peggy Chism 5-16-1833 (5-17-1833)
Brown, Eliphalet to Nancy Sain 1-6-1834 (1-9-1834)
Brown, Harrison to Serilda Doughty 12-8-1838 (12-10-1838)
Brown, Henry H. to Mary Ann Dotson 2-11-1835
Brown, Henry W. to Mary A. Fowler 7-4-1831 (7-7-1831)
Brown, Hiram N. to Martha Johnson 1-27-1845
Brown, James L. to Sarah J. Holly 9-11-1854 (9-12-1854)
Brown, Jas. H. to Mahala Gunter 6-28-1832
Brown, John Calvin to Elizabeth Tillman 1-3-1852 (1-11-1852)
Brown, John H. to Kissiah H. Pipkins 12-28-1853 (12-29-1853)
Brown, John T. to Angeline Wood 12-18-1841 (12-19-1841)
Brown, John W. to Narcissa Jane Brint 12-13-1853 (12-15-1853)
Brown, John to Clara M. Coleman 1-14-1832
Brown, John to Mary Wilkeson 3-15-1836
Brown, L. W. to Mary E. Hensly 12-23-1858
Brown, Lawson W. to Elizabeth M. Hood 9-19-1843
Brown, Perry to Nancy Thrailkill 4-18-1848 (4-20-1848)
Brown, Robert to Ann Eliza Pipkin 11-23-1857
Brown, Ruffin to Martha Pankey 7-22-1851 (7-24-1851)
Brown, Thos. K. to Elizabeth Ann Sellers 2-3-1847 (2-4-1847)
Brown, W. G. to Caroline Pankey 12-11-1850
Brown, Wesley C. to Lucy Kennedy 10-28-1836
Brown, William T. to Mary W. Mauldin 2-24-1851 (2-27-1851)
Brown, William to Mary Hullum 6-19-1829 (6-25-1829)
Brown, William to Minney Jane Howell 5-14-1857
Brown, William to Racheal Lewdermilk 1-21-1834 (1-23-1834)
Brown, William to Sarah Cox 7-22-1834 (7-24-1834)
Brown, Wm. J. to Lydia M. Grantham 8-1-1857 (8-4-1857)
Brown, Wm. James to Frances Parker 11-13-1860 (11-15-1860)
Browning, George W. to Harrett Adams 10-16-1840 (11-17-1840)
Bruhl, Edward to Ann Mulby 10-29-1859 (11-1-1859)
Brumbelow, John to Theay Stamps? 8-28-1834
Brumley, W. J. to Eliza Jane Morphus 8-27-1861 (8-29-1861)
Bryan, Ellen F. to Mary Jourdan 12-31-1829
Bryan, William O. to Mary S. Harris 12-16-1833 (12-18-1833)
Bryant, A. W. to Louisa G. Davis 10-13-1847 (10-14-1847)
Bryant, James E. to Amanda S. Fortune 9-1-1858 (9-2-1858)
Bryant, Jesse to Mary L. Hicks 9-30-1856 (10-2-1856)
Bryant, John to Jane McDaniel 9-16-1850 (9-17-1850)
Bryant, N. A. D. to Virginia C. Ingram 5-27-1856
Bryant, Thomas J. to Mary(Nancy) Walpole 12-29-1856 (1-1-1857)
Bryant, Washington to Mary Elizabeth Usery 4-30-1854
Bryant, Wm. A. to Nancy J. Elmore 10-22-1851 (10-23-1851)
Bryant, Wm. to Jan M. Glass 9-1-1845 (9-16-1845)
Bucke, James G. to Mary Ann E. Reynolds 12-26-1854 (12-31-1854)
Buding?, Thomas to Mary Carter 1-9-1838
Buffalo, Mathew T. to Kezziah Brown 5-13-1839 (5-15-1839)
Bulger, Cornelius to Emily Waxter 6-20-1861 (6-21-1861)
Bullard, Christopher to Mary Moon(Moore) 11-6-1844 (11-?-1844)
Bullington, B. F. to Mary M. Rose 3-31-1855 (4-?-1855)
Bullington, Josiah C. to Mary A. C. McKinly 11-8-1850 (11-14-1850)
Bullington, Lewis Jackson to Parilee Box 7-4-1850 (7-11-1850)
Bumpass, Benjamin to Lucinda Short 3-30-1829 (4-5-1829)
Bumpass, Gabril to Susan Hateley 9-22-1844
Bumpass, Moses to Nancy Brantley 7-14-1826 (7-16-1826)
Burford, F. M. to Cordelia A. Shaw 10-22-1849 (10-25-1849)
Burford, Jesse S. to Martha M. White 5-9-1842
Burkett(Burkhead), Thomas O. to Nancy Willoughby 2-7-1839 (2-8-1839)
Burkhead, Andrew H. to Mamena? Willoughby 11-28-1844
Burkhead, Eliazer to Rhoda Jane Nailor 1-1-1856 (1-3-1856)
Burkhead, Geo. G. to Sarah Roark 12-30-1847
Burleson, Aaron to Minerva Jane Seaton 8-21-1838 (8-23-1838)
Burleson, Jacob to Elizabeth Burleson 12-24-1828 (1-8-1829)
Burleson, Jonathan to Elizabeth Nichols 2-4-1833 (2-7-1833)
Burleson, Joseph to Ally M. Seaton 10-8-1827 (11-1-1827)
Burnes, Nathan M. to Mary Jane Tipler 7-31-1846 (8-4-1846)
Burnes, William A. to Cyntha May 10-28-1837 (10-31-1837)
Burnet, Geo. L. to Amanda J. Gatewood 2-6-1858 (2-7-1858)
Burnett, Charles J. to Nancy Vinson 2-24-1841 (2-26-1841)
Burnett, Glenn O. to Sarah M. Rogers 1-4-1830 (2-1-1830)
Burnett, Peter H. to Harriett W. Rogers 8-13-1828 (8-20-1828)
Burnett, William P. to Caroline Gatewood 12-26-1860
Burns, Charles to Louisa Williams 1-10-1861
Burns, Nathan M. to Hannah T. Harrison 1-13-1840
Burris, Thomas to Precilla Wright 3-5-1825 (3-6-1825)
Burrow, R. G. to Emily Lewis 12-23-1844
Burrow, Robert A. to Melora S. Pledge 7-25-1852 (9-8-1852)
Burrow, Starling to Dicy Barker 11-4-1837 (11-5-1837)
Burrow, Sterling to Ruth Zamples 2-6-1834
Burrus, Charles to Elizabeth Thompson 3-16-1835 (3-19-1835)
Burt, Williamson N. to Cintha Boydston 7-19-1838
Burton, Jerimiah to Nancy Issabella Stevenson 12-10-1850 (12-13-1850)
Burton, John F. to Nancy Griffith 10-14-1850 (10-17-1850)
Burton, William to Cynthia Baker 9-12-1829
Butcher, Joseph to Jane Burnes 5-6-1829
Butler, Carrol to Mary E. Johnson 2-2-1856 (2-5-1856)
Butler, David T. to Ann A. Young 6-18-1852 (6-23-1852)
Butler, Jacob H. to Sarah W. Nelson 12-23-1858
Butler, James to Mary Biddy 12-9-1829 (12-10-1829)
Butler, Thomas to Wilmurth Grooms 10-28-1824
Butts, Leroy D. to Mary Faw? 8-25-1851 (8-28-1851)
Byram, Ralph to Nancy E. Durner 2-6-1860 (2-9-1860)

Cabell, Samuel J. to Elizabeth Harvill 6-1-1827 (6-3-1827)
Caborne, James to Sarah Shipman 4-25-1826
Cage, E. R. to Sarah F. Minter 1-20-1847 (1-21-1847)
Cagle, M. G. to Susan C. Barkley? 5-24-1836
Cain, Dyes to Mary Harris 12-15-1832 (12-27-1832)
Cain, John H. to Percilla Washburn 10-18-1829
Cain, Obediah to Catharine Muse 1-25-1847
Caine, Calloway to Martha A. Nabors 4-13-1841
Caldwell, E. S. to Margaret Jane Galoway 12-23-1857 (12-24-1857)
Caldwell, J. F. to Tabitha A. McCommon 2-20-1849 (2-22-1849)
Caldwell, John to Mary Ann Harris 10-12-1827
Caldwell, Saml. S. to Elizabeth Ray 1-1-1856 (1-3-1856)
Caldwell, Wilie to Kesiah Hanks 7-11-1827
Callahan, A. M. to Eighty Eveline Neelly 3-1-1826 (3-7-1826)
Callahan, R. M. to Susan A. Cox 1-28-1860 (1-29-1860)
Callihan, Doke to Elizabeth Cariker 11-29-1852 (11-30-1852)
Campbell, Alex G. to Angelin R. Ashby 9-14-1852 (9-15-1852)
Campbell, Alexander to Martha A. Walker 9-6-1856 (9-7-1856)
Campbell, Archabald to Louisa Skinner 12-24-1847 (12-30-1847)
Campbell, Calvin to Pheby Stockton 11-3-1848 (11-9-1848)
Campbell, Claiborne to Lucinda Hester 1-25-1836 (1?-7-1836)
Campbell, Daniel to Elvira E. Guise 12-21-1857 (12-23-1857)
Campbell, G. D. to Tabitha Brigman 6-23-1857
Campbell, Garner D. to Elizabeth Rankin 11-11-1850 (11-14-1850)
Campbell, George L. to Jane Molloy? 7-24-1828 (7-29-1828)
Campbell, James to Sarah Ann Sadler 12-22-1859
Campbell, John to Anny Yeary 7-10-1828 (4-6-1829)
Campbell, Joseph to Aura? Love 1-30-1835
Campbell, Moses to Ann Eliza Camp 2-14-1854
Campbell, Robert to Elizabeth Vails 2-27-1847
Campbell, Wm. to E. C. H. Holland 10-7-1845
Candell, Buckner to Polly Craton 2-18-1828
Cane, Henderson to Lucy Boothe 2-3-1843 (2-2?-1843)
Cannon, Bryant to Margaret Murphy 10-10-1843 (10-12-1843)
Cannon, Daniel S. to Joana B. Gayler 1-13-1857
Cannon, Elija to Louvenia Higgs 5-25-1850 (5-26-1850)
Cannon, Gabrial to Lavinia Gately 6-11-1841 (6-12-1841)
Cannon, Wm. to Caroline Tillman 6-11-1861 (6-13-1861)
Caps, Andrew to Sarah Ann Coleman 12-1-1855 (12-6-1855)
Caraway, John to Sarah Brown 5-30-1835
Cardwell, Wm. A. to Sarah J. Ussery 1-12-1857
Caricker, Charles to Nancy Brown 7-28-1854 (7-30-1854)
Carithers, John A. to Mary Rudolph 8-22-1831
Carley, Jesse to Letty Roberts 8-17-1849 (8-19-1849)
Carley, John W. to Milly Boothe 10-1-1840 (10-4-1840)
Carley, John to Elizabeth Davis 1-27-1849 (2-4-1849)
Carley, John to Polly Ann Savage 9-26-1840 (9-27-1840)
Carley, Luke to Louisa Barham 4-21-1852 (4-22-1852)
Carley, Peter K. to Susannah Liggett 1-26-1843
Carley, William to Malinda Binkley 8-10-1839
Carley, William to Sarah Carley 10-1-1840 (10-2-1840)
Carnes, David B. to Mary Steel 10-7-1828 (10-9-1828)
Carnes, Robert W. to Prudence E. Steele 11-10-1842
Carnes, Thomas to Elizabeth McBride 6-26-1835 (6-28-1835)
Carouth, Aquilla H. to Emily E. Robertson 5-23-1850
Carpenter, Dangerfreld? to Ellin Kyle 3-7-1835 (3-8-1835)
Carper, Alexander to Mary Huffman 5-19-1857 (5-22-1857)
Carper, William to Margaret Goforth 2-2-1861 (2-5-1861)
Carr, Hardy to Mahulda Duberry 2-29-1840 (3-1-1840)
Carraway, Henry to Abacilla McKinnie 3-14-1843
Carraway, Jas. M. to Susan C. Casey 11-23-1858 (11-25-1858)
Carricker, Geo. M. to Mary E. Phillips 9-16-1857
Carricker, George M. to Elizabeth Gray 8-7-1852
Carrington, J. B. to Elizabeth Springfield 6-21-1861 (6-22-1861)
Carrington, Luke to Nannie Toone 12-10-1858 (1-11-1859)
Carrington, Wiley A. to Martha Pirtle 4-30-1859 (5-2-1859)
Carroll, Allen to Jane Jones 2-2-1826 (2-4-1826)
Carroll, Francis M. to Frances M. Lowe 7-25-1838 (7-26-1838)
Carroll, John D. to Racheal Rennick 1-28-1828
Carroll, R. H. to Caroline M. Thurmond 3-21-1836 (3-24-1836)
Carroll, Washington B. to Martha L. Mathis 1-1-1828
Carruth, J. J. to Mary Jane Clark 5-27-1858 (8-10-1858)
Carson, A. J. to Eliza A. Rosson 3-4-1856 (3-6-1856)
Carson, Andrew J. to Matilda Tedford 2-28-1854
Carson, Wm. S. to Martha A. Jenkins 4-17-1860 (4-22-1860)
Carter, D. R. to Sarah E. Pled;ge 11-26-1855 (11-27-1855)
Carter, Green B. to Nancy Ann Crews 1-3-1839
Carter, James to Salina Dean 4-27-1836
Carter, Jesse A. to Anna Johnson 9-19-1857
Carter, Jos. John to Sarah Ann Sheckels? 12-27-1842 (12-28-1842)
Carter, Robert to Rozy Ann Jones 9-5-1844
Carter, Thomas L. to Mary Ann Pirtle 9-10-1859
Cartmell(Cartwell?), R. H. to Mary Jane Baldwin 3-26-1850 (3-27-1850)
Cartwright, Robert to Sarah Hamblin 4-7-1828
Carvan, Will to Lucinda Vails 1-1-1853 (1-2-1853)
Case, Martin to Barbry Jackson 1-2-1845
Case, Thomas to Mary Jackson 6-24-1840
Casee, Mizo to Mary Brantly 2-16-1839 (2-23-1839)
Casey, Hiram D. to Ann Lax 5-21-1847 (5-23-1847)
Casey, James A. to Margaret Honel 5-5-1829
Casey, James G. to Jane Harris 9-30-1861 (10-6-1861)
Casey, James to Jane Savage 8-4-1829
Casey, John L. to Harriett Nunnelly 11-23-1836 (11-24-1836)
Casey, John L. to Marilda Stewart 8-8-1844
Casey, Joseph to Nancy Westbrook 7-16-1850 (7-21-1850)
Casey, R. D. to Cynthia G. Joyner 12-31-1857 (1-5-1858)
Casey, Randolph to Gilly Dean 5-25-1828 (5-26-1828)
Casey, S. W. to S. J. Holloway 10-18-1861
Casey, Solomon C. to Eliza Ann Hicks 9-8-1856 (9-11-1856)
Casey, Zadoc to Amanda Foster 3-6-1841
Casey, lHiram to Sydney M. Hale 6-4-1861 (6-6-1861)
Cash, Benjamin to Mildred S. Dandrige 7-23-1838 (8-1-1838)
Cassitt, F. D. to L. F. J. Malone 12-10-1844
Casson, John to Julia Armstrong 12-2-1833
Castell, Abram to Rachel Hays 8-2-1826
Castellaw, Alfred to Priscilla Fort 7-8-1833
Castor, W. W. to Sarah K. Rose 1-21-1861 (1-24-1861)
Cates, William to Parthena Parrish 11-18-1839
Causeby, John to Jane Norton 3-3-1825
Cavenor, William B. to Margaret E. Meeks 5-25-1853 (5-26-1853)
Cavens, A. B. to Elizabeth Burton 12-22-1860 (12-24-1860)
Caviness, Daniel H. to Eliza Jane Bailey 12-23-1851 (1-1-1852)
Cerly, Jesse to Martha Davis 1-18-1849
Cesterson, Camel to Arina Bass 12-12-1832 (12-23-1832)
Chaddick, James W. to Cyntha Mills 3-20-1837 (3-30-1837)
Chaffin, Talafaro B. to Jennet Riddle 12-27-1831 (12-29-1831)
Chambers, Thomas to Martha Mask 10-23-1846 (10-28-1846)
Chambliss, Daniel R. to Sarah Ellen Overton 10-8-1849 (10-9-1849)
Chambliss, John N. to Nancy M. Walker 6-4-1852 (6-6-1852)
Chambliss, T. W. to C. J. Drinnon 6-3-1848 (6-4-1848)
Chambliss, Thomas to Adelia C. Bell 9-7-1853 (9-8-1853)
Champion, Jack Thomas to Harriet A. Walls 3-10-1849 (3-13-1849)
Champion, James to Parthena H. Champion(Anderson) 10-2-1833
Champion, William to Catherine Robertson 11-25-1826
Chandler, R. T. to Susan L. Foreman 1-21-1861 (1-23-1861)
Chandler, William Hutson to Mary Blount 8-15-1839 (8-15-1839)
Chandler, Wm. F. to Martha Burney 7-21-1859
Chapman, Albartis to Matilda Gray 11-20-1828
Chapman, Alexander to Nancy Godlin 6-5-1846 (6-6-1846)
Chapman, Eli to Equilla Portis 3-1-1850 (3-3-1850)
Chapman, James C. to Mary Biebers 9-5-1845 (9-?-1845)
Chapman, Robert D. to Rebecca Hodges 10-6-1836
Chappel, Christopher to Ann Green 12-31-1838 (1-1-1839)
Chappell, John P. to Patsy Davis 12-14-1839 (12-15-1839)
Cheairs, David B. to Eliz. Ann Wooley 11-30-1841 (12-1-1841)
Cheairs, Nathaniel to Eliza Mask 3-7-1853 (3-10-1853)
Cheairs, Wm. T. to P. Hitchcock 9-6-1847
Cheak, William to Elizabeth M. Rogers 1-30-1846
Cherry, John to Mary Myers 4-1-1832 (4-5-1832)
Cheshier, John to Nancy C. Fortune 11-28-1849 (11-29-1849)
Cheshier, Johnathan to Ann E. Clements 2-15-1860 (2-16-1860)
Cheshier, Washington D. to Rebecca Ann Pankey 8-31-1846 (9-1-1846)
Cheshire, Hezekiah to Sarah J. McKinne 10-2-1854 (10-3-1854)
Childress, Ellison to Sarah Simms 7-13-1829
Childress, John W. to Martha A. McCarter 5-15-1859 (6-16-1859)
Childress, Stephen to Elizabeth Allen 2-29-1840 (3-3-1840)
Childress, Will H. to Abigil Johnson 7-17-1856 (7-20-1856)
Childress, William to Lucinda Johnson 8-6-1847 (8-8-1847)

Childs, Robert H. to Mary Bailey 1-29-1854 (1-19?-1854)
Chism, Vann R. to Elizabeth Ann Dillingham 6-18-1836
Chisum, Henry T. to Jane Park 10-26-1829
Chisum, John D. to Mary R. Davis 12-24-1860 (12-27-1860)
Chisum, John G. to Louisa Jane Purtle(Pirtle?) 6-3-1839 (6-6-1839)
Chisum, John to Sarah Robinson 12-29-1834
Chisum, Thomas G. to Belinda Chisum 11-19-1829
Chisum, William to Mary Ann Chisum 2-24-1828
Chowning, Tinsley to Julia Ann M. Taylor 5-11-1839 (6-12-1839)
Chronister, Adam to Tinsey Garrison 1-5-1826
Clark, Andrew J. to Sarah P. Lyle 4-15-1843
Clark, Harrison to Elizabeth Williams 1-30-1841 (2-14-1841)
Clark, Harvy S. to Cleopatra Robinson 9-16-1854 (10-19-1854)
Clark, John R. to Malinda Sweeton 4-13-1832 (4-15-1832)
Clark, John S. to Lucinday Ann Covington 11-2-1838 (11-4-1838)
Clark, John to Smithy Burden 8-23-1853 (9-8-1853)
Clarke, Benj. F. L. to Harriet Thompson 2-13-1847
Claunch?, Jerimiah S. to Harriet A. Hullum 4-24-1835 (4-27-1835)
Claxton, Francis M. to Cary Ann Freeman 2-24-1857
Clay, Jackson M. to Cynthia G. Guynn 12-14-1839 (12-15-1839)
Clayton, Alfred N. to Ann Maria Peters 9-10-1846 (10-16-1846)
Clayton, Calvin to Winniford Jones 1-6-1842
Clayton, William to Elizabeth Floyd 12-28-1836
Cliburn, Patrick H. to Elizabeth S. Epps 1-11-1833 (1-13-1833)
Clifft, B. A. to Sabella Prewett 2-19-1859 (2-22-1859)
Clifft, Barnet to Alsey Allsup 1-23-1828 (1-24-1828)
Clifft, Thomas J. to Lydia Ann Gay 2-11-1860 (2-13-1860)
Clift, Thos. J. to Mary Ann Barkley 4-4-1842 (4-7-1842)
Clift, Willie to Temperance A. Sherron 11-30-1854
Clifton, J. D. to Nancy House 9-1-1851 (9-4-1851)
Clifton, John to Hannah Strothers 12-23-1841 (12-30-1841)
Clifton, John to May Webb 9-28-1858 (10-7-1858)
Clifton, Thomas B. to Adaline Cupp 1-1-1855 (1-5-1855)
Climer, Carrol to Mary E. Vandygriff 1-22-1853 (1-30-1853)
Clinton, David to Rebecca McKearly 6-11-1833 (6-13-1833)
Clinton, Robert to Sarah Coonrod 3-8-1826 (3-9-1826)
Clinton, William S. to Sarah Ann Coates 1-22-1850
Cloud, Jason to Elizabeth Adams 1-2-1830
Cloud, Joseph F. to Jane M. Vaughn 1-22-1832
Cloud, Joseph to Elizabeth Short 2-24-1836
Clyne, Hiram to Elizabeth Miller 3-13-1843
Coates, Caswell to Mary Allen 12-27-1841 (12-30-1841)
Coates, John to Adaline Coffey 10-31-1846 (11-11-1846)
Coates, John to Mary Ann Jernigin 9-8-1847 (9-19-1847)
Coates, John to Nancy C. Johnson 2-20-1839
Coates, Thompson C. to Amanda S. M. Luggett 12-17-1845
Coates, William C. to N. E. Lile 7-13-1846
Cobb, Jesse B. to Lucy Ann Jones 12-22-1847 (12-28-1847)
Coburn, James L. to Margaret Bradford 7-5-1855
Coburn, Wm. H. to Margaret A. Doyle 3-20-1861
Cocke, Harmon to Celia Tudor 12-28-1829 (12-31-1829)
Cockeram, Henry to Ruth Johnson 7-30-1828 (4-6-1829)
Cody, James to Janie Colbert 4-19-1826 (4-20-1826)
Cody, Thomas D. to Lucinda Nichols 8-3-1831
Coffey(Coffer?), James to Adalin Murry 3-2-1840
Coffey, Elijah to Polly McConell? 3-22-1847
Colbert(Colvard), Wade H. to Lathey Gage 1-30-1830
Cole, Will H. to Caroline Fortner 9-16-1846 (9-20-1846)
Cole, William H. to Sarah Adams 11-4-1861
Cole, William to Eliza Stockton 6-17-1835
Cole, William to Harriet Simpson 8-31-1858
Coleman, A. A. to Louisa Neely 7-6-1859
Coleman, James to Ellen David 1-4-1853 (1-5-1853)
Coleman, Joshua to Elizabeth McBride 11-24-1855 (11-26-1855)
Collier, Carter C. to Louisa Neelly 3-4-1824
Collier, Telemicus H. to Sarah Cobb 10-10-1849 (10-11-1849)
Collins, Peter A. to Ann Tims 1-18-1842
Collins, Thomas J. to Armasa King 1-11-1841 (1-13-1841)]
Collins, Thos. L. to Sarah Fort 6-15-1847
Colvard, Pleasant to Jane Bailey 6-28-1826 (6-29-1826)
Coly, James to Sarah Hopkikns 12-20-1834
Combs, William to Louisa Granby 3-22-1847 (3-25-1847)
Comer, Elijah to Mary Wood 10-25-1837
Comer, Henry M. to Lucy E. Daniel 10-25-1842
Comer, Wm. C. C. to Wincey C. Richardson 11-14-1860 (11-15-1860)
Compton, David R. to Tabitha Lax 8-8-1853 (8-10-1853)
Conlee, Henderson to Sarah Williams 12-30-1835
Coodey, Edward to Catharine Rainer 5-28-1829
Cook, James D. to Nancy Atwell 1-8-1850 (1-9-1850)
Cook, Leroy to Olive W. Farguson 1-22-1840
Cooksey, James to Isbele Waldrup 6-15-1832
Cooksey, Vincent to Elizabeth Terry 9-28-1842 (9-29-1842)
Cooper, B. H. to Clarissa F. Wilkinson 1-3-1861 (1-7-1861)
Cooper, Edmund to Mary E. Stephens 10-22-1844
Cooper, J. J. to Virginia Kirkland 12-22-1857 (1-7-1858)
Cooper, James to Mary A. E. Jones 4-5-1855
Cooper, John to Winney Wright 8-28-1833
Cooper, Sidney to Eliza Jones 3-24-1835
Cooper, Solomon E. to Emily H. Blalock 12-23-1861 (12-26-1861)
Cooper, William D. to Susan T. Bishop 1-19-1833 (1-20-1833)
Coor, Charley to Levina Morris 6-20-1843 (6-22-1843)
Coor, Chas. A. to Eviline Rhodes 8-10-1854 (8-11-1854)
Coor, Willie to Frances J. Smith 5-2-1836 (5-5-1836)
Cope, Caleb jr. to Martha(Maletha?) J. Davis 7-1-1856 (7-2-1856)
Copeland, William to Hannah McBee 1-26-1825 (2-27-1825)
Coppadge, G. J. to Mary J. Bishop 1-7-1856 (1-10-1856)
Cordle, Thomas R. to Sarah Moore 3-1-1855
Corley, John to Elizabeth Hudson 12-29-1834 (12-30-1834)
Cornelius, William to Patsy Bolling 1-21-1834
Cortner, John to Jane Hays 7-5-1824 (7-7-1824)
Cossitt, F. G. to Sarah Frances Taylor 8-29-1861 (8-30-1861)
Costello, Uriah to Elizabeth Shipman 11-15-1826 (11-16-1826)
Cothran, Erasmus R. to Rosanna Shinault 1-10-1838 (1-11-1838)
Couch, Saml. to Rebecca Needham 2-10-1842
Counsel, WilliamH. to Cinthia W. Rucker 1-10-1832
Covington, John M. to Charity Johnson 12-17-1838 (12-20-1838)
Cowan, David to Nancy Davis 11-7-1846 (11-8-1846)
Cowan, George to Amanda Hargrove 12-16-1853
Coward, William to Agness E. Shaw 6-7-1845 (6-12-1845)
Cox, Abram to Polly Rook 10-24-1830 (11-3-1830)
Cox, Alfred to Sarah Bishop 9-11-1839 (9-12-1839)
Cox, Allen to Lillie Ann Hudspeth 3-11-1833
Cox, Allen to Mary Ann Parker 10-15-1858 (10-3?-1858)
Cox, Asa to Nancy Harris 12-21-1835 (12-22-1835)
Cox, Bryant to Cornelia Bailey 10-17-1851 (10-23-1851)
Cox, Cader to Edny Bishop 12-16-1835 (12-17-1835)
Cox, Caleb to Elizabeth Hicks 8-4-1832 (8-9-1832)
Cox, Charles J. to Charlotte Horn 4-24-1844 (4-25-1844)
Cox, Cunningham to Mary Galloway 12-30-1834 (1-2-1835)
Cox, Eli to Elizabeth Young 4-19-1847 (4-20-1840
Cox, Eli to Jane Parkes 10-1-1832 (10-?-1832)
Cox, Eli to Precilla W. Brown 8-2-1848
Cox, Eli to Virtuous? C. Grant 8-2-1836
Cox, Jacob to Elizabeth Herne? 2-27-1834
Cox, James to Harriet Kilpatrick 5-19-1855
Cox, Jesse to Zilpha Boyt 7-14-1832 (7-?-1832)
Cox, John Allen to Martha Horne 12-13-1847 (12-17-1847)
Cox, John B. to Amanda M. Reynolds 5-23-1843 (5-25-1843)
Cox, John to Mary M. Pankey 8-11-1852 (8-12-1852)
Cox, Johnathan to Elizabeth Macon 10-31-1850 (11-7-1850)
Cox, Joseph to Sally Rogers 12-19-1837 (12-21-1837)
Cox, Marshall W. to Nancy Gately 11-21-1840 (11-26-1840)
Cox, N. J. to M. E. Dishough 11-12-1860
Cox, Thomas to Sophronia W. Farned 1-18-1858 (1-19-1858)
Cox, W. B. to Catharine Denton 1-2-1860
Cox, William G. to Martha Jane Lamber 4-25-1853 (5-5-1853)
Cozby, Jacob A. to Mary Ann Cearly 2-17-1847
Cozby, James L. to Rebecca Womack 2-21-1839 (2-25-1839)
Cozby, John to Violett O. Ozburn? 11-30-1846 (12-1-1846)
Cozby, Mathew to Jane Hutson 6-12-1833 (6-15-1833)
Cozby, Robert A. to Sarah Carley 12-17-1847 (12-28-1847)
Cozby, Robert to Elizabeth Murdaugh 8-5-1835
Craddock, John R. to Louisa E. Nappier 6-5-1845
Craft, Archibald to Jane E. Renolds 11-19-1838
Craig, Andrew to Jane E. Lambeth 3-17-1845 (3-18-1845)
Crain, Giles B. to Caroline Fulgum 2-15-1832 (2-16-1832)
Crain, Thomas to Sally Hopper 8-31-1829
Crain, William to Drucilla Fowler 5-24-1830
Crates, Wm. J. to Lucy A. Bishop 4-29-1861 (5-1-1861)
Crawford, Alexander to Harriett Shackleford 4-8-1828

Crawford, Ashly R. to Elizabeth J. Ward 2-26-1848 (3-2-1848)
Crawford, Edwin to Jane Reagan 2-24-1824 (2-26-1824)
Crawford, Isaac W. to Sarah Lillard 8-10-1846 (8-12-1846)
Crawford, James B. to Cyntha A. Williams 6-7-1852
Crawford, James to Mary Ann Tackett 2-20-1861 (2-21-1861)
Crawford, John R. to Amanda Powell 1-12-1850 (1-24-1850)
Crawford, Peter P. to Margret Hudson 8-22-1845
Crawford, Pitser M. to Ellen E. Ray 2-6-1860 (2-9-1860)
Crawford, Raiford to Nancy Coor 7-1-1839 (7-15-1839)
Crawford, Rufus P. to Jane Milisse McCrory 10-2-1848 (10-4-1848)
Crawford, Russell J. to Nancy G. Neely 11-5-1827
Crawford, Russell P. to Ruan J. Warford 5-7-1858 (5-11-1858)
Crawford, W. R. to Amy C. Wood 12-20-1859 (12-21-1859)
Crawford, William to Martha A. B. Vinson 11-3-1853
Crawford, Wm. F. to Martha Ann Ward 5-10-1845 (5-22-1845)
Crenshaw, N. M. to Elizabeth Boothe 1-20-1849 (1-24-1849)
Crews, Eppy to Syrena Carter 2-9-1837
Crews, Isaac T. to Elizabeth A. F. Tisdale 11-5-1853 (11-7-1853)
Crews, John to Elizabeth Wright 10-31-1832 (11-1-1832)
Crews, John to Mary Jane Tisdale 12-31-1849 (1-10-1850)
Crews, Jonathan to Elizabeth Bumpass 9-26-1827
Crews, Peter R. to Mary Adams 8-30-1854
Crews, Wm. H. to Arpy? Tisdale 2-7-1855 (2-8-1855)
Criner, Robert L. to Martha Gunter 12-28-1835
Crisp, Charles A. to Nancy Crisp 4-7-1842
Crisp, Clinton to Mary Cheshier 9-28-1854
Crisp, Hiram C. to Martha Bates 10-20-1842
Crisp, Lemuel M. to Ann J. Norton 1-1-1857
Crisp, Moses P. to Angeline B. Lawhorn 9-18-1855
Crisp, Tilman A. to Rebecca Couch 4-8-1848 (4-9-1848)
Crittenden, Wm. H. to Ann E. Collins 1-3-1843
Crocker, James to Amanda M. Morphis 6-20-1846 (6-21-1846)
Crofford, William H. to Hannah E. Williams 5-19-1845 (5-20-1845)
Cross, Elijah W. to Martha E. Irwin 11-9-1842 (11-10-1842)
Cross, Milton P. to Mary Moore 3-1-1841 (3-3-1841)
Cross, William to Eliza Ann Hobbs 10-23-1837 (10-24-1837)
Cross, Wm. T. to Sarah A. Crowder 9-15-1855
Crouse, Jesse to Amanda L. Mills 11-5-1847 (11-7-1847)
Crouse, John to Sarah Carver? 5-17-1849
Crouse, Joseph to Harriett Mills 6-22-1843
Crow, J.W. to Minerva Mahern(Mahan) 2-20-1832 (2-21-1832)
Crow, John to Isabel Henry 9-22-1829
Crow, R. M. to Eliza A. Morril 2-10-1862 (2-12-1862)
Crowley, Samuel to Elizabeth E. White 4-23-1851 (4-24-1851)
Crowley, Strong to Olvizara? Nuckolls 6-24-1839
Crowly, Matthew to Rosusey Fine Parker 12-16-1843 (12-17-1843)
Cruise, James to Hester Ann White 3-2-1844 (3-6-1844)
Cruise, Lemuel W. to Milinda Jones 10-1-1833
Crum, Elias to Fainy Kenedy 2-15-1831
Crunk, John to Louise May 5-24-1826
Cruse, William to Rebecca Road 8-2-1833 (8-7-1833)
Cumings, William to Agelina Fewtrill 1-26-1853 (1-27-1853)
Cup, Stephen to Cornelia A. Caviness 8-30-1850 (9-1-1850)
Curl, Dempsey E. to Mary M. Higgs 12-4-1858 (12-5-1858)
Currin, W. D. to Nancy A. Campbell 8-7-1854 (8-14-1854)
Curtis(Carter?), Green B. to Martha J. McMahan 1-11-1848 (1-12-1848)
Curtis, Green B. to Louisa J. Allen 8-23-1841
Curtis, John F. to Ailsy Eaton 4-28-1855 (5-1-1855)
Curtis, John M. to Nancy Eaton 6-23-1855 (6-25-1855)
Cuthbertwson, Thomas M. to Philpina Jarman 4-1-1824 (4-3-1824)
Dabb, Richard to Betsy Harper 6-22-1826
Dabbs, C. H. to S. S. Hunt 12-5-1834
Dale, Anderson to Elizabeth Stone 1-9-1830
Dalton, D. L. to Mary Ann Wilkins 8-23-1849 (8-28-1849)
Damon?, Noah to Amanda L. Scott 11-14-1849 (11-15-1849)
Damson?, George to Mary Ann Low? 5-19-1836 (5-22-1836)
Daniel, Isaac M. to Mary E. Jackson 12-10-1857 (12-13-1857)
Daniel, John B. to Visa Ann Davis 1-24-1852 (1-26-1852)
Daniel, R. L. to Jane Myrick 6-30-1860 (7-3-1860)
Daniel, W. H. to Mary L. Dougherty 7-15-1860 (7-17-1860)
Daniels, Isaac M. to Elizabeth Ann Hardy? 4-3-1852 (4-4-1852)
Darnell, John to Martha Matthews 7-13-1861
Daugherty, Wm. S. to Elizabeth Atkinson 1-9-1846 (1-11-1846)
Davis, A. M. to Ellen V. Harbin 5-14-1861 (5-21-1861)
Davis, Andrew to Sarah Alingny? Linsey 7-23-1836
Davis, Benj. W. to Mary Jane Grace 2-24-1847
Davis, Benjamin to Catherine Jones 9-1-1831
Davis, Bryant to Nancy A. J. Rose 12-24-1855 (12-26-1855)
Davis, Cyrus to Olivia Rucker 4-8-1844 (4-9-1844)
Davis, George to Cena M. Black 11-2-1844 (11-4-1844)
Davis, George to Miss Sarah Spears 1-12-1852 (1-14-1852)
Davis, German W. to Cela A. Maxwell 4-16-1858 (4-18-1858)
Davis, Hughie to Elizabeth Jones 10-7-1830 (10-14-1830)
Davis, Jacob to Mary A. Ables 2-21-1859 (2-23-1859)
Davis, Jarman W. to Sarah J. Flenn 1-5-1858
Davis, Jesse to Priscilla Kennedy 6-5-1828 (6-14?-1828)
Davis, Jno. C. to Nelly Cerly 11-28-1849
Davis, John E. G. to Mary J. Russey 8-13-1840
Davis, John M. to Martha A. F. Jones 11-27-1824
Davis, John to Hollen Dougherty 8-13-1836
Davis, John to Martha Hudson 7-17-1846
Davis, S. R. to Sarah Foster 1-28-1862 (1-29-1862)
Davis, Thomas to Elizabeth Rogers 10-14-1826 (11-20-1826)
Davis, V. A. to Jane Whitehorn 3-14-1837
Davis, Willie to Polly Tedford 8-14-1830 (8-16-1830)
Davis, Willis to Elizabeth M. Duncan 8-2-1845 (8-3-1845)
Davis, Zachariah to Rosanna Shinault 5-22-1824
Dawson(Damson), Stephen H. to M. J. King 1-20-1845
Dawson, James C. to Sarah Brown 1-7-1839 (1-8-1839)
Dawson, James L. to Martha Low 2-18-1843
Dawson, James O. to Barbara B. Johnson 1-9-1839 (1-11-1839)
Dawson, John to Christianna G. Smith 12-19-1838 (12-20-1838)
Day, Richard G. to Julia V. Armstead 12-19-1856
DeBerry, Wm. H. to Polly Hendricks 6-23-1828 (6-24-1828)
Dean, W. Jasper to Martha E. Bradford 10-25-1859 (11-2-1859)
Dean, W. R. to Elizabeth Dunn 2-19-1859 (2-26-1859)
Deason, John to Olive Hall 10-30-1828
Deason, Samuel to Hester Piles 11-1-1834
Deaton, George W. to Catharine I. Dubois 1-7-1835
Deaton, M. M. to Agnes P. A. Anderson 10-1-1851
Deaton, Philip to Delila Wilson 3-2-1836 (3-6-1836)
Deeson?, Abraham to Mahaly Davis 12-18-1826
Deming, J. W. to Mary C. Bradford 2-3-1860
Deming, J. W. to Nancy Jones 12-15-1845 (12-23-1845)
Deming, Wilie to Harriet Ann Jones 10-18-1853
Dennies, Wheetly to Hester A. Minter 6-18-1855 (6-24-1855)
Dennis, Adolphus G. to Elizabeth E. Minter 4-20-1849
Dennis, Charles to Pamelia Jane Smith 4-17-1854 (4-18-1854)
Denny, Robert to Louisa Lyons 11-24-1836 (11-25-1836)
Deraberry, P. M. to Susan C. Carper 9-18-1857 (10-2-1857)
Deshaze, Edmund to Elizabeth Jourdan 6-19-1837 (6-20-1837)
Devenport, William S. to Mary Jane Hatfield 11-27-1848 (11-28-1848)
Devinport?, Hiram G. to Mary R. Abernatha 11-23-1846 (11-26-1846)
Dew?, Joseph I. to Martha Greenleaf 7-23-1831 (7-24-1831)
Dial, Wm. T. to Lucinda C. Jackson 1-19-1857 (1-20-1857)
Dickens, Mathew to Martha A. Clifft 10-31-1857 (11-3-1857)
Dickerson, Almeron to Susanna Wilkerson 5-24-1829
Dickins, Jno. R. to Mary S. Hunt 2-21-1842 (2-22-1842)
Dickins, Samuel to Virginia Hunt 2-21-1842 (2-22-1842)
Dickson, Edward to Sarah Pugh 11-30-1842 (12-1-1842)
Dickson, Henry to Frankey Machaum(Michum) 7-4-1827 (7-5-1827)
Dill, John to Minny E. Henson 3-7-1856 (3-9-1856)
Dillard, Allen to Lucretia Lynch 5-11-1831 (5-15-1831)
Dillard, Gabriel to Arrena Vails 12-26-1837
Dillard, Owen to Sarah Dillard 7-13-1833 (7-14-1833)
Dillard, Owen to Sarah Ewing 1-7-1828 (1-8-1828)
Dillard, Willis to Martha L. Dillard 9-3-1834
Dishough, Isaac R. to Nancy Bostwick 12-15-1841 (12-16-1841)
Dixon, Edward to Martha Pugh 7-21-1841 (7-22-1841)
Dixon, J. C. to M. J. McCommon 1-1-1861
Dixon, Linnear to Sarah Dillard 9-10-1836
Dodson, James E. to Rebecca W. Ingram 4-7-1851 (4-9-1851)
Dodson, Robert T. to Mary P. Flynt 12-31-1849 (1-8-1850)
Dodson, Wm. to Ophelia J. Crews 3-19-1857 (3-17?-1857)
Doile, Solomon to Polly Ann Norton 12-27-1847 (12-28-1847)
Donaldson, John B. to Sarah Fulgum 3-21-1833
Dongan, Robert S. to Louisa S. Ritchie 2-28-1839
Donnell, George to Mary Jane Daniel 2-24-1851
Dorris, E. H. to Teressa Ann Bradford 11-10-1853

Dorris, Eldrige W. to Mary M. Binkly 1-21-1846
Dorris, J. G. to Frances R. Sills 2-14-1861
Dorris, N. B. to Lucretia Nuckolls 12-28-1857
Dorris, W. F. to Nancy P. Young 12-4-1851
Douglass, Addison H. to Martha Adeline Robertson 2-2-1842
Dowdy, John J. to Lucy T. Thompson 11-10-1853
Dowdy, Martin V. to Matilda Jane Laws 5-3-1859 (5-4-1859)
Dowdy, Robert to Martha A. Dial 1-1-1857 (1-8[18]-1857
Dowdy, W. K. to Jane Dial 3-19-1856
Dowdy, W. K. to Marcilla E. Dial 9-3-1860 (9-4-1860)
Dowdy, William K. to Eliza C. Crawford 10-31-1855 (11-1-1855)
Doyle, Geo. W. to Sarah T. Cosby 9-29-1860 (9-30-1860)
Doyle, J. R. to Mary Ann Stone 1-18-1860 (1-20-1860)
Doyle, Matthew to Mary Ann Inman 12-9-1843 (12-17-1843)
Doyle, Saml. J. to Jerusha A. Sexton 1-7-1860 (1-10-1860)
Dranna, William to Polly Lorance 5-29-1838
Dubois, J. G. to A. E. Cooper 10-9-1845 (10-10-1845)
Duese?, W. M. to E. S. Belote 6-24-1857
Dugan, G. M. to Mary A. David 2-2-1857
Dugger, Jesse P. to Phebe A. Aulford 5-14-1845 (5-15-1845)
Duke, Edmund F. to Elizabeth A. Price 5-18-1849 (5-20-1849)
Dukes, RLobert B. to Jane Edwards 6-30-1847 (7-1-1847)
Dunahoe, Calvin H. to America Fish 3-4-1856 (3-6-1856)
Dunaway, John to Sarah Colverd 7-14-1828 (7-17-1828)
Duncan, Albert D. to Mary D. Jarman 8-5-1831 (8-10?-1831)
Duncan, Crawford A. to Elizabeth Harvey 4-11-1838
Duncan, E. G. to Mary Ann Little 6-14-1855 (6-15-1855)
Duncan, E. S. to Siddy J. Springfield 9-5-1859 (9-6-1859)
Duncan, Elijah G. to Jane Null 1-5-1829
Duncan, Henry W. to Margaret M. Ruddle 1-2-1849 (1-3-1849)
Duncan, Henry W. to Mary Burlesson 10-24-1827 (10-27-1827)
Duncan, James to Sinah P. Hannis 7-7-1831
Duncan, John F. to Margaret Brotherton 10-20-1828
Duncan, John to Malinda Duncan 2-17-1830 (2-18-1830)
Duncan, Samuel to Mary James Smith 12-27-1855
Duncan, Thomas L. to Susan Brotherton 6-11-1829 (6-21-1829)
Duncan, Thomas L. to Susan Rosson 6-6-1854 (12-5-1854)
Duncan, William C. to Mary Jane Anthony 12-17-1849
Duncan, Wm. C. to Elizabeth J. Wiley 7-17-1861 (7-18-1861)
Dunlap, N. H. to Mary J. Lake 1-20-1861
Dunn, A. J. to Elizabeth Young 10-7-1853 (10-9-1853)
Dunn, Bartholomew to Catharine Whittier Bond 5-27-1834 (5-29-1834)
Dunn, Cullen to Abbe Boyte 3-8-1833
Dunn, John R. to Elizabeth Campbell 10-7-1847
Dunn, William to Hannah Mathis 10-24-1859
Dunn, William to Margaret Cook 2-14-1851 (2-16-1851)
Durden, William to Jane Bryant 11-30-1854 (12-3-1854)
Durrum, Henry H. to Anny Martin 10-5-1826
Dyal?, Greenberry to Nancy M. Wilson 6-13-1836
Dyke, Thomas B. to Peggy Rogers 1-26-1838 (1-8?-1838)
Dyson, Hezekiah to Mary Clark 2-14-1860 (3-18-1860)
Easom, John to Matilda Alsop 8-20-1851 (8-24-1851)
Easter, Jackville R. to America Whitaker 6-27-1833 (6-30-1833)
Easterwood, Wm. W. to Susan Lee 12-30-1844 (12-31-1844)
Eastlack, Joseph M. to Caroline Carroll 2-5-1844
Eastman, Charles F. to Elizabeth Colbert 7-28-1834 (7-29-1834)
Easum(Eastham?), H. O. to Elizabeth Robinson 3-29-1848
Eaton, David W. to Amanda Newman 10-9-1855
Eaton, J. L. to Mary J. Cearley 2-8-1862
Eaton, John sr. to Sarah C. Johnson 9-13-1858 (9-14-1858)
Eaton, Wm. to Nancy J. Freels 9-21-1860 (9-23-1860)
Eddlemon, F. J. G. to Susan F. Adams 3-3-1856 (3-6-1856)
Edmonson, William to Nancy L. Leech 12-2-1833
Edmundson, D. M. to Lavanda Shaw 9-15-1832 (9-18-1832)
Edwards, Amos A. to Mary Elizabeth Stephenson 8-5-1850 (8-6-1850)
Edwards, Benj. J. to Martha R. Stephenson 10-28-1854 (10-29-1854)
Edwards, David K. to Mary Jane Crawford 4-30-1853 (5-1-1853)
Edwards, Harbert H. to Nancy C. Webb 11-10-1853 (11-13-1853)
Edwards, Jacob L. to Sally Boydston 2-7-1824 (2-8-1824)
Edwards, James A. to Nancy Murphy 5-30-1848 (6-1-1848)
Edwards, James B. to Elisa Virginia Wilkinson 10-29-1827 (10-30-1827)
Edwards, James to Elizabeth Edwards 11-5-1849 (11-8-1849)
Edwards, Jas. to Eliza J. Simmons 12-18-1843

Elerson, Green? B. to Susannah Glenn 11-18-1845 (11-20-1845)
Elgin, John to Nancy O. Hughes 3-24-1839 (3-25-1839)
Elgin, Robert to Mary A. Norment 3-19-1827 (3-21-1827)
Elkins, Hiram to Margaret Henson 12-24-1850 (12-29-1850)
Elkins, Miles to Caroline Coor(Coon) 7-31-1838 (8-2-1838)
Elks, F. to P. Reecks? 3-22-1860
Elks, William B. to Sarah Jane Holliday 7-16-1850 (7-21-1850)
Elliott, Andrew C. to Alphia Johnson 10-18-1828 (10-19-1828)
Ellis, JSames F. to Cornelia Nixon 5-12-1827
Ellis, Nathl. D. to Elizabeth Adams 12-3-1833 (12-5-1833)
Ellison, John to Dorothy H. Teague 2-20-1843 (2-21-1843)
Ellison, Timothy to Elizabeth Lackey 7-18-1839
Elmore, J. W. to Georgeanna Robinson 11-27-1850 (11-28-1850)
Elmore, Thomas G. to Ann Burns 4-28-1834
Embrey, Rubin A. to Jane Townsend 3-7-1835
Enis, Saml. to Cathanne(Catharine) Gray 2-18-1858
Erven, William C. to Margarett Eveline Mills 2-6-1847 (2-7-1847)
Ervin, Theophilus to Jane Dillard 1-22-1861
Ervin, William C. to Ann T. L. Bell 7-12-1855 (7-15-1855)
Ervin, William to Lucinda Burleson 7-23-1835
Ervin, Wm. C. to Catharine W. Parker 5-19-1841
Eskew(Askew?), Nathan Berry to Mary Brown 3-6-1849
Eskew, Alford to Orphy Dority(Daugherty?) 3-9-1846 (3-11-1846)
Eskew?, Enoch to Sarah Ann Crawford 4-22-1847 (4-18?-1847)
Eskue?, Enoch to Mary Matilda Ross 7-29-1841
Estes, Andrew J. to Julian Lambert 1-30-1850 (1-31-1850)
Estes, Asa to Minerva Long 11-29-1827
Estes, Erwin to Sarah Waller 9-9-1861
Estes, Joshua to Martha Carley 6-8-1838 (6-10-1838)
Estes, Joshua to Martha Wood 3-25-1843 (3-26-1843)
Estes, Major to Rhoda Wood 10-23-1845
Estes, P. N. to Nancy Sweeton 10-3-1861
Estes, Reubin to Martha J. Lambert 1-6-1846 (1-6-1846)
Eubanks, J. T. to Mary E. McGowan 12-20-1858 (12-24-1858)
Evans, David to Elizabeth Donnell 2-6-1843 (2-9-1843)
Evans, David to Mary Ann Elkins 12-24-1861 (12-26-1861)
Evans, G. C. to Virginia A. Cross 2-7-1857 (2-12-1857)
Evans, Henry to Mary Deason? 12-4-1839
Evans, Serel to Minerva Wilson 8-31-1833 (?-19-183-)
Evans, Wm. H. to Mary Davis 10-4-1859 (10-6-1859)
Evens, Thomas to Nancy A. Marsh 9-13-1848 (9-14-1848)
Evens, William Henry to Susan Young 2-11-1851 (2-13-1851)
Everett, James A. K. M. to Margaret Williams 11-13-1860
Ewell, R. H. D. to ElizabethS. Sheppard 11-2-1843
Ewing, Newton A. to Nancy N. Lorant 12-15-1829
Fackler, C. W. to Hattie A. Watkins 1-15-1859
Faison, Wm. to Temperance Crawford 2-2-1846 (2-5-1846)
Falls, H. H. to Seragh Jane Scott 10-27-1852 (10-28-1852)
Faris, Anderson to Eliza C. Reaves 7-29-1840 (7-30?-1840)
Faris, Moses B. to Nancy Savage 10-26-1842 (10-28-1842)
Farley, William W. to Mary Jane Redd 4-17-1851 (4-20-1851)
Farned, Wm. M. to Tabitha A. Floyd 11-12-1857 (11-15-1857)
Farris, James to Eighty Scott 5-15-1848
Farris, Thos. J. to Sarah T. Steward 12-23-1856 (12-25-1856)
Farris, W. N. to Mary Ann Johnson 10-4-1838
Faucett, John M. to Sarah Ann Cox 3-26-1853 (3-29-1853)
Faucett, Josiah T. to Malinda Huddleston 5-13-1853 (5-17-1853)
Fausett, William T. to Sarah A. Murrell 12-24-1850
Fawcett, Wm. E. to Ardenia F. Grace 7-26-1859
Feagan, Thomas H. to Martha I.? Gray 11-14-1843 (11-15-1843)
Fellow, William to Penny Spurlin 6-3-1831 (6-12-1831)
Fennel, Charles Fox to Sallie F. Hartsfield 11-22-1859 (11-23-1859)
Fenner, Joseph F. to Mary M. Gossett 8-31-1852 (8-30?-1852)
Fentress, James to Mary T. Perkins 8-24-1859
Fentress, John R. to Anne E. Fitzhugh 6-15-1848
Ferguson, F. W. to Margaret Lawrence 2-4-1837
Ferguson, J. L. to E. J. Bailey 11-29-1850
Ferguson, J. T. to F. E. Camp 10-17-1861 (10-22-1861)
Ferguson, James L. to Telitha C. Hood 11-28-1855 (11-29-1855)
Ferguson, T. J. to A. E. Dixon 9-12-1861 (10-21-1861)
Ferguson, Will F. to Marietta Howell 11-27-1854 (11-29-1854)
Ferrell, James to Dosha Riplogle 6-21-1851 (7-24-1851)
Ferrell, John B. to Malinda Gaddy 8-28-1856
Ferrell, Wm. B. to Catharine Marsh 11-17-1851 (11-19-1851)
Ferrill, Thomas to Nancy Rogers 10-7-1853

Fewell, WilliamH. to Mary E. West 2-8-1844 (2-9-1844)
Field, Billam? to Mahaly Williamson 12-4-1830
Field, James M. to Frances Z. McKinnie 8-11-1855 (8-12-1855)
Fields, James W. to Margaret Ramsey 6-18-1838
Fields, Jefferson M. to Diena M. L. Hunter 1-8-1851 (1-9-1851)
Finch, W. A. to Martha J. Smith 11-12-1849 (11-14-1849)
Finley, Jacob to Nancy Parker 11-14-1826
Finley, Richard to Obedience Parker 11-24-1836
Fish, Edwin to Mary J. Cozby 8-13-1855
Fish, James to Olivia C. Parker
Fish, John to Centhia Hicks 9-24-1844 (9-26-1844)
Fitch, John J. to Clarinda Callahan 12-28-1854
Fitzgerald, Clinton to Jemina Hopper 3-9-1833 (3-19-1833)
Fleet, James M. to Susan Prewett 6-14-1843
Fleet, John J. to Emeline Mullikin 1-9-1847
Fleet, Wilie D. to Sarah Knox Barkley 12-24-1850 (12-25-1850)
Fleet, Wm. C. to Caroline Ham 12-15-1842
Fleming, James O. to Elizabeth C. Brown 2-3-1851 (2-4-1851)
Fleming, Joseph to Sarah Core 9-16-1854 (9-21-1854)
Fleming, Thomas to Rachael C. Kirkman 2-12-1859 (2-19-1858?)
Fletcher, Jessee to Sally Ann Cornelius 11-17-1838 (11-18-1838)
Flin, Isaiah to Rhoda Teague 12-31-1828
Flowers, Ickabad to Jane Partridge 12-21-1833
Floyd, John C. to Nelly McNeely 12-29-1839 (1-2-1840)
Floyd, Thomas to Nancy Reynolds 2-29-1840 (3-4-1840)
Floyd, Thomas to Sarah Horn 9-11-1838 (9-13-1838)
Folts, Harrison G. to Mary Jane White 6-7-1841
Folts, J. C. to Sophronia E. Poston 12-23-1844
Forbers, H. J. to Fred E. Bagley 8-31-1861 (9-5-1861)
Forbis, John to Julian Childress 12-5-1832
Forbush, Overton to Martha M. Moore 10-6-1834 (10-10-1834)
Ford, Augustin P. to Pearcy Ann Lee 8-9-1849
Ford, Jefferson to Polly Cain 6-31?-1828 (7-3-1828)
Ford, John F. to Margarett E. Williams 10-13-1828
Ford, Robert to Mary Murphy 10-8-1836
Ford, William to Martha Magee 12-7-1840
Forehana, Solomon to Telitha Ammons 11-29-1837
Foren, Moses to Ciely Reagan 4-27-1824 (4-29-1824)
Forte, Elias to Nancy Simmons 10-13-1825 (10-15-1825)
Fortenberry, Wm. J. to Annisy Allen 8-10-1842 (8-11-1842)
Fortner, Benjamin to Elizabeth C. Bryant 12-15-1847 (12-21-1847)
Fortner, David to Mary Jackson 9-10-1859 (9-11-1859)
Fortner, Efel D. to Margaret Nabers 6-23-1838 (7-1-1838)
Fortner, George W. to Martha Elizabeth Anthony 12-22-1852 (12-23-1852)
Fortner, James M. to Frances J. Cross 2-5-1850 (2-10-1850)
Fortner, Robt. J. to Elizabeth Grantham 8-6-1856 (8-7-1856)
Fortner, Sample A. to Nancy (Jane) Rankin 1-9-1858 (2-11-1858)
Fortune, E. F. to Frances Johnson 11-17-1855 (11-6?-1855)
Fortune, James V. to Mary E. Thompson 8-4-1856 (8-7-1856)
Fortune, NiNicholass to Racheal Pascal 4-30-1834
Fortune, Wm. N. to Susan E. Stewart 5-15-1861
Foster, A. D. S. to Elizabeth J. Punch 4-26-1856 (4-27-1856)
Foster, Amos to Eliza Parks 9-30-1826 (10-3?-1826)
Foster, Braddock to Marcilla C. Brown 2-11-1860 (2-14-1860)
Foster, Bryant to Nancy Ann Tilmon 12-2-1841
Foster, Daniel D. to Martha S Lemings 12-17-1860 (12-27-1860)
Foster, Joel to Margaret Nixon 9-22-1829
Foster, John C. to Samira C. Craven 12-22-1854 (12-24-1854)
Foster, John to Frances A. McKee 1-6-1851 (1-7-1851)
Foster, John to Sarah Ann Simpkin 5-5-1830 (5-6-1830)
Foster, L. W. to Elizabeth Wilkinson 12-28-1852
Foster, W. B. to Eliza Rogers 5-1-1851
Foster, W. B. to Martha Somers 8-31-1860 (9-2-1860)
Foster, William B. to Ann Rogers 5-1-1835 (5-14-1835)
Foster, William J. to Lavina J. Craven 12-27-1854 (12-28-1854)
Fowler, J. C. H. to Jane Darnell 11-1-1850
Fowler, J. C. H. to Jane Darnell 7-14-1853
Franklin, C. M. to M. E. Thurmond 10-22-1859 (10-27-1859)
Franklin, Jesse B. to May C. Wilson 11-10-1845
Franklin, Jessee D. to Amelia L.(S?) Thurmond 1-25-1849 (1-30-1849)
Franklin, Robert A. to Livinia Jane Wilson 6-29-1842
Frederick, H.K. to Nancy A. Thompson 9-22-1860 (9-23-1860)
Freeman, Aaron to Elizabeth S. Thomas 1-18-1853
Freeman, Aaron to Polly Kindrick 8-23-1853 (8-24-1853)
Freeman, Charles to Allis Anderson 11-15-1845 (11-18-1845)
Freeman, Charles to Melinda Morris 8-28-1843 (8-29-1843)
Freeman, Clark to Harriet Core 5-2-1843 (5-5-1843)
Freeman, John G. to Elvira E. Coburn 2-7-1842 (2-8-1842)
Freeman, John to Liney(Siney) Scott 4-4-1831 (4-14-1831)
Frye?, Shadrach Sl. to Elizabeth Burns 6-28-1834 (7-3-1834)
Fulgham, Pearce to Hester A. Hines 3-3-1832 (3-6-1832)
Fulgham, Wm. to Martha Donnelson 3-10-1831 (3-16-1831)
Fulghum, Benjamin R. to Merinda Crawford 6-22-1840 (6-25-1840)
Fulghum, Raiford to Susan Craig 11-26-1836 (11-27-1836)
Fulps, William G. to Amanda M. Ayers 2-21-1854
Fulton, Eliphlet G. to Eliza A. Davidson 7-21-1845
Furgason, Will O. to Lavender D. Edmonson 10-12-1838 (10-14-1838)
Furguson, Joel to Sarah M. Flint 2-6-1834 (2-11-1834)
Futrel, Isaac to Nancy Alford 3-23-1843 (3-30-1843)
Futrell, Berry to Elizabeth Saul 7-25-1853 (7-28-1853)
Futrell, Isaac to Sarah A. Stewart 2-4-1839 (2-5-1839)
Futrell, Wilie to Sarah Chandler 7-7-1855
Gadd, D. F. to Mary Ann E. Powell 12-9-1857
Gaddy, Wm. H. to Hannah M. Phillips 1-29-1861
Galling(Gatling?), Enoch S. to Elizabeth Champion 9-2-1845
Galloway, Robert to Martha McCrory 8-7-1839 (8-8-1839)
Galloway, William to Rebecca Cox 12-20-1837 (12-21-1837)
Gally, D. B. to Leonora S. O'Brien 6-11-1861
Gamble, Andrew Jackson to Sarah Eliza Robertson 1-6-1852 (1-7-1852)
Gamble, Ephraim B. to Winaford Gray 12-6-1853
Gamble, William to Martha Holder 3-10-1851 (3-13-1851)
Gardner, Henry to Lydia Gardner 11-11-1843 (11-16-1843)
Gardner, Thomas J. to Sarah G. Lawhorn 5-4-1847 (5-?-1847)
Gardner, Thos. J> to Lucy J. Crisp 6-14-1843
Garland, Reubin F. to Susan Ann Elizabeth Greer 7-25-1853 (7-26-1853)
Garner, Brice L. to Susan Anderson 12-16-1840
Garner, John A. to Eliza G. McAlexander 5-4-1850 (5-16-1850)
Garner, John A. to Frances E. Thompson 6-29-1852
Garner, John T. to Rebecca Dillard 8-29-1832 (8-30-1832)
Garner, William to Nancy Richardson 6-2-1835
Garrett, Jacob to Mary Polk 9-12-1829 (10-3-1829)
Garrett, Matthew D. to Joycy Ann Wilkinson 3-6-1843
Garrett, Thomas S. to Elizabeth Jane Mitchell 12-19-1848 (12-21-1848)
Garrett, Turner to Martha A. Fletcher 11-26-1860 (11-27-1860)
Garrison, William B. to Belinda Shipman 12-2-1826 (12-7-1826)
Gates, David A? to Sarah L. Hervell? 11-9-1850
Gates, James F. to Emiline Webster 12-15-1846
Gates, John H. to Eliza M. C. Avent 11-23-1852 (11-25-1852)
Gatewood, John F. to Nancy McDonald 11-3-1840 (11-15-1840)
Gatewood, Wm. to Martha E. Simms 8-1-1858
Gatlin, Andrew S. to Jane West 10-22-1836
Gatlin, John A. to Isabella Woodson 9-17-1854
Gatlin, John A. to Lucy Ann Cross 9-26-1849 (9-27-1849)
Gatlin, John A. to Nancy E. McDaniel 5-19-1855 (5-27-1855)
Gatlin, Riley to Martha C. Shelly 4-26-1835 (4-29-1835)
Gaugh, Eleazar to Maria J. Powell 8-2-1856 (8-3-1856)
Gaugh, Eleazar to Sarah E. Adams 6-25-1861
Gay, B. F. to Marselia Bass 5-21-1857 (5-24-1857)
Gay, Edwin to Margaret McKay 4-3-1829
Gay, Edwin to Margarette Jones 7-19-1855 (11-11-1855)
Gay, Gary to Elizabeth Overall 5-9-1831 (5-10-1831)
Gay, Gary to Minerva Wells(Wills?) 1-29-1850 (1-31-1850)
Gay, John H. to Margaret Y. Biles 12-19-1831
Gay, Lemmon B. to Margaret Cox 12-22-1852 (12-29-1852)
Gay, Lemon to Eliza Wilkerson 1-2-1834
Gayler, Atheriah to Catherine Tiger? 12-3-1834
Gayler, Stephen S. to Polly Ann Murphy 12-14-1839 (12-19-1839)
Gazzam, Charles W. to Clementina Lea 11-29-1827
Gee, Geo. W. to Sarah Lambert 3-10-1852 (3-11-1852)
Gee, James to Nancy Casey 12-18-1847 (12-19-1847)
Gee, Nathan to Diannah Mayfield 11-23-1853 (11-24-1853)
Gentry, Robert to Emily Rhodes 9-29-1851 (9-30-1851)
Geoghegan, John to Mary McDaniel 6-30-1856 (7-1-1856)
Gibson, Archibald to Jane Rogers 11-13-1844
Gibson, George S. to Nancy Henson 1-27-1828 (1-29-1828)
Gibson, Hiel to Sarah Henson 12-23-1846 (12-24-1846)

Gibson, Stephen to Cela A. Highfield 5-28-1856 (5-29-1856)
Gibson, Stephen to Mary Henson 11-1-1836
Gibson, William P. to Ariminta R. Belotte 11-29-1852 (12-16-1852)
Gibson, William to Susan V. Parris 2-28-1861 (3-7-1861)
Gillam, A. P. to E. O. Neal 1-19-1858
Gillaspie, Mathew to Mary Cozby 8-29-1835
Gillet, Amasa to Rebecca McCord 1-9-1844 (1-11-1844)
Gilman, James S. to Martha Meeks 4-10-1857 (4-16-1857)
Gilmore, John S. to Angeline A. Graham 8-28-1860
Gilmore, Richard to Louisa Faughton? 1-9-1837 (1-15-1837)
Givens, John J. to Martha O. Dennis 11-29-1854 (11-29-1854)
Glasgow, G. to Minerva Childress 11-30-1830
Glass, Isaac to Elizabeth Pool 9-11-1848 (9-14-1848)
Glass, James H. to Nancy L.(S.) Davis 1-18-1858 (1-21-1858)
Glass, James S. to Jane Vickers 4-29-1843 (5-4-1843)
Glen, David to Margarett Bookart 9-4-1834
Glenn, James L. to Martha Pace 6-18-1861 (6-23-1861)
Glenn, Lewis to Priscilla Brown 8-9-1836
Glenn, W. L. to Ann Treese 7-26-1859 (7-28-1859)
Glidell, James to Polly Reynolds 9-23-1856
Glidewell, Anderson to Mary Biddy 4-13-1835
Glidewell, Jesse to Polly King 11-7-1842 (11-8-1842)
Glidewell, Robt. to Eliza Jane King 8-5-1845 (8-10-1845)
Glidewell, William W. to Jane Cozby 9-10-1851 (9-28-1851)
Glidwell, Timothy to Mary Ann Timms 8-18-1853
Goad, James M. to M. J. Riggs 7-22-1856 (7-23-1856)
Goad, John A. to Elizabeth Beaver 9-17-1852 (9-22-1852)
Goff, Jessee T. to Elizabeth Sexton 4-11-1848
Goforth, H. M. to Mary Carper 6-20-1859 (6-23-1859)
Goforth, Samuel J. to Martha E. F. Hendricks 10-31-1853
Goforth, W. H. to Elizabeth Gurly 12-8-1854
Goodwin, John to Martha Saunders(Launders?) 3-22-1828
Gordon, Charles R. to Elizabeth Ruddle 4-11-1855 (4-12-1855)
Gordon, John K. to Mary E. Prewett 1-1-1861
Gore, Thomas to Sarah Box 1-8-1840 (1-9-1840)
Gossett, Andrew to Rody E. Muldan 12-26-1831
Gossett, Harvy M. to Elizabeth Roberts 9-15-1841
Gossett, James L. to Priscilla Thompson 3-29-1829
Gossett, John to Frances C. Hatley 1-15-1840
Gossett, V. D. to Mary N.? Hatley 3-21-1825 (3-24-1825)
Gould, John W. to Laura V. Napier 10-17-1853
Grace, J. M. to Ruth Fawcett 3-8-1859
Graham, Elihue G. to Evelina Willouby 8-24-1850 (8-25-1850)
Graham, Elija to Eliza C. Pankey 2-27-1850 (2-28-1850)
Graham, Jo L. to Nancy L. Kerr 11-6-1860 (11-27-1860)
Graham, John C. to Lucinda E. Coburn 1-18-1851 (1-27-1851)
Graham, John M. to Betsy Brantley 5-5-1826 (5-20-1826)
Graham, Nimrod to Mary Jane Macon 8-17-1851
Graham, Thomas G. to Mary Parker 2-8-1838
Graham, Wm. E. M. to Nancy C. Payne 8-16-1843
Grant, Alston to Rebecca Hodges 1-7?-1834
Grantham, Alvin to Mary Ann Carter 12-25-1849
Grantham, Chalkley to Abegill Grantham 5-29-1841 (5-31-1841)
Grantham, G. W. to Elizabeth Flemming 6-30-1858 (7-4-1858)
Grantham, James to Sarah Jane Hale 4-17-1850 (4-24-1850)
Grantham, Joel to Mehala Musgrave 1-1-1829
Grantham, Josiah to Marry A. Harris? 11-3-1859
Grantham, Lewis to Martha L. Fortner 10-11-1853
Grantham, Moses H. to Mary J. Bailey 5-18-1860
Grantham, Richd. to Emily E. Goad 12-5-1844 (12-12-1844)
Grantham, Scion to Betsy(Elizabeth) Rogers 9-29-1838 (10-3-1838)
Grantham, Sion to Clarky Grant 8-31-1833 (9-1-1833)
Grantham, Thomas R. to Mary A. Bizzell 12-16-1857 (12-17-1857)
Grantham, Thomas to Edy Ann Cole 6-23-1841
Grantham, William to Malinda Bell 8-30-1849
Granthan, Solomon to Emily Sacer(Sasser) 9-8-1838 (9-9-1838)
Grave, George E. to Elizabeth Adams 10-25-1829 (11-5-1829)
Graves, Elijah W. to Kezirah Perry 7-7-1845
Gravett, Obediah to Mary L. Ruffin 12-22-1856 (12-24-1856)
Gray, Alfred W. to Elizabeth Laney 4-12-1854 (4-19-1854)
Gray, Alfred W. to Susan Gamble 8-26-1851 (8-27-1851)
Gray, Daniel to Mary A. Glass 1-29-1848 (2-1-1848)
Gray, George to Casandra Rutherford 1-10-1833
Gray, Hugh A. to Martha E. Haily 10-26-1857
Gray, James M. to Mary Grantham 9-5-1850 (9-8-1850)
Gray, James P. to Phetama Phillips 1-31-1843 (2-7-1843)
Gray, Jesse to Minerva Jenkins 3-20-1832
Gray, Thomas D. to Mary A. Harvey 7-13-1838
Gray, Thomas D. to Nancy Gamble 12-23-1848
Gray, William to Lucy A. Gambell 2-7-1839
Green, A. H. to Nancy J. Atkinson 1-15-1855 (1-18-1855)
Green, Sherwood to Lucy K. Macon 6-30-1837 (7-3-1837)
Green, William to Mary Cooksey 1-14-1847
Green, dJohn to Elizabeth Jorden 9-16-1838 (9-18-1838)
Greenly, William to Zilpha Warren 10-12-1834 (10-15-1834)
Greenwood, Malcom H. to Elizabeth C. Boney 6-29-1838 (7-1-1838)
Greer, J. J. H. to Mary A. Goode 7-9-1860
Greer, P. E. to Nancy Mitchael 7-3-1854 (7-4-1854)
Gregg, Charles C. to Mary Hines 2-12-1838
Grice, Jesse G. to Bathis Hart 11-14-1827
Griffin, James R. to Martha Ann James 8-9-1848 (8-10-1848)
Griffin, Jonathan B. to Virginia W. Petigrue 12-30-1852
Griffin, Michael to Mahala Sweeton 4-19-1860
Griggs, H. C. to Elizabeth Murphy 9-9-1854 (9-13-1854)
Griggs, William M. to Elizabeth A. Riddle 1-31-1849 (2-1-1849)
Grimmet, Charles to Cynthia C. Ross 8-27-1860 (8-28-1860)
Grisham, James to Thiaza Autry 5-8-1830 (5-15-1830)
Grissom, Enons J. to Elizabeth Campbell 7-4-1846 (7-9-1846)
Grove, James H. to Jane H. Harris 1-29-1850 (1-31-1850)
Grove, John L. to Margaret Thompson 1-2-1860 (1-24-1860)
Grove, William B. to Emeline C. Rivers 12-22-1831 (12-23-1831)
Groves, William R. to Mary Martha Malery 7-1-1848 (7-2-1848)
Gruber, M. W. to Mary E. Carper 8-9-1859 (7?-14-1859)
Guffey, John to Malinda Williams 12-28-1835
Guin, Danl. M. to Olivia Ricks 9-13-1832
Gullender?, John C. to Racheal Davis 1-18-1835
Gunter, James M. to Elender Jones 4-7-1828 (4-13-1828)
Gurley, James H. to Frances E. Robertson 7-29-1848 (8-1-1848)
Guthrie, Daniel to Nancy Rainey 1-17-1848 (1-18-1848)
Guthrie, Orin to Eliza Davis 1-23-1829
Guthry, Orrin to Nancy Boyd 1-20-1827 (1-21-1827)
Gwyn, Hugh A. to Sally G. Dickinson 6-7-1852 (6-9-1852)
Gwyn, R. R. to Mary C. Dickinson 11-1-1854 (11-9-1854)
Hackney, Joseph D. to Malinda Pirtle 11-15-1852
Hail, Shadrich to Amanda Brown 8-2-1837 (8-3-1837)
Haile(Hails?), Fleming to Silphia Williams 5-25-1829 (5-1?-1829?)
Hailey, Gastin to Margaret J. Todd 12-14-1859 (12-15-1859)
Hainline, Benjamin R. to Nancy Chesher 7-27-1847 (7-29-1847)
Hainline, Benjamin to Marcella Frances Drake 6-13-1857 (6-16-1857)
Hainline, Jacob to Mary Jane D. Muse 12-26-1839 (1-16-1840)
Hale, Alexander to Martha Sanders 7-22-1831 (7-?-1831)
Hale, James B. to Mary E. Savage 10-18-1851 (10-30-1851)
Haley, Franklin to Tabitha J. Cox 9-4-1858 (9-5-1858)
Hall(Hale), D. W. to Catharine Childress 6-19-1837 (6-20-1837)
Hall, Albert A. to Dorthey E. Whitaker 11-6-1826 (11-14-1826)
Hall, George H. to Margarett Thompson 9-13-1834
Hall, James W. to Eliza B. Carnes 3-16-1840
Hall, Josiah to Mary Jane Laney 4-22-1854 (4-23-1854)
Hall, Laban to A. P. Carr 12-21-1857
Hall, M. W. to Mary A. E. Barnes? 5-27-1858 (6-10-1858)
Hall, M. W. to Nancy T. Hadden 4-27-1861 (4-29-1861)
Hall, W. S. to S. J. Nelson 12-19-1861
Hall, William to Nancy Elmiria? Barker 5-7-1842 (5-8-1842)
Haltom, B. F. to Elizabeth Barrett 9-24-1856
Haltom, Benj. F. to Julian Suggs 12-15-1855 (12-19-1855)
Haltom, N. P. to Martha J. Henson 10-10-1861 (10-13-1861)
Halton, Eli to Nancy J. Garrett 11-10-1856 (11-12-1856)
Ham, David F. to Harriett A. Moore 7-11-1840 (7-17-1840)
Ham, William to Maria Moore 12-3-1850 (12-4-1850)
Ham, Willie to Susan S. Moore 5-1-1844 (5-2-1844)
Hamblin, Benjamin to Susannah Newton 12-18-1831 (12-23-1831)
Hamblin, William to Elizabeth Croslin 7-23-1824
Hamer, A. M. to Laura J. Hardison 11-29-1858
Hamer, A. M. to Sarah Ann Janes 12-2-1854 (12-5-1854)
Hamer, Milton J. to Mary Ann Shepperd 11-7-1838 (11-8-1838)
Hamer, P. O. to Mary J. Moss 1-18-1854
Hamer, Thomas to Sarah Mask 11-10-1856 (11-19-1856)
Hamilton, Alexander to Emily Huddleston 10-16-1852 (10-17-1852)
Hamilton, J. A. to Mary Ann Nail 9-16-1837 (9-19-1837)
Hamilton, James to Elizabeth Breeding 1-2-1830

Hamilton, James to Mary Mills 7-19-1845 (7-20-1845)
Hamilton, James to Nancy Burney 10-6-1856
Hamilton, John to Nancy Grantham 9-24-1842 (9-25-1842)
Hamilton, Randle to Frances Spurling 12-11-1833
Hamilton, Thomas to Ruthy Steel 11-29-1828 (12-4-1828)
Hamilton, William to Narcissa Jane Wilks 7-27-1835
Hamlin, John to Nancy Bennet 9-8-1828 (9-9-1828)
Hamlin, William to Lydia Ann Brown 7-10-1847 (7-18-1847)
Hamlin, William to Lydia Ann Kinard 12-7-1846
Hammers, Joel to Lydia Tims 8-31-1846 (9-3-1846)
Hammon, Isaac to Elizabeth King 11-2-1830
Hammonds, E. D. to Elizabeth Thomas 9-24-1859
Hammons, Thomas D. to Lucinda Thomas 12-19-1837
Hammons, William H. to Mary Jane Mashburn 2-26-1853 (2-27-1853)
Hancock, Thomas H. to Sarah Usher 2-9-1848 (2-10-1848)
Hancock, Thos. H. to Elmira J. Anderson 2-24-1859
Hancock, W. F. to Catharine M. Mask 9-10-1855 (9-13-1855)
Haney, Benjamin to Thursday Matilda Littrull? 7-14-1849 (9-7-1849)
Haney, Lindsey to Eliz R. Futill 8-12-1839 (8-13-1839)
Hanis, Martin L. to June Mitchell 12-16-1845
Hank, Hansford to Susan Foster 1-7-1829 (1-11-1829)
Hankins, Thos. D. to Ruth G. Casey 1-7-1860 (1-8-1860)
Hankins, W. D. to Satira Savage 6-1-1861 (6-2-1861)
Hanks, Allen to Elizabeth Wolverton 1-23-1833 (1-24-1833)
Hanna, James to Nancy Stewart 4-9-1842
Hannis, David S. to Charlotte Caraway 12-26-1849
Hannis, Samuel to Mary Taylor 4-10-1824 (4-11-1824)
Hannis, William D. to Tabitha D. Carricker 7-15-1848 (7-20-1848)
Hansard, James to Lydia Allen 6-23-1849 (6-24-1849)
Hansford, G. W. to R. E. McCarver 4-10-1856 (4-16-1856)
Hardage, John B. to Malinda Dean 11-6-1837
Hardcastle, John to Sarah Moon(Moore) 6-26-1830
Hardeman, John M. to Mary Hardeman 5-13-1828
Hardin, John C. to Elly Jane Robinson 1-2-1858
Hardin, Martin L. to Helen C. Harriss 6-22-1846 (6-25-1846)
Hardison, Asa J. to Martha Land 3-18-1858
Hardison, William B. to N. A. C. White 3-18-1851 (3-19-1851)
Hardridge, Wm. to Martha Cain 12-24-1831 (12-?-1831)
Hardwick, Robert C. to Margaret C. Moon(Moore?) 2-28-1850 (2-7?-1850)
Hardy, Henry H. to Melvina Moss 10-21-1846
Hardy, Rufus S. to Isabela Jane McDowell 9-9-1847
Hardy, William to Sally Ann Williams 2-1-1847 (2-4-1847)
Harehaw, S. M. to Sarah S. Bogue 9-1-1860
Hargrove, L. M. to Nancy Farriss 11-14-1857 (11-16-1857)
Hargroves, Jackson to Ann Johnson 8-2-1839 (9-2-1839)
Harkins, Hugh to Jane Myrick 2-3-1847
Harley, John to Menerva Shipman 1-5-1829 (1-8-1829)
Harley, Thomas to Martha R. A. Beard 7-2-1849 (7-11-1849)
Harlin(Hardin?), Ellis to Synthia Sweeton 8-14-1826 (8-15-1826)
Harlon, Wyatte to Julia Ann Tuning?(Luning?) 9-19-1850
Harlow, James to Mary E. McGuire 9-16-1848 (9-18-1848)
Harper, Danl. to Mary D. Jones 10-14-1825
Harper, Moses to Ruth Box 2-14-1843 (2-15-1843)
Harper, Samuel B. to Ann S. Jones 12-27-1827 (1-1-1828)
Harrell(Howell), Joab to Anide May 1-11-1834 (1-13-1834)
Harrell(Howell?), Thomas C. to Elizabeth E. Howell? 10-13-1846
Harrell, James W. to Nancy Jane Pace 8-20-1855 (8-21-1855)
Harriman, Jos. to Elizabeth R. Vinson 9-17-1859 (9-18-1859)
Harriman, Stephen to Parrylee Ellen Harty 9-6-1858 (9-12-1858)
Harrington, Saml. J. to Elizabeth N. Jarman 1-28-1846 (1-30-1846)
Harris, Eli to Elizabeth Owen 12-13-1832
Harris, Eli to Susan N. McKinnie 7-22-1848 (7-27-1848)
Harris, G. P. to Mary C. Chisum 5-16-1860 (5-23-1860)
Harris, George W. to Martha W. Lake 5-7-1836
Harris, Gillum to Sarah Parker 9-2-1834
Harris, Isaac R. to Elizabeth Turner 6-18-1850
Harris, James B. to Mary Ann Robb 4-22-1835
Harris, James to Martha Fenler? 12-15-1834
Harris, Jerimiah to Catharine King 3-22-1836
Harris, John C. to Sarilla Thompson 10-17-1827 (10-18-1827)
Harris, John to Jane Sulivan 7-10-1854 (7-18-1854)
Harris, Loami to Frances K. Bonds 11-13-1854 (11-14-1854)
Harris, Orris to Lucille W. Price 8-30-1858
Harris, Samuel B. to Exy(Elizabeth) S. Elkins 1-14-1834 (1-14-1834)
Harris, Thomas D. to Ann E. Haltom 12-15-1860
Harris, Thomas L. to Fannie W. Ray 10-19-1859 (10-26-1859)
Harris, Thomas to Lucinda Cheshier 10-17-1838 (10-18-1838)
Harris, Thomas to Margaret Willoughby 12-3-1835
Harris, Turner J. to Ann E. V. Bates 4-1-1854 (4-2-1854)
Harrison, Cris R. to Sarah R. Adams 4-22-1845
Harrison, David to Elizabeth Forsyth 10-1-1840 (10-4-1840)
Harrison, Francis M. to Mary Ann Cole 8-13-1852 (8-14-1852)
Harrison, Harmon to Rebecca J. Doyle 12-21-1858 (12-22-1858)
Harrison, James C. to Margaret Cole 8-13-1852 (9-19-1852)
Harrison, James Hutson to Alvira Cheshier 4-1-1844 (4-2-1844)
Harrison, John B. to Elizabeth McGee 10-27-1842
Harrison, John W. to Manervia Ann Dial 7-23-1844 (7-24-1844)
Harrison, L. M. to Sarah Jane Craig 10-15-1857 (10-18-1857)
Harrison, Robert to Nancy Duboyce 3-1-1830 (3-2-1830)
Harrison, Wm. R. to Milley Forsythe 4-29-1840 (4-30-1840)
Harrison, Wm. to Polly Irvin 2-18-1830
Harriss, Benjamin A. to Rebecca Pirtle 12-27-1837 (12-28-1837)
Harriss, Eli to Martha M. Forbuss 2-25-1846 (2-26-1846)
Harriss, J. B. to Mary E. Rogers 10-12-1857 (11-8-1857)
Harriss, James H. to Isabella Adams 10-28-1847
Harriss, Jesse to Percilla Simmons 9-20-1856 (10-1[7]-1856)
Harriss, West to E. J. Clinton 10-29-1857
Harriss, West to Mary Ann Palmer? 11-25-1846 (11-26-1846)
Harty, Jacob to Alsy Eaton 9-26-1845 (10-1-1845)
Harty, John R. to Juda E. Scoggins 8-16-1855
Harvard(Howard?), James W. to Winneford C. Moore 2-3-1842
Harvey, Abner to Minney(Winney) W. Duncan 2-12-1836 (1?-17?-1836)
Harvey, Albert G. to Martha G. Joyner 5-16-1848
Harvey, James M. to Margret Murphy 4-14-1845
Harvey, Jesse S. to Mary A. Hamlett 8-14-1855 (8-15-1855)
Harvey, Oney S. to Elizabeth C. Murphy 12-29-1847 (12-30-1847)
Harvey, Samuel to Sarah Vaught 8-1-1844 (8-20-1844)
Harvey, Thomas to Jane Cartwright 5-20-1859 (5-22-1859)
Haskins, James V. to Elisabeth Smith 11-30-1857 (12-10-1857)
Hassal, James to Mary King 8-31-1840
Hatch, Henry to Sarah Wilson 9-21-1858 (9-23-1858)
Hatley, Richard to Mary Reagan 1-5-1825 (1-9-1825)
Haulton, Elisha to Amanda Roark 6-25-1850 (6-28-1850)
Hawkins, Bray to Sarah King 4-16-1840
Hawkins, Ralph to Susan Jane Erwin 9-14-1861 (9-16-1861)
Hays, Andrew J. to Sarah Brock 9-11-1841 (10-12-1841)
Hays, H. Scruggs to Elizabeth J. Cozby 6-4-1856 (6-5-1856)
Hays, Isaac to Eliza Kennedy 11-19-1832 (11-22-1832)
Hays, Larkin to Giley Kernay? 12-17-1829
Hays, Robert to Eliza Hart 6-4-1827 (6-7-1827)
Hays, Samuel E. to Hannah Scott 2-6-1835 *
Hays, Samuel E. to Hannah Scott 2-6-1836 (2-11-1836)
Hays, Wm. G. to Nancy Henson 3-7-1833
Haywood, Egbert to Sarah Johnson 5-7-1828 (5-10-1828)
Haywood, William to Eliza Jones 3-27-1836
Hazlegrove, George W. to Cary Alsop 12-18-1847 (12-23-1847)
Hazlewood, Joshua to Catharine Tate 5-27-1826 (6-7?-1826)
Hazlewood, William to Mary Ann Tate 5-29-1827
Heaslet, James A. to Emily Philpott 5-3-1827
Heatcock, Ruebin to Julia Ann Hopkins 5-22-1838
Heckon?, James L. to Harriet E. Webb 12-20-1858
Hendley, Leonard W. to Syrena McDanile 12-10-1839
Hendly, Joseph to Susan Patridge 2-24-1839
Hendricks, John B. to Mary Elizabeth Morgan 10-20-1828 (10-25-1828)
Henley, William to Elizabeth Terry 10-6-1853 (10-7-1853)
Henly, William to Rebecca Cooksey 11-19-1834 (11-20-1834)
Henry(Heniny), A. J. to Anna Hughes 9-28-1829
Henry, C. W. to Mrs. S. B. Wilkerson 11-28-1851 (12-10-1851)
Henry, George W. to Nancy R. Kindrick 2-17-1855 (2-21-1855)
Henry, Thomas to Roberta D. Alexander 3-3-1859
Henry?, William B. to Mary Garrett 4-7-1847
Henslee, Enoch to Maranda Box 1-6-1859 (5-29-1859)
Hensley, George W. to Margaret Crawford 6-7-1843 (6-13-1843)
Hensly, Martin to Rachel M. C. Thrasher 1-22-1846 (1-23-1846)
Henson, Andrew T. to Margaret E. Babb 1-28-1850 (1-29-1850)
Henson, Daniel to Mary J. Ross 10-19-1860
Henson, George to Mary E. Carley 1-24-1861

Henson, Jesse to Sarah Sperling 3-7-1827 (3-14-1827)
Henson, John sr. to Charlotte Patterson 3-28-1859 (3-29-1859)
Henson, John to Arrena Odum 10-21-1848 (10-22-1848)
Henson, John to Polly Phillips 12-19-1856
Henson, Joseph J. to Sarah C. Rogers 2-22-1851 (3-5-1851)
Henson, Saml. to Susan King 10-17-1838 (10-18-1838)
Henson, Samuel to Lotty Cozby 9-21-1849 (9-23-1849)
Henson, Will to Elizabeth Jones 2-21-1835
Henson, Wm. to Talitha Pipkins 6-2-1856
Herndon, B. R. to S. A. Sadler 11-24-1849
Herndon, Wm. H. to Margaret Y. Martin 2-20-1841
Herrell, Wm. to Nancy Lewis 8-5-1857 (8-11-1857)
Herriman, Stephen to Nancy Welch 1-25-1851 (1-26-1851)
Herryman, Joseph to Louisa Jane Harty 11-10-1842
Hervey(Harvey?), Thomas R. to Lucinda Jones 5-29-1848 (6-1-1848)
Hervey, Calvin M. to Temperance H. Williams 12-14-1841
Hester, Robert H. to Judah Anderson 9-30-1846
Hester, Thomas to Mary Gay 9-30-1850
Hester, Wyatt to Eliza B. Jones 12-2-1823 (12-4-1823)
Hewett, W. H. to M. A. Norton 5-17-1858 (5-20-1858)
Hickman, Thomas to Margrett K. Ross 3-9-1847 (4-8-1847)
Hickman, Wyatt to Mary A. Thompson 2-16-1838 (2-20-1838)
Hicks, C. H. to Luch sH. Ingram 10-6-1848
Hicks, Green B. to Sally Hicks 3-26-1844 (3-28-1844)
Hicks, John T. to M. E. Robertson 12-28-1859
Hicks, N. B. to Exes Jane Mauldin 2-29-1840 (3-12-1840)
Hicks, Thos. J. to Rebecca Jane Casey 12-22-1856 (12-23-1856)
Hicks, W. W. B. to Mary A. Ray 12-30-1857
Hicks, William to Mary Cox 3-14-1828 (3-18-1828)
Higgs, Reuben to Rebecca Mangum 11-6-1844 (11-10-1844)
Higgs, Theophelus to Margaret B. Chears 1-24-1856 (1-31-1856)
Higgs, Thomas to Margret Rosson 12-30-1845
High, James to Ann Adeline Brown 9-8-1838 (9-10-1838)
High, William to Ann Eliza Hester 8-8-1837
Highfield, Bennett to Margrett Johnson 12-29-1846 (12-31-1846)
Highfield, Hezekiah to Tempe Rook 9-17-1829
Highfield, Jerimiah to Malinda Nabers 11-10-1851 (11-11-1851)
Highfill, James to Martha Jackson 4-22-1833 (4-25-1833)
Highfill, William H. to Celia A. Patterson 9-11-1852 (9-19-1852)
Hightower, Stephen to Mary Ann New? 12-19-1836
Hill, Benj. M. to Mary Howell(Harrell) 8-9-1833 (8-15-1833)
Hill, James K. to Nancy S. Smith 5-12-1840 (5-13-1840)
Hill, Jno. C. F. to Mary Owen 12-8-1837
Hill, Josiah M. to Lucinda Caldwell 3-6-1843 (3-7-1843)
Hill, Lewis to Margarett Jackson 12-16-1848 (12-17-1848)
Hill, Napoleon to Mary M. Wood 7-7-1858 (7-8-1858)
Hill, Richard C. to Mary Ann Crews 11-27-1849 (11-29-1849)
Hill, Smith H. to Newoma Harvey 1-13-1844
Hill, Thomas G. to Sarah A. Smith 2-7-1848 (2-8-1848)
Hill, William J. to Edy Turner 2-27-1843
Hillhouse, Benjamin M. to Rachel Norton 12-20-1833
Hines, James W. to Caroline Carter 2-23-1847
Hines, James to Hannah Matilda Beaton 12-27-1848 (12-28-1848)
Hines, James to Mary Beaden 12-21-1860 (1-1-1861)
Hines, Sherrod to Mary Ann Chapman 9-9-1844 (9-?-1844)
Hines, Thomas to Mary Ann Thompson 11-17-1846 (11-19-1846)
Hines, Zephaniah to Sarah Kelly 2-10-1841 (2-11-1841)
Hinson, lHiram G. to Martha J Reagan 9-28-1846 (9-30-1846)
Hizer, Jasper to Mary Ray 2-23-1857 (2-26-1857)
Hobson, J. N. B. to Margaret Pankey 2-13-1860
Hodges, Able to Susan Chapman 7-12-1836
Hodges, James T. to Elizabeth Rogers 12-26-1848 (1-4-1849)
Hodges, John T. to Ann E. Coates 1-9-1850 (1-11-1850)
Hodges, John T. to Mahala Bailey 3-11-1836
Hodges, Jonathan to Winney E. Ammons 1-4-1851 (1-16-1851)
Hodges, William to Eliza Jane Stephenson 12-13-1841
Hogue, J. A. to M. E. Wallace 1-3-1861 (1-4-1861)
Hogue, Samuel A. to Mary F. Smith 3-22-1851 (3-27-1851)
Holcomb, Beverly L. to Eugenia D. V. Hunt 6-25-1829 (7-2-1829)
Holder, John to Nancy Gray 1-30-1854 (2-2-1854)
Holford, John W. to Fannie N. Crews 3-14-1859 (3-15-1859)
Holford, William to Martha Ann Minerva Sylvester 12-22-1840 (12-24-1840)
Hollad, Benjamin to Mary T. Allen 12-1-1831
Hollady, Jeremiah to Elizabeth Smith 6-5-1847 (6-13-1847)
Holland, Charles to Nancy Taylor 8-24-1832
Holland, Charley to Mary Hodge 8-30-1838
Holland, John to Amanda Matthews 4-9-1861
Holland, John to Jullia Ellis 4-1-1859
Hollaway, James P. to Sarah Ozment 4-20-1854 (4-24-1854)
Holley, Calvin J. to Sarah Ann Rogers 10-9-1830 (10-10-1830)
Holley, John D. to Avy Core 4-20-1833
Holley, William to Ann Willheight 4-20-1833
Holliday, Andrew J. to Mary A. McCrewry 12-30-1857
Holliday, Jeremiah to Mary W. White 8-28-1827 (8-31-1827)
Holliday, Martin to Catharine Sims 8-8-1859 (8-9-1859)
Holloway, James P. to M. Pryor Dixon 8-24-1861
Holloway, Nathan to Mary A. Thompson 9-24-1861
Holly, Henry to Mary S. Poiner 9-10-1838 (9-11-1838)
Holly, Hoyle to Sophia Flake 5-12-1835
Holyfield, S. B. to Caroline Guise 2-6-1861 (1?-10-1861)
Holyfield, Wm. R. to Elizabeth C. Ayers 7-8-1839
Hood, Danl. B. to Margaret Ann Davis 9-8-1857 (9-10-1857)
Hood, J. W. to M. A. Sexton 11-17-1860 (11-18-1860)
Hood, John R. to Susan E. Ferguson 12-24-1855
Hood, Robert to Esther A. Ferguson 7-31-1849
Hooks, Robert D. to Charlotte N. Fulgham 3-16-1828 (3-18-1828)
Hooper, F. M. to Malvina E. Patterson 1-21-1861 (1-22-1861)
Hooper, Jeremiah to Eleonor Gilmore 12-30-1841
Hooper, Jeremiah to Mary Murley 12-18-1846 (12-20-1846)
Hooper, John to Cathanne Patterson 2-10-1858
Hooper, Wm. W. to C. A. Marlar 2-19-1845
Hooper, Wm. W. to Martha Marler 8-7-1843
Hopkins, John E. to Judith E. A. Martin 6-30-1838
Hopkins, John E. to Sarah G. Darnell? 9-7-1847 (9-9-1847)
Hopper, Barzillai to Sarah A. W. Jones 5-24-1859 (5-25-1859)
Horn, Willis to Sarah Mullins 7-7-1856 (7-13-1856)
Hornesby, A. G. to Elizabeth Price 2-29-1860 (3-1-1860)
Hornesby, Kimbro E. to Mary C. Bradford 1-2-1860
Hornsby, Kimbro to Martha Ann Sebastian 4-6-1833
Horton, William to Rebecca Thompson 12-24-1834 (12-26-1834)
House, Archibald B. to Eliza Wilks 11-21-1840
House, David to Jane House 12-22-1843
House, John to Elizabeth A. Wilkes 10-15-1860
House, Timothy T. to Sarah Jane Minter 9-12-1853
Houston, Felix to Cynthia Gillespie 6-6-1832
Howard, Andrew J. to Susan S. Ham? 7-23-1850 (7-24-1850)
Howard, Hartwell to Marry Holman 5-17-1829
Howard, Permanis to Mildred Mitchell 1-1-1851
Howard, Wardlaw to Mary Polk 12-29-1834
Howell, David C. to Nancy Jane Jones 12-12-1851 (12-18-1851)
Howell, James to Elizabeth A. Roundtree 7-10-1833 (7-14-1833)
Howell, John R. to Merilla H. Johnson 6-3-1840 (6-4-1840)
Howell, K. P. to Nancy Farris 7-25-1859
Howell, R. W. to Winefred Fulgham 2-15-1835 (2-26-1835)
Howell, Rufus R. to Elizabeth Brown 11-19-1850 (11-24-1850)
Howell, W. R. to Nancy Brown 5-19-1842
Howell, Wm. H. to Amanda M. Hooper 11-29-1861
Howell, Wm. P. to Nancy L. Estes 7-5-1858 (7-8-1858)
Hubbard, Isaac B. to Mary Ann Pirtle 1-3-1849
Hubbard, Isaac M. to Ailsy Warren 6-1-1849 (6-3-1849)
Hubbard, John C. to Clemintine Harris 10-24-1837
Huddleston, David M. to Catharine Huddleston 11-26-1855
Huddleston, Nelson to Charlotte Wilson 10-8-1849 (10-10-1849)
Huddleston, William H. to Mahala Huddleston 3-27-1850
Hudson, G. W. to Susan Cox 12-17-1859 (12-15?-1859)
Hudson, Giles G. to Martha J. S. Hammons 7-1-1853 (7-3-1853)
Hudson, Jarman to Mary Ann Rogers 12-17-1842 (12-20-1842)
Hudson, John to Ellen Smith 11-27-1830 (12-2-1831)
Hudson, John to Mary S. Price 9-4-1845
Hudson, Joshua to Mary Ross 1-12-1842 (1-19-1842)
Hudson, Thomas D. to Rebecca F. Roark 2-9-1854 (2-21-1854)
Hudson, Thos. W. to Elizabeth C. McKinnie 5-7-1846
Hudson, Washington to Lucinda Rutherford 8-19-1836 (9-16-1836)
Hudson, William L. to Nancy C. Litrell 7-11-1853 (7-13-1853)
Hudson, Wm. C. to Lucy E. Humphrey 3-31-1845
Hudspeth, John C. to Nancy E. Cocke 8-30-1834
Huffman, Vance to Sarah Wright 3-26-1857 (3-27-1857)
Hughes, Alexander L. to Jane Park 4-2-1851 (4-3-1851)
Hughes, John C. to Samantha E. Hubbard 3-3-1857

Hughes, William F. to Mary E. Boyd 8-10-1844
Hughes, William to Louisa Joyner jr. 5-18-1854
Hughes, William to Nelly(Ellen) Cox 9-28-1829 (10-2-1829)
Hughey, Jacob to Jane Journagan 8-28-1839 (8-29-1839)
Hull, David to Isabella Matthews 12-5-1842 (12-13-1842)
Hull, J. F. to Elizabeth W. Murphy 3-2-1843
Humphrey, David to Mary Ann Thrift 11-21-1842
Humphrey, E. O. to Julia A. Bunting 12-18-1852 (12-30-1852)
Humphrey, James F. to Angerona Warr 8-16-1852
Humphrey, M. C. to Sallie J. Hall 3-15-1858 (3-17-1858)
Humphries, Ezekial to Mary McKenzie 8-27-1837
Hundley, Calvin C. to Emily J. Jones 5-27-1861 (5-29-1861)
Hunnel, Peter to Mary Savage 1-21-1836
Hunnell, Moses to Maranda Martin 10-8-1838 (10-18-1838)
Hunphreys, Bryant to Pritena Hardwick 4-16-1839 (5-1-1839)
Hunt, B. F. to Elizabeth Cook 10-29-1831 (11-3-1831)
Hunt, Charles W. to Lucy Ann Ruffin 9-2-1834
Hunt, Daniel to Sarah Thurmond 3-21-1833 (3-26-1833)
Hunt, E. N. to Sarah M. Lowe 5-22-1857 (6-4-1857)
Hunt, James W. to Nancy Ann Greenwood 4-19-1843 (4-20-1843)
Hunt, John S. to Catharine Simpson 1-16-1849 (1-17-1849)
Hunter, Geo. J. to Drucilla V. Champ 10-16-1850
Hunter, John to Sarah Fields 5-19-1850 (6-19-1850)
Hurley, John to Mary Gunter 12-28-1835
Hursh, H. H. to E. J. Prewitt 1-23-1862 (1-28-1862)
Hurst, Henry to Amanda Preston 1-11-1850
Hutcheson, Charles W. to Agnes A. B. B. Baugh 2-27-1841 (3-4-1841)
Hutchison, Joseph to L. J. Lallier(Sallier?) 2-21-1857 (2-22-1857)
Hutson, Richard D. to Permelia Dillenham 10-10-1828
Ingram, James F. to Charity Springfield 6-29-1850 (6-30-1850)
Ingram, Needham to Jane Simpson 12-18-1830 (12-23-1830)
Ingram, Samuel P. to Rebecca Scott 11-6-1841 (11-12-1841)
Ingram, Thomas M. to Mary T. S. Jones 10-30-1850 (11-14-1850)
Irion, Thomas to Delila F. Baldwin 5-6-1851
Irion, William to Frances White 1-7-1851 (1-16-1851)
Irvin, James B. to Elizabeth White 12-14-1835 (12-15-1835)
Irvin, James C. to Sarah Herryman 2-4-1836
Irvin, Saml. to Susan W. Rainey 10-2-1837 (10-12-1837)
Irvine, F. W. to Clemintine B. Carnes 11-16-1850 (12-18-1850)
Irwin, Green? L. to Cordelia L. Poiner 12-18-1844
Irwin, Jesse H. to Elizabeth Foster 7-20-1861 (7-22-1861)
Isbell, Johnson to Emilia Duncan 10-15-1827
Isbell, Nathaniel S. to Ally Hicks 11-4-1846 (11-9-1846)
Isbell, R. H. to Elizabeth Hamm 4-24-1841 (4-29-1841)
Isbell, Thomas D. to Frances E. Holyfield 11-10-1838 (11-13-1838)
Isom, John to Elisa Thomas 9-3-1828
Jackson, Andrew to Jane Allen 7-6-1850 (7-10-1850)
Jackson, Andrew to Matilda Tisdale 12-27-1845 (9?-30-1845)
Jackson, Calvin to Martha Patridge 3-23-1852
Jackson, Harmon O. to Cinderralla Hunnell 11-30-1833 (12-4-1833)
Jackson, Harmon to Elizabeth Johnson 12-28-1853 (12-29-1853)
Jackson, Henry to Elizabeth Moon(Moor) 8-2-1832
Jackson, Isaac to Betsy Brooks(Polk?) 10-22-1828 (10-29-1828)
Jackson, James A. to Barbra Cantwell? 11-26-1845 (11-27-1845)
Jackson, James M. to Mary M. Glidwell 5-5-1856 (5-13-1856)
Jackson, James N. to Sarah E. Tims 2-15-1848
Jackson, John to Fanny Gambell 4-18-1845 (4-25-1845)
Jackson, John to Nancy Hill 8-11-1851
Jackson, Needham to Hannah Casy 1-25-1834 (1-26-1834)
Jackson, Robert D. to Melinda King 10-5-1835
Jacobs, Henry to Jane Dillard 5-14-1826 (5-15-1826)
Jacobs, Henry to Mary Fortune 10-11-1854 (10-12-1854)
Jacobs, James M. to Martha Anderson 12-13-1843 (12-14-1843)
Jacobs, James M. to Parmelia Harris 12-2-1858 (12-8-1858)
Jacobs, John J. to Julia Ann Jordan 12-12-1859 (12-15-1859)
Jacobs, John to Martha Lewis 12-9-1829 (12-10-1829)
Jacobs, Solomon to Olive Crawford 1-30-1838 (2-1-1838)
Jacobs, William R. to Jinnetta A. Fortune 12-10-1855 (12-13-1855)
Jacobs, William R. to Martha Whitaker 12-17-1849 (12-20-1849)
Jacobs, William to Sarah Bass 8-4-1824
James, Buckhanan to Jula Ann Poyner 12-20-1845 (12-23-1845)
James, Thomas to Jane G. Lacy 11-1-1836
James, William to Mary Mallery 5-7-1844 (5-21-1844)
James, William to Sarah Barker 1-5-1836
James, William to Sarah E. Williams 3-13-1843
Janes, Andrew F. to Martha Keith 5-15-1861 (5-16-1861)
Jarmon, Richard B. to Tebitha H. Kilpatrick 12-19-1829 (12-24-1829)
Jarmon, Robert F. to Rosanna S. Jarmon 11-14-1845 (11-18-1845)
Jarnigan, James to Jane Philips 10-21-1851
Jarratt, John A. to Harriet Neely 5-7-1857
Jarrett, John A. to Jane C. Durrett 11-30-1842 (12-1-1842)
Jarvis, Regis to Parella Yarbrough 1-5-1836
Jenkins, J. L. to A. M. Prewett 12-24-1860
Jenkins, James G. to Eleanor Terry 8-9-1830
Jenkins, John N. to Susan Fulgham 9-5-1826
Jenkins, Thomas to Sarah C. Roberts 12-6-1841 (12-15-1841)
Jenkins, W. H. to Roena M. Meeks 5-2-1853 (5-10-1853)
Jerman, Jefferson to Mary McKinsey 2-3-1826 (2-7-1826)
Jernigan, James to Margaret A. Howell 2-27-1854 (3-2-1854)
Jernigan, William C. to Mary Ann Taylor 8-16-1849 (8-19-1849)
Jernigan, Wrigdon to Martha Howard(Howell?) 1-28-1848
Jeter, Jessee to C. M. Mitchell 12-2-1849
Jewell, James H. to Sarah M. Park 1-5-1850 (1-6-1850)
Job, P. D. to Mary C. Parks 3-12-1858 (3-16-1858)
Jobe, Henry C. to Amarintha Hudson 2-22-1858 (2-24-1858)
Johnson, Benjamin G. to Mary A. Clark 8-7-1847 (9-12-1847)
Johnson, Berry to Nancy Read 6-10-1834 (6-12-1834)
Johnson, Bryant to Elizabeth Fish 5-9-1849 (5-17-1849)
Johnson, E. L. to C. A. Reasens? 7-15-1846
Johnson, Green B. to Martha C. Orrell? 8-26-1857
Johnson, Henry to Mary Ann Coates 1-3-1857 (1-4-1857)
Johnson, J. H. to Sarah Prewitt 1-4-1849
Johnson, James to Melvina Crisp 8-22-1829 (8-23-1829)
Johnson, John G. to Rebecca Wilkins 2-23-1852 (2-24-1852)
Johnson, John H. to Charity Moore 5-16-1860
Johnson, John M. to Margaret Philips 8-27-1849 (8-29-1849)
Johnson, John P. to Jnnu? Ratliff 5-7-1845 (5-14-1845)
Johnson, John to Elizabeth Jones 12-15-1826 (1-6-1827)
Johnson, Joseph to H. A. Fish 11-19-1859 (11-20-1859)
Johnson, Joshua to Altha Birdsong 10-28-1851 (11-5-1851)
Johnson, Martin to Mary Jones 6-15-1828 (6-19-1828)
Johnson, Michael to Mary A. Holloway 3-30-1857
Johnson, N. K. to Kiziah Brush 12-15-1849 (12-16-1849)
Johnson, Nathan to Eleanor E. Nealy 5-23-1861 (6-2-1861)
Johnson, Nathan to Margaret S. Neely 11-30-1854
Johnson, O. H. P. to Melissa A. Stricklin 7-7-1857 (7-8-1857)
Johnson, William P. to Jane Parks 11-24-1857 (11-26-1857)
Johnson, William to Ann Childress 3-29-1841 (4-1-1841)
Johnson, Wm. C. to Frances Moon(Moore?) 6-1-1846 (6-11-1846)
Johnson, Wm. L. R. to Anna D. Avant 8-22-1861
Johnson, Wm. M. to Margaret J. Johnson 1-4-1862 (1-5-1862)
Jones, Abraham to Matilda Hale 10-4-1834 (10-7-1834)
Jones, Atlas to Mary F. Cheairs 3-7-1853 (3-10-1853)
Jones, Buckner to Jane Cozby 2-28-1829
Jones, Cladius C. to Lucinda G. Bailey 9-1-1834
Jones, David B. to Minerva A. Ladd 10-27-1860 (10-28-1860)
Jones, Henry M. to Lydia Ann Kenneday 8-30-1843 (9-2-1843)
Jones, J. A. to Martha A. Norton 8-24-1858
Jones, James H. to Susan Wells 1-1-1850
Jones, James M. to Jane James 12-16-1841
Jones, James M. to Rebecca Casey 3-18-1835
Jones, James W. to Clemency Jane Jones 10-2-1851
Jones, James to Winaford Duncan 10-5-1848 (11-7-1848)
Jones, Jesse to Unetta? E. Carruth? 8-13-1847 (8-15-1847)
Jones, John A. to Mary Ann Townsend 8-5-1840 (8-9-1840)
Jones, John T. to Martha Swindle 4-13-1836
Jones, John to Lucinda Bates 12-26-1835
Jones, John to Malinda Williams 1-12-1837
Jones, John to Polly Ann Martin 10-26-1826
Jones, Jonothan to Evelina Brown 7-15-1825
Jones, Lemuel to Elisabeth Young 8-6-1846
Jones, Leolen to Susan Dixon 12-10-1857
Jones, Louallen to Eliza V. Bordman 12-20-1844 (12-22-1844)
Jones, Montezuma to A. E. Wood 10-11-1849
Jones, Moses N. to Elisabeth Magby 3-7-1838 (3-11-1838)
Jones, Paul T. to Jane M. Wood 2-26-1849 (3-1-1849)
Jones, Phillip R. to Mary Jane White 9-22-1841 (10-5-1841)
Jones, R. D. to Mary Reeves 2-28-1856 (3-5-1856)
Jones, Robert Alexander to Nancy J. Haynes 7-31-1856
Jones, Robert to Melinda Yewing(Ewing) 4-2-1827 (4-5-1827)

Jones, Samuel D. to Julia Ann Allen 1-5-1843
Jones, Stephen B. to Elizabeth C. Roberts 9-9-1839
Jones, Stephen jr. to Margaret Fitzgerald 9-19-1832 (9-27-1832)
Jones, Stephen to Surany? Matthews 11-11-1836 (11-13-1836)
Jones, Thomas C. to Mary C. Irons 5-17-1837
Jones, Tignell to Mary E. Lankford 3-8-1861
Jones, Wilie to Minnerva A. Estes 9-21-1849 (9-23-1849)
Jones, Wilie to Sarah Holliday 12-26-1837
Jones, William E. to Fanny M. Kirkland 9-3-185 (9-6-1855)
Jones, William J. to Minervia Campbell 6-8-1848 (6-11-1848)
Jones, William L. to Mary C. Joyner 12-7-1843
Jones, William to Martha A. Wilbanks 12-28-1860 (1-1-1861)
Jones, William to Mary E. Cavinar 7-12-1850 (7-14-1850)
Jones, William to Neomi Robertson 4-19-1838 (4-26-1838)
Jones, Wm. B. to Delelah Short 4-25-1846 (4-30-1846)
Jones, Wm. H. to Ann Adams 10-26-1842 (11-3-1842)
Jones, Wm. T. to Sarah Comer 12-5-1855
Jordon, James to Lucinda Robertson 1-20-1846
Joslyn, John to Joysy W. Thomas 11-15-1833 (11-21-1833)
Josslyn, Silas M. to Elizabeth A. Thomas 9-10-1833 (9-19-1833)
Jourdan, C. P. to Zilphy Cherry 10-26-1847 (10-28-1847)
Jourdan, James S. to Wincy Macon 1-3-1848 (1-6-1848)
Jouvenat, E. to Minnie Morris 1-15-1862
Joy, Christopher G. to Ellen D. Nappier 12-22-1842
Joyce, Archibald to Louisa Denny 1-1-1838
Joyce, Hardin to Mary Smalley 4-16-1838 (4-19-1838?)
Joyner, J. R. to S. A. Janes 11-5-1860 (11-8-1860)
Joyner, Jonathan to Mary Jane Crews 4-14-1858 (4-20-1858)
Joyner, Mathew to Mary Ann Nutt? 7-3-1837 (7-4-1837)
Justice, Daniel to Frances A. Webb 2-16-1856 (2-17-1856)
Justice, John W. to Lucy W. Shearin 12-23-1858
Justice, Samuel H. to Arlesa Yarbrough 3-16-1853 (3-17-1853)
Justice, William A. to Susan H. Felts 1-5-1854
Justice, Wm. M. to Bethuenia P. Rogers 12-25-1861 (1-1-1862)
Kearney, Philip I.? to Sarah Ramsey 1-6-1829
Keith, A. D. to M. O. Stockton 9-14-1854
Kelly, Alfred to Malinda Shelby 2-16-1835
Kelly, Daniel G. to Susan E. Field 4-3-1843 (4-5-1843)
Kelly, John to Marinda Pain 2-22-1834
Kelly, Saml. to Charlotte Harmon(Hannon) 12-16-1833
Kendel, William Clark to Martha Ann Eliza Barry? 3-11-1841
Kennedy, Irvin to Selina Meshow? 6-26-1834
Kennedy, John to Ailsy E. Boyte 8-21-1839 (8-29-1839)
Kennedy, Saunders to Polly Box 4-14-1827 (4-19-1827)
Kenney, John to Sarah M. Wells 5-21-1857
Kenney, Thomas to Ann Sammons 4-11-1840
Kenny, George to Lucinda Tucker 1-11-1834 (1-13-1834)
Kerkendall, Abner to Maria Duff 12-8-1829 (9-30-1830)
Kerr, Thomas to Issabella Treese 10-17-1854 (10-18-1854)
Kerr, William to Louisa G. Mitchell 7-8-1837 (7-13-1837)
Kerr, Wm. A. to Elizabeth Murray 3-1-1861
Kesterson, John to Belinda Dorsey 2-1-1827 (2-?-1827)
Key, James B. to Leeann E. Pickens 5-14-1856
Kiernan, Braxton W. to Harret? Comer 11-20-1845
Killman, Henry to Frances Hooper 6-20-1846 (6-21-1846)
Killough, John to Sarah Jones 10-12-1830
Kimball, Lunsford L. to Frances D. Maroney 12-28-1829 (12-29-1829)
Kimber, Joshua to Mary Blackamore 10-10-1851 (10-12-1851)
Kimbrough, Albert to Virginia Smith 5-1-1843
Kinchey?, Woodson to Celia McArver 5-8-1828
Kindrick, William H. to Nancy M. Henry 2-17-1853? (2-21-1855)
King, A. J. to Clara Ann Moore 12-9-1854 (12-6?-1854)
King, Anderson to Jane Gilmore 1-4-1849 (1-7-1849)
King, Andrew Thomas to Alpha Jane Parris 3-7-1852 (3-9-1852)
King, Enoch to Leah? Ragan 3-14-1837 (3-15-1837)
King, Enoch to Mary Womack 6-12-1841
King, Gillard to Malissa Hendly 2-3-1836
King, Haliard to Polly Jarnigan 11-25-1856
King, Jesse to Rachael Osment 9-28-1859
King, Jesse to Sarah Jane Savage 7-5-1841 (7-6-1841)
King, Joberry to Bethinia B. Naylor 10-26-1852 (10-27-1852)
King, L. B. to Melisa Ann Weedin 6-18-1844
King, Thomas to Elizabeth Butler 6-12-1824
King, Vinson to Lioty(Sioty?) Crouse 7-5-1847
Kinnard, George to Lyda Brown 2-25-1840 (2-26-1840)
Kinnard, James P. to Manerva Ann Harland 8-10-1832 (8-13-1832)
Kinnard, James to Margaret Norris 11-10-1841
Kirk, George M. to Nancy Sassems 8-9-1826 (8-10-1826)
Kirkland, John W. to Sarah Ann Jones 1-1-1855 (1-4-1855)
Kirkland, Joseph B. to Nancy J. Blaylock 1-9-1858 (1-13-1858)
Knight, Henry to Sarah Jarrett 9-11-1844 (9-12-1844)
Knight, Jos. T. to SophiaH. Cheairs 12-11-1860
Knight, S. C. to Susan Simpson 2-20-1855 (2-21-1855)
Knolton, Horrace C. to Mary A. Stone 8-15-1848 (8-17-1848)
Knott, Marcellas to Meranda Yarbrough 3-17-1860
Knott, Sydney S. to Rachael Murdough 1-10-1861
Knott, William L. to Martha J. Murdaugh 1-19-1858
Knox, Robert to Catharine Kirk 11-30-1823 (11-31?-1823)
Kyle, Robt. to Elizabeth Martin Tull(Taber?) 12-16-1835
Lacefield, Martin V. to Rebecca Lineberry 4-18-1861
Lacey, Joseph H. to Jane Howard 6-25-1833 (6-26-1833)
Lackey, Benjamin F. to Clemintine Lawson 1-4-1854 (1-5-1854)
Lackey, Ephraim A. to Nancy T. Lawson 5-13-1854 (5-14[18]-1854)
Lackey, John to Florida McVey 11-22-1853 (11-23-1853)
Lackie, Theodore to Elizabeth Steele 12-27-1836 (12-28-1836)
Lacy, John B. to Ann B. Smith 12-15-1853 (12-16-1853)
Lake, Joseph E. to L.? A. Nabors 12-29-1845
Lake, Joseph E. to Laura H. Alexander 11-7-1860 (11-8-1860)
Lake, M. H. to M. F. Moore 12-20-1856 (12-23-1856)
Lake, Richard to Mary Jane McLarty 12-19-1853 (12-22-1853)
Lakey, James H. to Elvira E. Addington 9-8-1860
Lakey, William to Jane Cordle 3-9-1856
Lamb, Richard to Elizabeth Pirtle 1-7-1828 (1-8-1828)
Lambert, James to Willey Gee 9-15-1859
Lambert, Jehu to Mincy Jane Huddleston 9-15-1854 (9-18-1854)
Lambert, John J. to Ailsy O. Harris 7-19-1848
Lambert, John J. to Mary Jane Cox 7-12-1858 (7-14-1858)
Lambert, Leonard to Sally Kerby 2-5-1829
Lambert, Orrin to Chatarine Kearley 3-13-1832
Lambert, Saml. H. to Martha C. Crews 4-14-1858 (4-15-1858)
Lambert, Saml. to Martha Barnett 1-11-1826 (1-12-1826)
Lambeth, A. G. to Sarah Jane Williams 3-11-1850 (3-21-1850)
Lambeth, Alfred M. to Carolin E. Campbell 4-8-1835 (4-16-1835)
Lambeth, F. to M. J. Pankey 8-16-1856 (8-17-1856)
Lamkin, William to Mary Glen 4-4-1840
Land, William T. to Mahuldy Ramsey 7-25-1827 (7-26-1827)
Lane, Absalem to Matilda Brown 7-10-1837 (7-15-1837)
Lane, J. D. to Polly Murray 8-6-1857 (8-20-1857)
Langster, George to Amanda Robertson 3-9-1856 (4-9-1856)
Langston, George R. to Winney Elkins 5-21-1841 (5-26-1841)
Langston, William to Tobitha Thomas 6-18-1825 (6-19-1825)
Lanier, John A. to Sarah Cox 12-15-1856 (12-18-1856)
Laraner, Jacob to Susannah Gage 9-19-1831 (9-?-1831)
Lassiter, H. L. to Clemintine Wright 2-28-1857 (3-5-1857)
Laster, Wesley to Mrs. Hulda Steward 1-2-1854
Laughhon, Aden to Dacare Moore 6-21-1825
Lawhorn, Albert H. to Clarisa? Caraway 4-5-1845 (4-24-1845)
Lawrence, Abraham to Martha Pickens 2-17-1837
Lawrence, William to Nancy W. George 4-11-1826 (4-12-1862)
Lawson, Jno. M. to Mary Bolden 5-21-1856 (5-22-1856)
Lax, Benjamin to Nancy V. Gates 3-2-1846 (3-5-1846)
Lax, Berryman to Georgiana Adams 12-27-1852
Lax, J. L. to Eliza Cook 12-7-1859
Lax, John jr. to Ann Usher 2-26-1849 (2-27-1849)
Lax, R. M. to Mary E. Shinault 12-26-1854 (12-28-1854)
Lax, Timothy to Mary H. Crews 12-17-1852 (12-19-1852)
Lay, J. A. to Georgia Andrews 11-30-1859 (12-2-1859)
Lay, James to Rebecca Carnes 2-21-1832 (2-23-1832)
Lea, James to Clarisa Morris 9-8-1828 (9-9-1828)
Lea, Lindsey to Sally Ann New 3-12-1828
Leathers, Geo. M. to Margaret C. Lany 7-24-1860
Leathers, Reubin to Elizabeth Roach 7-28-1852
Lee, Jeremiah to Sarah Murphy 2-2-1841 (2-4-1841)
Lee, John W. to Catharine T. Perry 3-5-1855 (3-7-1855)
Lee, John W. to Hulda E. Mashburn 12-22-1846 (12-23-1846)
Lee, William to Sarah Wilson 10-26-1860 (10-28-1860)
Lee, Wm. T. to Martha A. Ussery 11-16-1860
Lee?, Joel to Melissa Ann Linsey 11-15-1837
Legate, William to Sarah Robinson 4-7-1827
Leggett, James to Rachel Carley 2-15-1844

Leggett, William S. to Mary Jane Ames 11-27-1845
Lennard, William N. to Lucy N. Polk 4-18-1827
Leslie, James to Elizabeth Ann Atkins 8-18-1832 (8-19-1832)
Lester, John E. to Frances A. Shore 12-2-1843 (12-3-1843)
Lewis, A. E. to E. F. Crews 7-16-1856
Lewis, Abram to Amanda Overton 12-17-1849 (1-20-1849)
Lewis, John to Susan Ogin(Agin) 8-25-1856
Lewis, Tavner to Lucindia Jordan 1-3-1853 (1-5-1853)
Lewis, Willis E. to Lucretia Dizen 3-12-1829
Lidy, Andrew to Sarah M. Reynolds 8-1-1831 (8-2-1831)
Liggett, Wm. S. to Elizabeth Savage 12-18-1841 (12-26-1841)
Lightforte, Robert L. to Ellen R. Montgomery 7-23-1851 (7-24-1851)
Lillard, James M. to Nancy Campbell 10-26-1841 (10-27-1841)
Linebarger, John to Rachael C. Campbell 12-19-1860 (12-25-1860)
Linvell, Worley to Racheal Pugh 3-23-1829
Litteral, James to Caroline Robson 10-27-1843
Little, E. S. to Nancy Davis 10-9-1858 (10-12-1858)
Little, James T. to Nancy E. Delk 6-16-1857 (6-18-1857)
Little, James to Eliza Pankey 8-11-1852 (8-12-1852)
Little, James to Nancy L. Johnson 11-24-1857 (11-25-1857)
Little, John W. to Mary J. Duncan 12-17-1856 (12-18-1856)
Little, John Wesley to Eliza Caroline Craven 9-2-1854 (9-3-1854)
Little, John to Eliza Coody(Cody) 10-9-1834
Littlejohn, William to Eliza Ann Chisolm 9-10-1833 (9-11-1833)
Littrell, Eli to Mary M. Barton(Baston?) 5-29-1846 (6-2-1846)
Littrell, Shelton to Bashiba Sims 12-29-1849 (12-30-1849)
Lloyd, Geo. M. to Mary T. Manson 2-13-1860 (2-15-1860)
Lockard, Miles N. to Williammetta Davis 11-20-1860
Lockett, Zachariah to Elizabeth C. Stewart 2-2-1846
Lockhart, Adam to Ann Scott 5-25-1861 (5-26-1861)
Lockhart, James to M. A. Pickett 2-7-1859 (6-20-1859)
Lockhart, Will to Elizabeth Scott 12-23-1837
Lofland, David to Elizabeth Tisdale 4-7-1824
Lokey, J. P. to Mary Ann Farriss 9-27-1854
Long, John A. to Lovenia Hervey 12-20-1848
Long, Tho. H. to Nancy J. Beaty 11-17-1859 (11-18-1859)
Looton(Tuoton?), Henry to Sarah Thornton 3-19-1858 (3-21-1858)
Lorance, A. H,. to Sally Maxwell 7-26-1848 (7-27-1848)
Loud(Land), W. H. to A. E. Purnell 12-14-1858 (12-16-1858)
Loudermilk, Jacob to Jane S. Rogers 10-23-1838
Lourance, Zophar to Eliza M. Lourance 4-15-1835
Love, Jas. C. to Mary A. Teague 12-24-1855
Low, Ezekiel E. to Mary A. L. Aitkin 9-3-1847 (9-5-1847)
Low, W. L. to Sarah C. Hawkins 2-23-1850 (2-26-1850)
Lowe, Sherwood to Hannah Matthis 1-24-1831
Lowery, Jacob to Mary Owens 4-26-1830 (4-27-1830)
Lowrance, Danil W. to Nancy J. Maxwell 9-29-1845 (10-11?-1845)
Lucade, Isaac J. to Mahala Forbess 12-16-1843 (12-20-1843)
Luckado, Wilson to Mary Dubois 2-3-1835
Lucky, John F. to Susannah Baker 8-16-1847 (8-26-1847)
Lumley, J. P. to Sarah Cavnar 1-31-1859
Lunsford, A. D. to America Nixon 5-23-1839
Lunsford, Thomas to Mary C. Nixon 10-19-1847 (12-24-1847)
Lunsford, William to Maria Rine 1-12-1837 (1-22-1837)
Lusk, Joseph to Minerva S. Bell 7-23-1833 (7-24-1833)
Luttrell, John W. to E. V. Thompson 1-20-1857 (1-22-1857)
Lux(Sax?), Benj. to Mary Hendricks 3-13-1860 (3-14-1860)
Lyer?, James to Mary Wilson 1-18-1836
Lyles, Dennis M. to Nancy E. Foltz 7-21-1840
Lyon, Richd. T.k to Phafama Elizabeth Hale 12-21-1854 (12-27-1854)
Lyons, Robert S. to Minerva Oakes 1-17-1842
Mace, John W. C. to Rebecca McCoy 7-16-1850 (7-18-1850)
Macklin, Jefferson to Mariah James 10-21-1851
Macon, Bailey to Martha Ann Fortune 11-25-1846 (11-26-1846)
Macon, David to Elizabeth Jacobs 11-20-1848 (11-23-1848)
Macon, Isaiah to Eldiss Cox 3-1-1844
Macon, John T. to Mary B. Fitzhugh 7-21-1842
Macon, Whitson to Jane Maria Jourden 2-7-1849 (2-8-1849)
Maddox, William to Fanny Goff 11-2-1846 (11-4-1846)
Maddox, William to Susan Mullikin 12-11-1849
Malam, Lennard to Mary Shinault 12-28-1839 (12-29-1839)
Malone, Benjamin to Nancy Dill 4-25-1845
Malone, Gabriel to Lucinda Hays 1-11-1839 (1-6?-1839)
Malone, Gilbert D. T. to Louisa C. Guy 10-17-1848 (10-25-1848)
Malone, Leonard to Ann Pullam 8-18-1849 (9-1-1849)
Mangrum, W. P. to Amanda E. Aldridge 1-27-1857 (1-29-1857)
Manuell, John C. to Polly Townsend 12-18-1827
March, Obediah to Elizabeth Beavers 10-29-1850 (10-30-1850)
Maris, William to Jane L. McGowan 12-1-1841 (12-2-1841)
Marler, James to Mary Casey 8-1-1838
Marler, Silas to Margaret Kerr 7-4-1842
Marler, Stephen to Elizabeth Hooper 4-6-1839
Marrs, John W. to Elizabeth Welch 12-17-1842 (12-18-1842)
Marrs, Robert J. to R. E. Hannis? 3-9-1848
Marrs, Wm. to Martha Vaughn 5-9-1846 (5-10-1846)
Marsh, Henry to Hannah Cain 9-17-1828 (9-18-1828)
Marsh, Hiram to Jane Martin 2-11-1839 (2-14-1839)
Marsh, James M. to Sarah Jane Whitford 12-20-1859
Marsh, James S. to Jane Murphy 1-12-1846 (1-25-1846)
Marsh, Munford S. to Caroline Jones 11-13-1829 (11-17-1829)
Marsh, R. A. to Elizabeth Norment 2-5-1844 (2-6-1844)
Marsh, Silas M. W. to Elizabeth J. Willoughby 11-8-1842
Marshall, J. J. to Anna Hopton 9-12-1859
Marshall, James H. to Sarah J. Avant 11-6-1854 (11-15-1854)
Martin, James M. to Margaret Worrell 9-16-1854 (9-21-1854)
Martin, Poleman to Elizabeth Dillard 8-16-1836 (8-17-1836)
Martin, Turner J. to Dycy? Anderson 12-31-1839
Martindale, Thomas J. to Martha Averett 7-8-1833
Martindale, William to Rispha Williams 5-19-1830 (5-21-1830)
Mashburn, Alfred to May Davis 4-19-1847
Mashburn, Hardy to Barbara Brown 1-9-1836 (1-10-1836)
Mashburn, John A. to Sarah Ann Hunter 3-13-1854 (3-16-1854)
Mashburn, Lewis to Vasty Mashburn 2-6-1839 (2-7-1839)
Mashburn, Moses J. to Vashti Cox 4-7-1828 (4-10-1828)
Mashburn, William C. to Mary Ann Webb 11-30-1849 (12-5-1849)
Mask, Hamilton to Amandy P. Whitmon 12-13-1847 (12-14-1847)
Mask, James M. to Elizabeth J. McKinnie 12-29-1851 (12-31-1852)
Mason, John to Elizabeth Corburn? 12-1-1834 (12-2-1834)
Mastin, Jno. E. to Mary E. Atkinson 10-20-1848 (10-26-1848)
Mathews, Edward J. to Rhoda N. Comwell? 12-6-1859
Mathews, Jeptha to Sarah Davie 4-20-1830
Mathews, Jeptha to Sarah Davis 4-20-1831 (4-21-1831)
Matthews, Abner S. to Mary C. Alexander 5-10-1842 (5-19-1842)
Matthews, Charles to Betsy J. Miller 7-28-1856
Matthews, John W. to Eliza R. Alexander 1-23-1839
Matthews, Joseph B. to Horpolacy? McGehee 3-3-1843
Matthews, Joseph W. to Sarah Hatley 1-1-1829
Matthis, Wm. B. to Martha Ann M. Fowler 6-3-1834
Mauldin, James C. to Martha Ann Lile? 11-30-1842 (12-1-1842)
Maury, Abram to Mary Jane Hancock 8-22-1859
Maxwell, John R. to Sarah C. Drennon 1-15-1850 (1-20-1850)
Maxwell, William C. to Sarah Hail 8-22-1832
Maxwell, William H. to Bethena Stephens 8-25-1825
May, Henry to Lila Baines 1-7-1828
May, Hiram C. to Louisa J. Waldrop 7-19-1858 (7-27-1858)
May, J. to Martha Park 12-26-1860 (12-27-1860)
May, Oliver C. to Lucinda Richardson 4-4-1836 (4-5-1836)
May, Paul to Amy Rook 1-2-1827 (1-4-1827)
May, Wm. C. to Emily P. Mohundro 7-24-1839] (7-28-1839)
Mayfield, Archibald to Mary Gee 11-1-1852 (11-2-1852)
Mayfield, Archibald to Nancy Lambert 10-3-1859
Mayfield, Bailey to Nancy(Ann) Partridge 8-1-1833 (8-7-1833)
Mayfield, Isrial to Margaret Allen 10-20-1835 (10-22-1835)
Mayfield, Joel to Louisa J. Champ 11-17-1854 (11-19-1854)
Mayfield, John E. M. to Sythia Pate 11-10-1836
Mayfield, Randolph to Elizabeth Thompson 11-6-1843
Mayfield, William to Terissa Faller 10-6-1828
McAfee, G. B. to Mary Fowler 3-24-1860
McAlister, J. F. to M. N. Ferguson 10-17-1861 (10-28-1861)
McAnaly, Jas. W. to Louisa Sullivan 7-21-1857 (7-22-1857)
McAnulty, Joseph S. to Margaret Ann Woods 11-17-1842 (11-18-1842)
McBride, E. R. to Elizabeth Cole 12-15-1849 (12-26-1849)
McBride, J. L. to Martha L. Harrison 3-19-1855 (3-21-1855)
McBride, James A. to Mary E. Harrison 2-28-1845 (3-6-1845)
McBride, Pleasant B. to Eady Ann Cole 9-14-1857 (9-15-1857)
McBride, William H. to Jane McKaughan? 8-14-1829
McBride, William Y. to Jane Ann Chambless 7-25-1852 (7-29-1852)
McCain, William to Narcissus C. McNeese 1-31-1853 (2-2-1853)
McCalap, Danl. J. to Sarah Faison 1-16-1839 (1-?-1839)

McCall, Robert R. to Mary E. Dawson 9-16-1846 (9-20-1846)
McCalla, James M. to Ann Eliza Irions 1-29-1842 (2-1-1842)
McCann, James to Willy Brewer 7-27-1841 (7-28-1841)
McCann, Thomas L. to Jane B. Black 8-14-1852 (8-17-1852)
McCarley, Alexander to Elizabeth S. Ozment 12-28-1848
McCarley, W. W. to Frances I? Robertson 3-12-1859 (3-15-1859)
McCarter, James to Elizabeth J. Lutrell 12-15-1858 (12-26-1858)
McCarter, Tho. to Sarah Ann E. Thompson 3-4-1857 (3-5-1857)
McCarty, Hugh B. to Mary Macon 4-4-1846
McCarty, Moses to Sarah Plant 8-31-1831
McCarver, Joshua to Elizabeth Drannon 10-25-1838 (10-26-1838)
McCary, Thomas to Benigna Johnson 9-19-1851 (9-21-1851)
McClain, William to Mary Pickins 12-4-1839 (12-5-1839)
McClain, Wm. F. to Mary Ritchie 4-8-1835
McClanahan, David to Betsey McCoy 7-28-1830 (7-28-1830)
McClanahan, Hamden to Lucy K. Green 1-27-1851 (2-4-1851)
McClanahan, Hamilton to Ann Jane Smith 11-5-1829
McCleland, Jno. H. to Mary E. Humphrey 11-4-1858 (11-10-1858)
McClellan, John H. to Mary G. McAnulty 5-29-1838
McClend(McLeod?), William to Mary Avent 3-21-1847
McClendon, David to Susannah May 8-1-1827 (8-3-1827)
McClendon, Geo. to Elizabeth McGlaughlin 12-22-1851 (12-23-1851)
McClendon, Thomas E. to Elizabeth A. Dixon 6-5-1856
McClory, lHenry to Susan Bennett 1-25-1862
McCommon, C. W. to A. C. Stricklin 10-6-1860 (10-11-1860)
McCommon, Geo. W. to Elizabeth D. Thomson 2-9-1853 (2-10-1853)
McCommon, George R. to Margaret Ann Glass 10-1-1852 (10-3-1852)
McCommon, Isaac N. to Elizabeth H. Rogers 6-19-1838
McCommon, James M. to Agness McClennand 1-2-1846 (1-6-1846)
McCommon, Jas. (Jos.) H. to Martha M. Wells 3-9-1858 (3-10-1858)
McCommon, John A. to L. C. Wafford 8-5-1857 (8-6-1857)
McCommon, Joseph A. to Isabella Lamar? 7-27-1835
McCommon, Reese to Catharine Lavina Sharp 3-24-1848 (3-28-1848)
McCommon, Seth Brownlee to Tebitha C. Cole 1-6-1841 (1-7-1841)
McCommon, Thos. R. to Eliza J. Ferguson 4-5-1859 (6-11-1859)
McCommon, W. H. to Nancy' Caroker 12-3-1851
McCommon, W. M. to Elizabeth J. Ferguson 12-21-1857 (12-22-1857)
McCommons, Stanhope? to Jula Ann Youngblood 12-29-1846 (12-31-1846)
McCord, Calvin E. to Ann E. V. Bates 3-7-1860
McCord, Richard H. to Frances A. Williams 1-11-1854 (1-12-1854)
McCowan, Jackson to Anna Box 4-11-1835 (4-16-1835)
McCoy, Joseph to Sarah Singleton 1-28-1832 (1-29-1832)
McDaniel, Abner to Unity Freeman 5-19-1847
McDaniel, Alexander to Mary Louisa Smith 2-8-1835 (2-12-1835)
McDaniel, B. A. to Ellen V. Harbin 4-28-1858 (5-11-1858)
McDaniel, C. C. to Elizabeth C. M. Rose 5-18-1859 (5-19-1859)
McDaniel, Cornelius to Hester Sain 12-9-1848 (12-14-1848)
McDaniel, Geo. E. to Louisa W. Rainer 4-24-1861 (4-25-1861)
McDonald, Alexander to Rebecca Avann 9-8-1837 (9-14-1837)
McDonald, John to Mary Ann Sullivan 7-8-1852
McDonald, John to Susan Cox 2-8-1836
McDonald, William A. to Frances C. Davis 3-10-1847 (3-11-1847)
McDowell, Erasmus Patton to Evelina S. McNeal 4-23-1838 (4-24-1838)
McElroy, Willson B. to Milly Crews 10-15-1838
McFall, John A. to Hannah Brown 8-9-1828 (8-10-1828)
McGee, John H. to Mary M. Mercer 8-18-1856 (8-19-1856)
McGee, T. L. to Sallie E. McKinnie 4-10-1858 (4-22-1858)
McGee, William to Louisa Martin 6-22-1833 (6-23-1833)
McGee, Wm. to Mary Ann Kerly 1-21-1833
McGehee, A. F. to Margaret Jane Ward 11-27-1854 (11-28-1854)
McGlothlin, Ephraim to Margaret J. Crane 3-12-1857
McGlothlin, John to Eunice Keller 11-2-1826 (11-4-1826)
McGlothlin, Wm. R. to Henrietta Thornton 1-6-1862
McGraw, Elhennan to Mary Rogers 10-31-1844
McGraw, Jno. H. to Elizabeth Sanders 8-12-1845
McGuire, George to Elizabeth McKay 1-5-1836
McGuire, James Y. to Elizabeth W. Turner 8-11-1845 (8-12-1845)
McGuire, John Y. to Harret? Scoot 10-13-1845 (10-14-1845)
McIntosh, John to Elizabeth Burton 12-13-1838
McIntyre, W. C. to Candia Johnson 2-21-1855 (2-25-1855)
McKalip, Andrew M. to Narcissa Koffman 5-23-1854 (5-24-1854)
McKaughan, John S. to Rachel B. Taylor 1-21-1848 (1-23-1848)
McKean, J. C. to Nancy A. Wilkinson 11-3-1830
McKee, James to Lucinda Whitby 11-17-1848 (11-24-1848)
McKee, John to Diana C. Goodwin 9-20-1832
McKee, John to Louisa Foster 12-22-1856 (12-23-1856)
McKee, John to Zelphi A. E. McKinne 12-12-1848 (12-16-1848)
McKehan, Wm. to Nancy C. Lasiter 5-28-1860 (5-30-1860)
McKennie, Jonathan to Semon Cozby 3-31-1836
McKey, T. B. to S. E. W. Rogers 9-18-1861 (9?-29-1861)
McKey, William to Kezier? Sellers 10-18-1847 (10-19-1847)
McKinie, Samuel Martin to Sarah Anders 9-4-1855 (9-6-1855)
McKinley, J. H. to Sarah A. McClarty 12-31-1851 (12-18?-1851)
McKinne, J. R. to Mary E. Kennedy 2-18-1856 (2-21-1856)
McKinnie, Arthur to Harriet D. Lee 3-23-1833 (3-26-1833)
McKinnie, Beverly R. to Zarina Williams 3-24-1839 (3-28-1839)
McKinnie, John R. to Susan F. Crawford 2-11-1830 (2-16-1830)
McKinnie, John to Elizabeth C. Reaves 3-8-1841 (3-11-1841)
McKinnie, Michial to Julia McKinnie 11-13-1832 (11-22-1832)
McKinnie, Saml. M. to Jane Martin 2-28-1848 (3-2-1848)
McKinnie, William W. to Billa E. Hammons 12-18-1855 (12-26-1855)
McKinnie, William to Susannah McKinnie 3-15-1826 (3-16-1826)
McKinnie, Wm. P. to Lucy Moon(Moore?) 10-5-1846 (10-6-1846)
McKinnie, Wm. P. to Sarah F. Crawford 12-1-1832 (12-5-1832)
McKinza, Asa to Matilda Condra 2-17-1828
McKissick, R. J. to Ellen Somers 10-6-1858 (10-7-1858)
McKizzick, Jno. W. to Sarah Thompson 12-14-1850
McKnight, Moses to Caroline C. Flynt 6-12-1852
McLain, John to Elizabeth Curley? 12-13-1837
McLaughlin, Thomas to Rachel McLaughlin 2-21-1824 (2-24-1824)
McLeary, W. T. to Amanda E. Pugh 9-14-1854 (10-3-1854)
McLemore, Wm. S. to Oregon N. Teague 12-21-1861 (12-24-1861)
McLeod, William M. to Sarah Bostick 6-7-1841 (7-29-1841)
McMahan, John to Lotty Golden 7-7-1851 (7-10-1851)
McMahan, Robt. B. to Martha Steagall 5-13-1846 (5-17-1846)
McMillan, James Howard to Nancy Jackson 3-22-1842
McMillan, Robert D. to Minerva Anderson 10-13-1836
McMillen, T. J. to C. R. Scott 9-10-1859 (10-10-1859)
McMillin, Addison to Mary Harris 5-18-1830
McNeal, Ezekiel P. to Ann Williams 1-22-1835
McNeal, William W. to Elizabeth W. Berry 11-26-1844
McNeely, John to Hester Brown 1-17-1843
McNees, Richard H. to Nancy H. Johnson 9-24-1828 (9-25-1828)
McNeill, John C. to Ann Polk 5-10-1859 (6-15-1859)
McNutt, S. F. to Ann White 1-5-1848 (1-11-1848)
McPherson, John to Abigal Scripson? 2-8-1834
McReaves(Reaves?), W. to Edmonia T. Neece 4-7-1859 (4-9-1859)
McSwain, William A. to Louisa Ann Justice 9-24-1852 (9-26-1852)
McWhirter, James B. to Paulina L. McWhirter 2-15-1832
McWilliams, James to Rhody Murphy 5-25-1847 (5-27-1840
Meador, Andrew J. to Sarah Ann Swindle 12-25-1860
Means, James P. to Malinda Neece 8-7-1848 (8-8-1848)
Medlock, Thomas to Mary J. Stinson 7-30-1838
Meek(Merk), John E. to Catharine Hughes 5-7-1838 (5-10-1838)
Meeks, Josephus to Elizabeth May 8-13-1838 (8-19-1838)
Mercer, Abner B. to Nancy Ann Robinson 4-12-1850 (4-16-1850)
Mercer, Joseph A. to Rebecca L. Robinson 2-20-1860 (2-23-1860)
Merlin, William to Edy Jackson 2-13-1827
Mesham(Mesbow?), John to Hannah Marsh 12-5-1834
Michell, Robert to Nancy Harrell(Howell?) 8-5-1828 (4?-6-1828)
Middleton, Hugh to Nancy Starky 2-29-1828
Middleton, John T. to Rosanna Pulliam 6-14-1858
Middleton, Saml. to Tempa Gocher 2-8-1860
Midlebrooks, William S. to Mary V. Lacy 12-25-1849
Miles, D. M. C. to Jane M. McCoyen? 9-13-1828
Miller, Austin to Mary Jane McNeal 10-22-1849 (10-23-1849)
Miller, Charles J. to Emma M. Jansen 12-3-1851
Miller, James L. to Sophia Darnell 3-2-1854
Miller, Josiah D. to Emily Adaline Swindle 9-14-1853 (9-15-1853)
Miller, Levi D. to Tabitha Dodd 1-22-1858 (1-27-1858)
Miller, Martin V. to Mary J. Gardner 4-17-1860
Miller, Pitser to Sarah Ann Stevens 12-19-1834 (12-21-1834)
Miller, William H. to Martha Conner 7-11-1837
Millikin, Leonard H. to Mary Levinia Moody 7-5?-1841
Mills, Andrew J. to Frances Morris 8-27-1850 (8-29-1850)
Mills, Elvy to Nancy Carley 9-11-1841 (9-12-1841)
Mills, Henry M. to Sarah Ann King 7-25-1849
Mills, Humphrey to Margaret Houston 12-29-1832 (12-30-1832)

Mills, Isaac to Maria Long 12-8-1827
Mills, James B. to Martha Vinson 1-24-1856 (1-26-1856)
Mills, James to Nancy? Jones 12-7-1836 (12-8-1836)
Mills, John to Dianah Bond 8-21-1832 (8-24-1832)
Mills, Sample to Bethenia Henry 11-24-1851 (11-27-1851)
Mills, W. R. to N. S. Steward 11-1-1859 (11-3-1859)
Mills, Wm. Y. to Mary Rodgers 8-16-1841 (8-17-1841)
Millsted, George C. to Frances E. Mullens 5-3-1849
Minter, Franklin to Lucinda Ham 1-19-1847
Minter, George W. to Louisa T. Warr 2-13-1849 (2-14-1849)
Minter, George W. to Martha R. Allen 11-28-1853
Minton, Joseph to Cytha Hines 5-19-1836
Misenheimer, Hampton C. to Emily Cummings 3-4-1848 (3-9-1848)
Misenheimer, Henry B. to Nancy B. McAnulty 3-2-1837 (3-7-1837)
Mitchel, James to Sarah Ann McGee 2-8-1831 (2-10-1831)
Mitchell, A. F. to Sarah Ann Philips 12-18-1844 (12-19-1844)
Mitchell, Houston to Martha V. Whitmore 11-30-1853
Mitchell, James M. to Elizabeth Henson 11-17-1858 (11-20-1858)
Mitchell, James to Mary Vaught 9-12-1835
Mitchell, Jno. M. to Olivia Ann Hornesby 2-25-1857 (2-26-1857)
Mitchell, John to Eliza Jane Birdsong 3-23-1848
Mitchell, M. P. to Cornelia Jackson 8-22-1861
Mitchell, Nathan M. to Martha C. McCommon 9-17-1842 (9-22-1842)
Mitchell, R. H. to Justianna Nelson 9-22-1861
Mitchell, Thomas J. to Nancy E. Scoggins 12-16-1858 (12-17-1858)
Moffitt, John to Mary C. Caviness 2-21-1853 (2-22-1853)
Moliter, C. F. to Martha Hallaburton 3-6-1857 (3-8-1857)
Monroe, W. H. to Christian Parmer 2-28-1850
Monroe, William to Pearcy Westbrook 11-8-1852
Montgomery, J. M. to Jane White 11-3-1834 (11-4-1834)
Montgomery, Leroy to Cassandria Yeary? 1-30-1827
Montgomery, Samuel W. to Malisa E. Strickland 1-7-1848 (1-9-1848)
Moon(Moore?), Wm. H. to Virginia Doxey 4-27-1846 (4-28-1846)
Moone, Levin B. to Elizabeth Williams 12-13-1828 (12-18-1828)
Moore, Abner to Mary Ann Anderson 6-21-1842 (6-22-1842)
Moore, Abner to Rebecca Black 1-2-1854 (1-3-1854)
Moore, Alfred to Nancy Eliz. Ellen Smith 1-23-1849 (1-30-1849) '
Moore, Andrew J. to Rachel Shull 6-8-1836
Moore, Andrew to Adline M. Anderson 3-9-1846 (3-10-1846)
Moore, Curtis to Frances Robertson 2-10-1845 (2-13-1845)
Moore, David S. to R. A. Robinson 11-22-1854 (11-23-1854)
Moore, Eli to Adeline M. Jacobs 7-16-1839 (7-18-1839)
Moore, Elias to Jackey Ann Perry 2-4-1850 (2-5-1850)
Moore, Hugh to Octavia D. Anderson 8-11-1859 (8-14-1859)
Moore, Isaac to Casey Lee Flower 7-12-1834 (7-17-1834)
Moore, J. S. to Susan L. O'Brien 10-25-1859
Moore, John A. to Elizabeth A. Dison 1-8-1852
Moore, John F. to Mary Ann Parks 9-13-1855 (9-15-1855)
Moore, John H. to Mary W. Orr 11-30-1840 (12-1-1840)
Moore, John P. to Elizabeth S. Harriss 12-23-1843
Moore, Lewis to Jane Anderson 8-5-1839 (8-7-1839)
Moore, Lewis to Parilee Wilkinson 12-20-1853 (12-21-1853)
Moore, Lodwick(Ridwick) to Mary Ann Turner 10-18-1848 (10-19-1848)
Moore, Martin to Martha Sammons 3-6-1841 (3-11-1841)
Moore, Masias J. to Elena Williams 9-9-1834 (9-10-1834)
Moore, Nathaniel B. to Sarah Campbell 7-25-1837 (7-31-1837)
Moore, R. P. to Mary M. Hubbard 10-25-1831 (10-27-1831)
Moore, Thomas D. to Sarah Crumply 2-9-1852 (2-10-1852)
Moore, Thomas E. to Elizabeth J. Joy 9-17-1846
Moore, Thomas to Ann Elizabeth Roshel? 10-31-1859 (11-1-1859)
Moore, Thomas to Sarah M. Hubbard 12-13-1848
Moore, Thos. H. to Lucy Brown 2-4-1839 (2-5-1839)
Moore, W. A. to Dicey Ann Dickens 1-11-1860 (1-12-1860)
Moore, William G. to Mary E. Moore 12-21-1853
Moore, William N. to Mary Ann Riggs 10-16-1850 (10-22-1850)
Moore, William to Almarinda Bennett 10-7-1850
Moore, Wm. A. to Susannah Bates 12-14-1842 (12-17-1842)
Moran, Geo. W. to Angeline McDaniel 3-28-1860 (3-29-1860)
Morphis, Alsy to Sarah Steward 2-13-1835
Morphis, John B. to Eliza J. Shelton 11-26-1855 (11-28-1855)
Morphys, J. L. to Mary J. Tannehill 6-27-1855 (7-5-1855)
Morris, Alex to Elizabeth Hooper 2-22-1858 (2-24-1858)
Morris, Hezekiah to Margaret Freeman 2-21-1843
Morris, Robert H. to Sarah Elizabeth Davis 6-10-1852
Morris, William to Sabrinah Jane Blunt 4-12-1858 (4-14-1858)
Morrison, Adli S. to Mary Bartlett 10-16-1833 (10-17-1833)
Morriss, Robert to Altetha E. Nixon 6-21-1841 (6-29-1841)
Morrow, Geo. N. to Darthula V. Price 3-23-1856 (4-1-1856)
Morrow, John T. to Margarett F. Marsh 9-9-1854
Morrow, Saml. R. to Melinda C. Gillespie 1-24-1842 (1-27-1842)
Morrow, Thomas to Susannah Clifft 11-29-1830 (11-30-1830)
Morrow, Thomas to Winsey Foster 9-16-1838 (9-22-1838)
Morrow, W. B. to Martha J. Smith 7-17-1855 (7-19-1855)
Morrow, William to Charity? Fargason 1-3-1837
Moss, Jno. to Sarah J. Brooks 10-13-1857 (10-14-1857)
Mott, John to Elizabeth Fort 3-7-1827
Mulherron, Charles to Ann C. Durham 12-12-1849 (12-13-1849)
Mulikin, Zeddack to Pernecy Noland 2-23-1839 (2-28?-1839)
Mullekin, Levi to Nancy Shickles 12-29-1846
Mullen, J. W. to W. L. Tate 8-2-1854 (8-3-1854)
Mullhall, James to Jane Nuckolls 12-28-1843
Mullican, Aquilla to Sarah Jane Parker 5-17-1853
Mundin, John to Sarah Bryant 7-15-1844
Munn, John S. to Sarah Jane Jones 7-26-1849
Muntz, Daniel to Lydia Wycoff 1-7-1825
Murchison, John to Hanah Ramsy 8-3-1829 (8-9-1829)
Murdaugh(Mordough), Samuel to Hannah Cearly 11-30-1848
Murdaugh, James to Lavanda Brooks 6-2-1859
Murdaugh, John to Mary Leggett 2-12-1840
Murdaugh, John to Matilda C. Binkley 1-1-1842 (1-2-1842)
Murdaugh, L. B. to Martha C. Hillhouse 12-1-1853
Murdaugh, Robert to Sarah Leggett 10-6-1840
Murley, Hamilton to Frances Jackson 12-9-1857
Murley, Hamilton to Jane Mills 2-4-1839 (2-7-1839)
Murley, William H. to Nancy Brown 7-24-1848 (7-26-1848)
Murphy, Andrew L. to Elizabeth Brenard 12-10-1828 (12-11-1828)
Murphy, Charles to Emily Harvey 12-29-1828 (1-1-1829)
Murphy, Eli to Rebecca Tuttle 7-4-1826 (7-5-1826)
Murphy, Ethan A. to Mary Broiles 2-25-1828 (4-5-1828)
Murphy, James to Elizabeth Hervey 10-31-1843 (11-2-1843)
Murphy, Jehu? to Selina? Nesbit 12-10-1829
Murphy, Tilmon to Sarah C. Smithwick 10-6-1845
Murphy, Walter M. to Martha A. F. Smith 1-10-1844 (1-11-1844)
Murphy, William to Charlotte Brown 11-13-1843 (11-15-1843)
Murrell, William to Nancy Mitchell 10-19-1829
Murry, John to Dorathy Bowlin 3-23-1846
Musgrave, Calvin to Maria Walden 7-21-1830 (7-29-1830)
Musgrave, Thomas to Sarah Maxwell 2-13-1828
Myers, John to Charlotte House 12-5-1848 (12-6-1848)
Myers, S. O. to Mary A. Mask 8-18-1852
Myers, William T. to Artimissa Dial 9-25-1850
Myrick, Alfred to Adelia Crawford 5-18-1844 (5-19-1844)
Myrick, Edward M. to Lucretia Harris 10-14-1840 (10-15-1840)
Myrick, Edward M. to Susan E. Moore 6-24-1844
Myrick, William to Jane Thompson 5-24-1842 (5-31-1842)
Nabers, Perry to Frances Brantly 1-21-1826
Nabers, Robert to Prudence Foster 11-21-1829
Nabors, Joseph to Malinda Garrett 8-2-1838
Nailor, Joshua D. to Mary Ann Burkhead 1-21-1857
Nappier, George F. to Mary Pricilla Green 11-29-1849
Naylor, Wm. A. to Lidia Blair 12-18-1855 (12-20-1855)
Neal, Alfred to Elizabeth Polk 9-16-1829 (10-3-1829)
Neal, Wm. to Martha Warford 1-25-1858
Nearin, E. L. to Elizabeth Leathers 2-21-1845 (2-23-1845)
Needham, Jeramiah to Racheal Spalding 10-23-1827
Needham, John to Mary(Polly) Lea 1-31-1835 (2-?-1835)
Needham, Rosell to Elizabeth E. Ramsey 10-26-1836
Needham, Solomon to Rebecca Dillard 12-3-1834 (12-4-1834)
Needham, William to Patsy Needham 4-17-1832 (4-19-1832)
Needham, William to Sarah M. Ruddle 9-10-1836
Neely, A. R. to Martha J. Kirk 1-5-1853
Neely, J. J. to Fanny M. Stephens 5-11-1848
Neely, James A. L. to Lucretia Lear? 4-1-1833 (4-14-1833)
Neely, Jno. M. to Clarissa Hunt 7-9-1833 (7-23-1833)
Neely, John J. to Maria(Mana) Marsh 7-1-1858
Neely, John K. to Rebecca T. Glass 11-29-1858 (11-30-1858)
Neely, John N. to Minirva Anderson 1-28-1833
Neely, Phillip J. to M. J. Smith 12-19-1859 (12-22-1859)
Neely, R. J. to Mary Hull 4-2-1851

Neely, Rufus P. to Elizabeth Lea 5-16-1829 (5-19-1829)
Neely, Samuel F. to Tirzah Caldwell 11-14-1837 (11-16-1837)
Neil, John to Pernisia Hays 11-26-1832
Neilson, A. D. to Martha Durrett 3-19-1851
Neilson, Alexander G. to Eugenia Polk 7-18-1827
Neilson, Jos. H. to Martha E. Hardy 5-26-1859
Nelems, John to Mary kSLusan McBride 6-19-1847 (6-21-1847)
Nellums(Nelms), William to Rachel Brooks 8-1-1840 (8-4-1840)
Nelms, A. C. to Sophronia O. Tedford 11-20-1843 (11-22-1843)
Nelms, Madison to Emily Rhodes 9-14-1853 (9-15-1853)
Nelms, Saml. to Martha Stephens 6-12-1838 (6-26-1838)
Nelms, Wm. R. to U. L. Clement 2-9-1860
Nelson, A. J. to Amanda J. Johnson 2-13-1856 (2-14-1856)
Nelson, Barnabas to Mary Dawson 12-15-1834 (12-18-1834)
Nelson, Braetin to Lucinda Childress 8-28-1834 (9-3-1834)
Nelson, John to Jane Matthews 9-7-1840 (9-17-1840)
Nelson, William W. to Mahaly Broyles 5-10-1826 (not endorsed)
Nevill, Andrew J. to Elizabeth Craft 2-9-1846 (2-11?-1846)
New, G. B. to Eliza Simmons 5-1-1830 (5-2-1830)
New, Nathan to Elizabeth Goodman 1-1-1838
New, William to Sally Ann Craft 9-21-1846 (9-22-1846)
Newbern, D. J. to Catharine L. Ramsy 11-18-1850 (11-19-1850)
Newbern, William Y. to Lavinia J. Wilson 3-16-1840
Newhouse, Benjamin to Susanah Pully 8-10-1829 (8-13-1829)
Newland, Chas. T. to Martha A. Hudson 3-24-1860 (4-3-1860)
Newland, Henson G. to Margaret Campbell 8-21-1839 (8-22-1839)
Newland, Joseph K. to Jane Campbell 11-2-1846 (11-4-1846)
Newland, Joseph K. to Sarah S. Crocker 10-28-1858 (11-10-1858)
Newland, William to Jane Stone 2-1-1845 (2-6-1845)
Newsom, John F. to M. E. Smith 8-6-1860
Newton, William M. H. to Hester Lea 1-4-1824
Nicholson, James to Jane Whitley 1-5-1837
Nicholson, Nathaniel to Mary Nicholson 9-8-1827 (9-12-1827)
Nietschke(Dietrike?), J.(P?) kD. to Harriet Alvorde 2-4-1851
Nixon, Elliote H. to Mary Lunsford 5-1-1837
Nixon, Granville to Annice Allen 1-17-1853 (2-8-1853)
Nixon, Lindsey G. to Nancy Ann Harper 8-22-1845 (8-28-1845)
Nolen, Geo. M.(W.?) to Mary J. Graves 8-3-1859
Nooner, Nathan to Elizabeth Gates 8-28-1828
Nordin, Alexander to Elizabeth Dodd 2-16-1828 (2-17-1828)
Norman, A. J. to Henrietta Hansen 5-19-1852
Norman, Albert? S. to Eliza J. Stinson 10-29-1845 (10-30-1845)
Norman, Kinard to Janella? Jones 7-1-1845
Norris, Calvin to Ajesty Smith 4-18-1839
Norton, Edward to Ann Short 9-27-1833
Norton, Isaac J. to Sarah Nabers 7-11-1837
Norton, Jacob N. to Elizabeth Curley(Carley?) 12-22-1838 (12-25-1838)
Norton, James W. to Nancy Highfield 1-26-1853 (2-2-1853)
Norton, Messer to Margarett Cosby 1-6-1829
Norton, Peter K. to Catherine Baker 1-9-1839 (1-10-1839)
Norton, William to Sophia Short 9-25-1832
Nowlin, James C. to Anlize Johnson 12-22-1837 (12-24-1837)
Nuckells, Starling to Narcissa McKinza 5-1-1832 (5-8?-1832)
Nuckolls, Richard to Lucinda D. Lillard 3-15-1855
Nuckolls, William jr. to Eliza Polk 9-5-1850
Null, Abner to Susan Mullins 12-21-1846 (12-24-1846)
Null, John to Elizabeth Rosson 3-22-1845 (3-23-1845)
Nunnelly, James S. to Parthenia Hitchcok 8-6-1852 (8-15-1852)
Oates, Wm. C. to Fanny S. Guy 10-11-1859 (10-12-1859)
Oatsfall, Jordan to Elizabeth McLain 2-5-1844
Olds, Daniel to Sarah Sherly] 9-11-1824
Oliver, James to Alethea Roberts 11-5-1850
Oliver, John to Eliza Jane Webb 11-26-1853
Oliver, John to M. Casy 9-10-1831
Oliver, Pleasant to Artemesia Cloud 11-5-1836
Oliver, Ruebin W. to Elizabeth W. Wilson 2-3-1836
Oliver, Shelton to Elizabeth J. Crisp 6-26-1850 (6-25?-1850)
Oliver, Thomas to Martha R.(P?) Crews? 1-14-1840
Oliver, William to Arsena King 10-21-1846 (10-22-1846)
Orr, Jones K. to Sarah Ann Young 5-15-1835 (5-21-1835)
Osborn, Thomas A. to Mary T. Woodfin 2-17-1853
Osborne, E. H. to Cynthia Crisp 6-24-1850
Osborne, J. H. to Ada Weatherford 11-7-1833
Osborne, Thomas A. to Sidney Jane Carruth 12-22-1858
Osment, Daniel to Sarah McCearly] 12-26-1846 (12-27-1846)
Oswell, William to Mary A. Ricks 5-22-1845
Overton, Absalom to Malinda Harrell? 1-18-1845 (1-23-1845)
Overton, Archibald to Sarah E. Anderson 8-16-1859 (8-17-1859)
Overton, Elija to Jane Monton 4-4-1846 (4-5-1846)
Overton, Elijah to Lucy Taylor 2-19-1838
Overton, Wm. to Mary J. Mashburn 9-30-1856 (10-2-1856)
Owen, H. S. to Nancy Hicks 3-21-1846
Owen, J. W. to Hennorah Boyle 2-3-1848
Owens, Benj. to Mary R. Harris(Hanis?) 5-29-1839 (6-1-1839)
Owens, Benjamin to Elizabeth Taggart 11-3-1830
Owens, Ezekiel to Juliann Wilkes 10-11-1847 (10-12-1847)
Owens, Samuel L. to Polly Carter 3-18-1829 (3-22-1829)
Owens, Winfrey to Sophia Duff 2-14-1827 (2-18-1827)
Owens, Wm. H. to Louisa Vails 12-29-1842 (12-30-1842)
Ozment, N. M. to Mary A. M. King 2-1-1860 (2-2-1860)
Ozwell(Oswald), Edward to Abedian Sanders 10-15-1856
Pace, W. H. to Mary Ann Leathers 9-16-1835
Pace, Wicke H. to Matilda W. Kirk 10-26-1836
Paine, James A. to Mary P. Poston 7-11-1856
Palmer, Jas. H. to Mary Ann Eliza Moon(Moore) 11-23-1844 (12-24-1844)
Palmer, Wm. F. to Nancy B. Hubbard 6-9-1840
Pankey, M. D. to Harriet Cross 2-20-1860
Pankey, Wilson N. to Louisa Cheisher 12-16-1844 (12-17-1844)
Panky, James P. to Delelah Davis 11-29-1845 (11-30-1845)
Pannell, E. M. to Martha Stone 5-16-1860
Pannell, Elihu S. to Martha J. Garrett 8-24-1859
Pare, William to Rebecca Dean 12-12-1837
Parham, E. G. to Sarah J. Bean 2-11-1862
Parish, J. R. to Mary Jane Herendon 3-18-1858
Park, Dugan to Martha Jane Yopp 10-26-1858 (11-3-1858)
Park, Eli to Darcus Cholwell 2-26-1840 (3-10-1840)
Park, James A. to M. F. Crawford 1-3-1856
Park, John M. to Mary Rankin 12-16-1848 (12-21-1848)
Park, Levi to Jane E. Devenport 12-7-1846 (12-8-1846)
Park, Robert to Margaret Jane Hogan 10-6-1841 (10-7-1841)
Park, Robert to Rhoda Abraham 3-13-1843 (4-2-1843)
Park, Samuel to Mary Ann Pitman 1-29-1848 (1-31-1848)
Park, Samuel to Mary Long 1-29-1834
Park, Syrus to Elizabeth Caldwell 11-16-1838
Park, T.C. to Mary A. Campbell 3-24-1849 (4-5-1849)
Park, Thomas C. to Carrie Scott 12-5-1857 (12-8-1857)
Parker, Asa to Lodoriska Hays 2-14-1834 (2-15-1834)
Parker, Benjamin to Tempie Isam 1-6-1827 (1-7-1827)
Parker, D. C. to Mary Jane Webb 11-27-1860 (11-28-1860)
Parker, Gamaliel to Rebecca Boyd 1-28-1829 (1-29-1829)
Parker, Giles to Elizabeth Isam 10-29-1828
Parker, Isaac to Annie Isum 10-25-1827 (11-18-1827)
Parker, J. A. J. to Jane Clary 10-7-1858
Parker, Jesse to Elizabeth Gregory 1-30-1841
Parker, Joel to Ann L.(T?) Moore 3-18-1835
Parker, John G. to Anne Ray 7-25-1850
Parker, John H. to Margaret Craton? 5-28-1833 (6-9?-1833)
Parker, John L. to Sophia Green 9-10-1833
Parker, John T. to Martha Ray 10-29-1856 (10-30-1856)
Parker, Payton L. to Eliza Jacobs 8-12-1840 (8-13-1840)
Parker, Payton to Emily Stephenson 6-17-1844
Parker, Sylvester G. to Louisa F. Jones 9-10-1851 (9-11-1851)
Parker, Thomas to Pamillia Ann Rook 8-12-1846 (8-16-1846)
Parker, Will to Mary Thomas 5-7-1836
Parker, Wm. G. to Mary E. Scott 6-14-1861
Parks, Eli to Clarinda Callahan 5-11-1859 (5-15-1859)
Parks, Ephraim to A. A. Leming 5-15-1861
Parks, John B. to Sarah A. Foster 2-2-1856 (2-5-1856)
Parks, Robert N. to Mary Ann Stewart 1-31-1842 (2-2-1842)
Parmer, J. C. to Sarah Ann Grove 9-29-1847
Parmour, John to Minerva Downs 11-26-1836 (11-27-1836)
Parr, James to Rena Caroline Davis 11-4-1833 (11-5-1833)
Parran, Thomas A. to Maria C. Wood 11-2-1848
Parris, Henry to Elizabeth Johnson 9-15-1849 (9-27-1849)
Parrish, Green to Julianna Lock 11-30-1825
Parrott, Albert G. to Mary Matilda Rainer 10-4-1849 (10-18-1849)
Partlow, William D. to Adelener H. Bowling 9-4-1831 (9-29-1831)
Pate, William to Barbay Boyte 10-8-1834

Pate, William to Jinnetta Irvin 6-23-1836
Patrick, Manian to Mary L. Mede Alford 6-21-1838 (6-26-1838)
Patrick, Thos. G. to Sarah J. Joyner 8-1-1844 (8-8-1844)
Patterson, James B. to Nancy Jane Gray 8?-22-1859 (8-23-1859)
Patterson, R. G. to Cynthia A. Lowe 4-11-1851 (4-15-1851)
Patterson, Raiford C. to Unicy? Miller 10-29-1842 (11-2-1842)
Patterson, Wm. to Susan Sparks 10-7-1857
Paul, M. H. to Catharine B. Casey 10-21-1850 (10-22-1850)
Paul, Travis to Charlotte Box 9-9-1834 (9-17-1834)
Peacock, Wilson N. to Martha C. Napier 2-17-1846 (2-18-1846)
Pearce, Levi to Susan Blount 5-15-1844 (5-16-1844)
Pearce, M. C. to Julia A. Humphrey 9-29-1860
Pebles, Thomas to Clarissa Roberts 10-5-1850
Peek, James to Susan Potts 5-1-1835
Peers, Jas. M. to Mary E. Pledge 3-28-1855 (4-2-1855)
Pegram, R. W. to Victoria Belote 1-2-1860
Pegram, Samuel G. to Harriett G. Jones 7-25-1836 (7-27-1836)
Pence, Jesse to Rebecca Hoke 6-22-1839 (6-23-1839)
Pennington, Abel to Mary Hurt 3-14-1841
Pennington, Archibald to Melissa Cooksey 11-16-1833 (11-17-1833)
Pennington, John M. to Abby Mills 12-28-1831 (12-29-1831)
Perkins, Peter to Mary Henry Hodge 1-20-1841
Perkins, Rufus to ____ Rouch 2-10-1860
Perkins, Williams to Sary Brown 7-10-1827 (7-12-1827)
Perry, John to Penelope Holiday 12-23-1852 (12-24-1852)
Perry, Nazerith to Mary Catherine L. McCommon 11-10-1853
Perry, W. F. to Charity Chapman 5-17-1858 (5-18-1858)
Perry, William S. to Prudence N. Perry 1-19-1848 (1-20-1848)
Perryman, John D. to Mary W. Napier 6-3-1843 (6-4-1843)
Pervis, George to Elizabeth Seate(Scott?) 6-29-1838
Peters, Edward J. W. to Mary Ann Sheets 3-11-1854 (3-12-1854)
Peters, Edward L. to Judah Hester 6-7-1848
Peters, Edward L. to Lettrice Parker 1-27-1827 (2-1-1827)
Peters, Edward L. to Rachel Murphy 6-30-1840 (7-2-1840)
Peters, George B. to Eveline L. McDowell 7-29-1841
Peters, George B. to Narcissa Williams 5-9-1839
Peters, Thomas to Ann Eliza Glasgow 6-15-1837 (6-22-1837)
Peters, Thomas to Sarah Jane Irions 10-28-1846
Pettigrew, Samuel to Nancy Nichols 7-17-1826 (7-18-1826)
Pettus, Henry L. to Eliza A. Ruffin 9-25-1851
Pevahouse, M. J. G. to Nancy J. Keer 6-24-1856 (6-25-1856)
Pew, John to Catherine Manerva Pew 11-21-1850
Pew, Wm. C. to Elizabeth Ann Williams 10-8-1838 (10-14-1838)
Phelps, Philip P. to Arkansas Overton 9-23-1848 (9-28-1848)
Philips, Alfred D. to Margaret McLendon 12-21-1853 (12-22-1853)
Philips, George R. to Caroline Meachum 7-19-1850 (7-25-1850)
Philips, William to Jane Wiggins 8-23-1856
Philley, Calvin to Lucretia Hanley 7-18-1827 (7-22-1827)
Philley, Miles to Mary Stinson 6-4-1838
Phillips, James W. to Rebecca E. Hannis 6-9-1849 (6-10-1849)
Phillips, Jas. M. to Martha A. Roberts 6-4-1859 (6-5-1859)
Phillips, Nathan to Catharine Breeden 8-21-1856
Phillips, Wm. M. to Julia A. Breedon 8-20-1859 (8-21-1859)
Philly, Calvin to Sarah Ann Stephenson 12-25-1838
Philpot, John to Mary Alexander 3-14-1831 (3-15-1831)
Philpott, Edward to Mary Ann Taylor 4-25-1829
Pierce, Josiah to Haley Goodwin 11-5-1836 (11-7-1836)
Pierce, Uriah to Judy Chandler 4-26-1833 (4-30-1833)
Piles, Hiram to Elizabeth Wright 12-30-1833 (1-3?-1834)
Piles, James M. to Minerva M. Pipkin 4-3-1861 (4-4-1861)
Piles, Lennard to Martha McIver 10-6-1827 (10-?-1827)
Pipkin, David H. to Elizabeth M. Yarbrough 9-28-1853 (9-29-1853)
Pipkin, Hinton J. to Sarah Jane Norris 5-23-1840 (5-28-1840)
Pipkin, Jesse to Sally Piles 1-4-1828 (1-6-1828)
Pipkin, John A. to Neety Jane Pugh 1-16-1848
Pipkin, William to Gila Ann Newman 1-17-1855 (1-21-1855)
Pipkins, David B. to Elizabeth Poyner 4-15-1848 (4-16-1848)
Pipkins, Needham to Henrietta Newton 12-8-1834
Pipkins, Stephen L. to Maria Jane Piles 2-20-1861
Pirtle, Benjamin W. to Harriett E. Dubois 12-29-1837 (1-4-1838)
Pirtle, Benjamin W. to Sarah Jane Leathers 9-16-1839
Pirtle, Isaac W. to Sarah E. Toone 11-12-1844 (11-14-1844)
Pirtle, Isaac to Eunisa Cunningham 12-13-1828
Pirtle, Jacob T. to Agness Overton 10-4-1852 (10-9-1852)
Pirtle, James to E. A. Priest? 5-5-1847
Pirtle, John A. to Mary B. Champion 8-19-1831 (8-24-1831)
Pirtle, John B. to Susan Priest 5-6-1850 (5-8-1850)
Pirtle, Lewis to Susannah? Jackson 10-8-1846 (10-13-1846)
Pirtle, Martin to Martha Jane Duboise 12-20-1833 (12-25-1833)
Pirtle, Peter B. to Sarah J. Brandon 12-22-1847 (12-23-1847)
Pirtle, Robert J. to Rebecca J. Toone 12-20-1848 (12-21-1848)
Pirtle, Robert to Elizabeth Bennett 9-19-1833
Pirtle, Robert to Mary Jane Taggart 3-13-1830 (3-17-1830)
Pirtle, William W. to Lucy Jane Robinson 5-14-1850 (5-16-1850)
Pitman, Ethelana to Elmina Jacobs 9-27-1829
Plank, James to Lucinda Taber 10-9-1833
Pledge, Lemuel M. to Mary W. Dodd 12-23-1826 (12-24-1826)
Polk(Pack), Thomas to Ann Morrow 12-18-1833
Polk, Alexander to Elizabeth Jackson 6-17-1829
Polk, Charles P. to Ellen M. Fitzhugh 10-7-1835
Polk, Edwin to Octavia R. Jones 7-29-1846 (7-30-1846)
Polk, Headly to Hetta Eliza Sebastin 6-3-1845
Polk, Horace M. to Ophelia J. Bills 6-15-1843 (6-20-1843)
Polk, Jackson J. to Elvira T. Boles 2-21-1835 (2-24-1835)
Polk, John to Sarah Croose 1-16-1830 (1-17-1830)
Polk, Johnathan to Agness Anderson 8-4-1851
Polk, Marshall T. to Evilina M. Bills 1-10-1856
Polk, Thomas W. to Sarah E. Brady 10-11-1838 (10-12-1838)
Polk, William to Elizabeth J. Bradford 10-24-1850
Pool, James to Nancy Neely 1-1-1830
Porter, D. H. to Louisa Drake 3-7-1851 (3-9-1851)
Porter, John M. to Sarah Rose 2-15-1848
Porter, William to Mary Wilson 12-7-1856
Porter, William to Susannah Rose 5-19-1841 (5-20-1841)
Portis, Benjn. H. W. to Equilla Bieber 6-20-1842 (6-?-1842)
Poterfield, Matthew A. to Mary Davis 10-4-1838
Powell, John to Mary Reason 7-19-1847 (7-27-1847)
Powell, Lemuel to Elizabeth Porter 3-25-1851 (3-27-1851)
Powell, Needham J. to Nancy M. Webb 11-24-1849 (11-27-1849)
Powell, Peyton to Ann H. Fowler 6-23-1835
Powell, R. H. to E. J. Gadd 1-10-1860 (1-11-1860)
Powell, Richard E. to Mary Gay 10-15-1836 (10-20-1836)
Powell, W. R. B. to Nancy M. Johnson 10-23-1857 (11-5-1857)
Power, Stephen F. to Maria S. Baskwell 9-13-1838 (SB 1839)
Power, Stephen F. to Maria S. Baskwell 9-13-1839 (9-26-1839)
Poyner, Lemuel to Elizabeth Smith 11-14-1840 (11-15-1840)
Prast?, J. A. to M. F. Jackson 7-12-1847
Prescott, Daniel to Anna M. Carver 5-18-1828
Prewett, A. N. to Caroline Bunting 11-15-1858 (11-18-1858)
Prewett, A. O. to Luvenia Bailey 2-16-1859 (2-17-1859)
Prewett, Daniel M. to Nancy Davis 6-6-1838 (6-12-1838)
Prewett, J. H. to Martha E. Hill 12-18-1858 (12-22-1858)
Prewett, James W. to Mary A. Hanis(Harris?) 1-21-1848 (1-25-1848)
Prewett, S. L. to M.F. Bass 9-29-1860 (10-24-1860)
Prewett, T. N. to Mary E. Harris 1-4-1860 (1-5-1860)
Prewett, W. H. to Martha A. Evans 10-19-1860
Prewitt, John P. F. to Malinda C. Brown 9-20-1843
Prewitt, Mastin to Polly Standly 2-26-1838 (2-27-1838)
Prewitt, Mathew Thomas to Rebecca Ann Glass 4-10-1848 (4-11-1848)
Prewitt, Milton W. to Mariah W. Prewitt 8-9-1847 (8-12-1847)
Price, Edwin H. to Maria A. Ruffin 4-27-1836 (4-29-1836)
Price, James W. to Elizabeth R. Toone 4-28-1852 (4-29-1852)
Price, John to Martha B. Reagan 8-1-1853 (8-15-1853)
Price, Michael to Elizabeth Brown 8-17-1837
Price, W. F. to Mary C. Breedon 3-21-1861
Priest, Benj. F. to Mary L. A. Jackson 1-31-1855 (2-1-1855)
Priest, Wm. C. to Helen Sloan 7-2-1860 (7-4-1860)
Pruete, James C. to Emblem Ham 9-23-1839 (9-26-1839)
Pruett, John to Rebecca Nail 2-7-1831 (2-9-1831)
Pruett, Stephen to Elizabeth Breeding 4-19-1827
Puckett, J. E. to Sarah A. Clifton 12-23-1858
Pugh, Andrew Jackson to Dovist? Ann Eatus 1-22-1852
Pugh, James R. to Charity M. Low 1-20-1840 (1-24-1840)
Pugh, James T. to Eliza B. Whitmore 8-21-1835 (8-27-1835)
Pugh, James T. to Salina Darnell 9-28-1853 (9-29-1853)
Pulliam, Clem to Martha Atkinson 12-30-1852
Pulliam, Tilman P. to Martha J. Hinson 12-20-1854
Pullum, Vachel W. to Martha M. Murphy 11-11-1848 (11-16-1848)
Punch, Mathew L. to Elizabeth Reagan 10-11-1838 (10-12-1838)

Putney, David E. to Elizabeth Harris 9-25-1831 (9-27-1831)
Pylant, Francis M. to Mary A. Collins 7-11-1849 (7-12-1849)
Pyles, Overton to Loty Robinson 2-19-1833 (2-?-1833)
Ragan, Nathaniel to Mary Vincent 2-9-1842 (2-10-1842)
Ragan, William B. to Nancy C. Rutherford 9-3-1847 (9-5-1847)
Ragan, William to Permelia Hynnell 12-9-1837
Ragan, Wm. B. to Martha Ann Hanniss 11-10-1838 (11-15-1838)
Raiford, Morris to Ann Boyte 12-12-1837 (1-4-1838)
Raiford, Needham to Rachel Sanders 8-13-1841
Rain, Cornelius to Martha Ann Field 4-11-1838 (4-12-1838)
Rainer, Eli to Eliza C. Sexton 1-18-1854 (1-19-1854)
Rainer, Joel to Polly Wellins 9-27-1837
Rainer, Joseph S. to Zilpha Greenlee 12-18-1851 (12-19-1851)
Rainer, P. M. to Arkansas Phelps 8-7-1858 (8-8-1858)
Rainer, Pitser R. to Martha J. Kelly 12-10-1850 (12-19-1850)
Raines, Joel S. to Elizabeth Yarbrough 8-27-1832
Raines, John H. to Eliza A. Bunting 12-22-1849 (12-23-1849)
Raines, Marshall to Emeline Chessher 4-8-1847
Raines, Thomas to Elizabeth Peck 10-29-1851 (10-30-1851)
Rainey, Alfred M. to Elizabeth J. Birdsong 7-11-1855 (7-12-1855)
Rainey, D. P. to Caroline Carricker 5-1-1848 (5-16-1848)
Rainey, James to Nancy S. Carricker 8-23-1852 (8-26-1852)
Rainey, Stephen Henry to Margaret Milissa Cloyd 8-26-1848 (8-29-1848)
Rainey, William T. to Talibhta C. McCommons 10-17-1848 (10-19-1848)
Rainey, Williamson B. to Matilda Dean 11-5-1841 (11-7-1841)
Rainey, Williamson E. to Rebecca Duberry 3-21-1843
Rains, George R. to Jane Yarbrough 1-5-1836
Rains, Wm. McD. to Clemintine M. Gossett 12-9-1840 (12-10-1840)
Rainy, Henry G. to June Riley 6-23-1846 (6-25-1846)
Rainy?, Wm. T. to Sarah A. Mashburn 9-4-1846
Ralph, Isaac to Lucindia McCarver 1-6-1842
Ramage, Josiah to Margaret McIver 9-9-1831 (9-15-1831)
Ramsey, Alexander to Sarah Black 12-?-1843 (12-22-1843)
Ramsey, Thomas B. to Elizabeth A. Newsom 10-10-1854
Ramsey, Thomas T.? to Virginia Mathews 7-29?-1858 (7-30-1858)
Ramsey, W. C. to Sarah Jane Brigman 2-25-1861 (2-26-1861)
Ramsey, William to Olive P. Patrick 1-16-1830 (1-17-1830)
Randolph, E.A. to Elleanor G. Riddle 10-3-1854
Randolph, John W. to Rutha Ann Baskwell 3-16-1853
Randolph, Richard B. B. to Elizabeth Perry 1-4-1842
Randolph, Richard B. B. to Elizabeth Perry 5-6-1844 (5-30-1844)
Rankin, James J. to Margaret G. Rolong 1-2-1856
Rankin, Robt. J. to Sarah F. Goforth 4-11-1859 (4-17-1859)
Ratten, William M. to Nancy Kremer(Creamer) 4-1-1835 (4-5-1835)
Ray, George to Frances Burrow? 11-7-1833
Ray, James M. to Matilda Delk 3-12-1859 (3-13-1859)
Ray, Lemuel L. to Elmira Kemp 5-4-1834
Ray, Moses to Susan Caroline Rosson 11-17-1836
Ray, Samuel to Amelia C. Wilson 12-19-1860 (12-10?-1861?)
Ray, Samuel to Oney Rogers 11-27-1833 (11-29-1833)
Raynard, Joseph S. to Martha J. Minton 12-10-1833 (12-17-1833)
Read, Bradford to Rebecca Burns 12-7-1833
Read, James to Catharine Vantrice 11-24-1828 (11-27-1828)
Read, Robert to Lucinda Norwood 5-29-1827
Read, Washington to Sarah Pool 11-28-1828 (11-30-1828)
Reagan, Charles to Lucinda Webster 6-16-1827
Reagan, Jessee to Polly Welch 12-20-1838
Reagan, John to Jane Davis 9-19-1833
Reaves, David to Elizabeth Tipler 12-28-1840 (12-31-1840)
Reaves, Edmund to Charlotte McKinnie 2-17-1838
Reaves, William to Nancy Carooth 12-23-1850
Reaves, Wm. to Lydia Crisp 5-14-1844
Reavis, Ashbey to Ann Mildred Mallory 12-21-1846 (12-24-1846)
Redd, W. J. to Mollie E. Montgomery 1-19-1861 (1-24-1861)
Reed, Finiss to Lugina Hopkins 7-28-1831 (8-4-1831)
Reed, James Y. to Mary J. Jones 3-23-1861
Reed, John Y. to Martha Ayres 2-18-1840
Reed, John to Elizabeth Truett(Pruett) 3-18-1828
Reedon, Samuel to Mahala Reedon 1-9-1862
Reeser, T. M. to S. E. Carter 12-23-1861 (12-27-1861)
Reeves, J. M> to Elizabeth Ussery 12-17-1860 (12-19-1860)
Reeves, William to Sarah Farris 4-3-1835 (4-7-1835)
Reeves, Willis G. to Mary J. Latta 11-6-1854 (11-8-1854)
Reynolds, Amos C. to Rebeccah Parker 1-16-1838
Reynolds, Joel J. to Sarah Cockram 11-27-1834
Reynolds, John C. to Martha Mashburn 5-29-1847
Reynolds, John W. to Margaret C. Blair 12-3-1859
Reynolds, Newnham to Julia Ruff 3-9-1859
Reynolds, Thurene E. to Mary Ann C. Rankin 12-14-1840
Reynolds, William to Tabitha Cookburn? 11-4-1830
Rhea, Joseph to Racheal Kelly 8-15-1835 (8-16-1835)
Rhodes, Alexander to Margaret Armor 7-17-1835
Rhodes, Cicero to Susan Bolt 11-25-1850 (11-28-1850)
Rhodes, Gilbert to Tilpha A. Brown 5-2-1857
Rhodes, James H. to Mary Cox 3-12-1832
Rhodes, James H. to Nancy Ann Rose 5-23-1844 (6-2-1844)
Rhodes, John F. to Rachael Chisum 7-19-1839 (7-29-1839)
Rhodes, John to Nancy Brown 8-13-1851
Rhodes, Pleasant to Malinda Brooks 2-17-1852 (2-19-1852)
Rhodes, Westley to Harriet R. Rollan 12-27-1855
Rhodes, Will W. to Lavicy Smith 4-4-1839 (4-10-1839)
Rice, Amasa to Rebecca Hodges 4-23-1836
Rich, Duncan T. to Elizabeth S. Bennett 9-2-1861 (9-3-1861)
Richards, B. T. to Sylvester Forte 10-3-1836 (10-4-1836)
Richardson, James M. to Catharine Jones 4-4-1855 (4-10-1855)
Richardson, Thomas to Elizabeth Nicholls 10-30-1841 (10-31-1841)
Richardson, Yimri? to Elizabeth Williams 5-26-1848 (5-22?-1848)
Richardson, Zachiriah to Lucinda Kesterson 10-6-1832 (10-?-1832)
Richie, Isaac P. to Nancy Murphy 7-29-1834 (7-30-1834)
Richmond, Ezekiel to Margaret Alexander 2-16-1832
Ricks(Riggs), John H. to Rebecca Colbert 5-2-1829 (5-7-1829)
Riddle, Wilie J.? to Ruth Bowers 7-29-1833 (8-8-1833)
Ridge, Samuel W. to Martha Pulla(Pully) 7-17-1829
Riggs, John W. to Mary C. Guthrie 11-8-1856 (11-9-1856)
Riggs, Reubin M. to Louisa I.? Delk 12-18-1850 (12-24-1850)
Riley, Joseph to Rebecca Lonsberry 8-24-1839
Ritchey, John to Sarah Love 4-23-1836
Ritter, Everett to Anna Goodwin 5-15-1828 (5-20-1828)
Ritter, Isham to M. Marler 3-3-1845
Roach(Roark?), William to Lucy Gregory 7-17-1844
Roach, Edward to Mary Riggs 11-10-1830
Roach, J. F. to Abigale Overton 10-23-1854 (10-26-1854)
Roach, J. F. to Martha A. Thomas 6-7-1858
Roades, Ashley to Nancy C. Boyt 5-30-1846 (5-31-1846)
Roark, John to Mary Murphy 2-14-1843 (2-15-1843)
Roark, William to Elizabeth B. Shepherd 12-27-1832
Robb, Washington G. to Julia Ann Thompson 12-11-1833 (12-12-1833)
Roberts, Henry M. to Clarissa Ann Ammons 5-16-1846 (5-17-1846)
Roberts, Lytle B. to Louisa Mills 2-8-1844
Roberts, Nathan to Mary P. Rosser(Roper) 10-20-1831
Roberts, Prestly H. to Margaret R. David 9-14-1853
Roberts, S.(L) B. to Catharine Waller 10-4-1850
Roberts, William to Kizziah Lampkins 10-16-1851 (10-16-1851)
Roberts, Wm. F. to Amanda M. Vails 12-12-1839
Robertson, A. T. to Martha Jane Vaden 10-27-1845 (11-2-1845)
Robertson, Charles S. to Lucinda E. Ayers 5-12-1852 (6-12-1852)
Robertson, Christopher to Nancy E. Taylo 11-1-1854 (11-2-1854)
Robertson, Edward to Harriett A. Barne? 4-4-1839
Robertson, Elisha to Elizabeth Woodward 5-24-1860
Robertson, J. M. C. to Elizabeth Watson 8-1-1832 (8-2-1832)
Robertson, James to Sarah Ann Stafford 5-31-1838
Robertson, Jerimiah W. to Mary Jane Patton 2-11-1854 (2-19-1854)
Robertson, John F. to Nancy Johnson 7-31-1827
Robertson, John H. to Vina Cornelius 11-4-1832 (11-6-1832)
Robertson, Jonas to Elizabeth Chisum 8-6-1828 (8-7-1828)
Robertson, Joseph R. to Mary A. Craig 6-26-1840 (7-7-1840)
Robertson, Theophulis S. to A. C. Dial 5-24-1847 (5-30-1847)
Robertson, Thomas J. to Delila A. Caviness 11-11-1854 (11-12-1854)
Robertson, Thomas to Emily Holliway 4-25-1855 (4-28-1855)
Robertson, Walter to Rebecca Hill 6-15-1824 (6-17-1824)
Robertson, Wm. R. to Jane C. Dial 12-26-1844 (12-28-1844)
Robinson, Alfred to Nancy Weaver? 7-23-1831
Robinson, Asa to Frances Cozby 12-29-1833
Robinson, Darius to Eliza J. Usher 1-17-1843
Robinson, Edward to Hellen E. Vernon 2-9-1850 (2-19-1850)
Robinson, Elisha to Barbara Chisum 1-5-1830 (1-7-1830)
Robinson, James H. to Sarah E. Wilson 1-24-1848 (1-25-1848)

Robinson, James to Mary Ann Burt 8-18-1832
Robinson, James to Nancy Vernon 3-26-1860
Robinson, John C. to Elizabeth J. Turner 12-23-1848 (12-26-1848)
Robinson, John to Levisa Grantham 8-28-1826 (8-28-1826)
Robinson, Patrick F. to Louisa I. Ayers 11-29-1850 (11-30-1850)
Robinson, Pleasant to Elizabeth Montgomery 12-21-1835
Robinson, R. W. to Delila Averett 8-22-1833
Robinson, R. W. to M. A. Lewis 3-1-1859 (3-13-1859)
Robinson, Robert W. to Mary Hall 5-10-1831
Robinson, Wm. E. to Virginia Bunting 10-14-1859 (10-18-1859)
Robison, John C. to Elizabeth Mercer 1-13-1852
Robley, John H. to Catharine Oswald 12-16-1858
Rodgers, Nathaniel to Mary Polk 2-23-1843
Rogers, Benjamin to Mary Strickland 4-23-1851
Rogers, David to Carolin Fletcher 10-9-1845 (10-12-1845)
Rogers, Elam to Margaret Forsheath 10-23-1844 (10-25-1844)
Rogers, George W. to Mary Ann Medford 2-3-1840 (2-4-1840)
Rogers, Henry J. to Malenda Highfill 12-6-1845
Rogers, Henry to Polly Hunnell 3-3-1831
Rogers, Irvin Q. to Sophronia Baskwell 12-28-1854
Rogers, Isaac to Mahala Elkins 3-18-1834
Rogers, James M. to Elizabeth S. Stone 2-26-1838 (3-13-1838)
Rogers, Jno. W. to Deliah L. Hansford 10-25-1858 (10-28-1858)
Rogers, John jr. to Eliza Cox 10-28-1835 (10-29-1835)
Rogers, John to Jane Mills 12-10-1845
Rogers, John to Mary Johnson 9-19-1861
Rogers, Lemuel to Clarissa Eliza Bowers 9-28-1833 (10-3-1833)
Rogers, Richard to Mary Riprogle 10-19-1858
Rogers, Robt. R. to Martha W. Absent 11-9-1859
Rogers, S. James to Caroline Hudson 3-22-1858 (3-25-1858)
Rogers, Saml. B. to Mary C. Yopp 2-4-1861 (2-7-1861)
Rogers, Saml. W. to Mary A. Woolberton 9-29-1860
Rogers, Sampson to Hollis Jackson 12-8-1830 (12-9-1830)
Rogers, Spier to Elizabeth Casey 10-27-1836
Rogers, Stephen to Polly Fulgham 12-8-1829 (12-10-1829)
Rogers, William R. to Nancy Robinson 5-7-1828
Rogers, William to Susan Mashburn 1-9-1829
Rogers, Willoughby to Sally Smith 1-4-1837
Rogers, Wm. R. to Joisey Hanks 9-8-1827
Rook, Amon Y. to Martha Kearley 1-15-1840 (1-22-1840)
Rook, Benjamin to Polly Smith 12-16-1829 (12-17-1829)
Rook, Grove to Biddy Huddleston 7-26-1845 (7-29-1845)
Rook, James Y. to Margaret Ramage 2-27-1828
Rook, William Y. to Elizabeth Eaver 12-23-1834
Roper, James to Ann M. West 5-25-1848
Roper, John S.(L?) to Sarah Mask 8-23-1838
Rose, Benjamin to Zilphia Coor? 7-20-1833
Rose, J. W. to Sarah Rogers 12-17-1856 (12-18-1856)
Rose, James A. to Eliza T. Crews 3-10-1852 (3-11-1852)
Rose, James to Elizabeth Maxwell 4-30-1832 (5-3-1832)
Rose, James to Prudence Littrell? 9-27-1848 (9-28-1848)
Rose, John P. to Mary Stout 8-12-1854 (8-13-1854)
Rose, John to Sarah Thompson 7-15-1835 (7-23-1835)
Rose, Kinchen L. to Jinnette C. Cherry 10-20-1853 (10-27-1853)
Rose, Kincheon L. to Susan Jane Covington 6-5-1841 (6-10-1841)
Rose, Thomas to Emeline Z. Brown 9-8-1856 (9-11-1856)
Rose, Wm. H. to Elizabeth Freeman 8-20-1860 (8-23-1860)
Ross(Rass-Russ), Enoch to Prudence Foster 1-14-1829
Ross, Alexander to Elizabeth Colbert 1-3-1826 (1-5-1826)
Ross, Andrew to Nancy Cody 6-6-1826 (6-7-1826)
Ross, Daniel A. to Elizabeth A. Wilkes 10-14-1860 (10-15-1860)
Ross, Hiram W. to Nancy Burns 7-7-1828
Ross, Jacob to Mariah Johnston 6-19-1825 (7-19-1825)
Ross, James F. to Sarah George 4-27-1841
Ross, John A. to Nancy Wilson 2-3-1843 (2-4-1843)
Ross, John W. to Louisa E. Cross 10-8-1859 (10-12-1859)
Ross, Thomas L. to Martha Wilson 2-1-1849 (2-4-1849)
Ross, W. F. to Willie Ann Parker 1-21-1861 (1-23-1861)
Rossen, William to Elizabeth Jacob 12-22-1824
Rosser, William to Melvina Hunt 5-29-1833
Rosson, Abner to Lucretia Holbut? 8-26-1836 (8-25?-1836)
Rosson, D. W. to Sarah A. Graves 3-14-1853 (3-16-1853)
Rosson, James to Deborah Crocker 1-23-1841 (1-26-1841)
Rosson, John to Delina Taylor 12-7-1853 (12-8-1853)
Rosson, Joseph L. to Mary Atkins 6-9-1858 (6-29-1858)
Rosson, Joseph L. to Ruth Ray 2-24-1851
Rosson, S. E. to Mary Whitfield 9-22-1837
Rosson, William to Polly Jobe 4-19-1826
Rowsey, W. H. to Eliana M. Sharpe 1-23-1851
Rucker, Linsey P. to Mary W. Tarver 11-15-1836
Rucker, W. J. K. to Elizabeth J. Chapman 11-23-1841
Ruddle, Robert K. to Dohorty J. Hankly 1-23-1849 (1-29-1849)
Rudisill, Joseph to Mary C. D. Champion 12-6-1832
Ruffin, James D. to Basina Ruffin 7-8-1834 (7-17-1834)
Ruffin, W. Brooks to Harriet Jones 3-9?-1833
Rummage, Joseph to Peggy Weaver 12-29-1825
Rush, William to Margaret E. Nailor 12-2-1850 (12-12-1850)
Russell(Russell), Stephen H. to Hannah Adeline Reed 9-8-1827
Russell, Isaac P. to Elizabeth Alsup 8-22-1828 (9-24-1828)
Russell, James L. to Elizabeth Mullins 8-10-1829 (8-11-1829)
Russell, John C. to Amanda Sauls 1-13-1857 (1-14-1857)
Russell, John H. to Ruth Casey 1-7-1829 (1-9-1829)
Russell, Robt. J. to Sarah J. Brown 8-24-1857
Russell, T. H. to Emeline Webster 8-1-1836 (8-23-1836)
Rutherford, B. B. to Sophronia A. Reaves 9-3-1861
Rutherford, John R. to Polina M. Grace 4-29-1851 (4-30-1851)
Rutherford, Linzy J. to Hetty Hodges 9-28-1830 (10-7-1830)
Sadberry, William to Hannah Jane Lorance 9-26-1843 (10-5-1843)
Sadler, B. W. to Mary E. Moore 12-26-1859 (12-29-1859)
Sain, Daniel B. to Mary E. Riddle 1-13-1838 (1-14(16)-1838)
Sain, Enoch to May Ann Elizabeth Panky 3-10-1847 (3-12-1847)
Sain, James to Louisa Macon 12-19-1843 (12-21-1843)
Sain, lPerry to Nancy McK. Jacobs 1-6-1845 (1-7-1845)
Sallier, N. B. to Mary Avant 12-18-1844 (12-19-1844)
Sammons, H. A. to Henrietta C. Wilkes 11-11-1859 (11-7?-1859)
Sammons, J. W. to Naoma T. Wilks 12-3-1858 (12-9-1858)
Sammons, John H. to Mary M. Wilkes 10-16-1854 (10-26-1854)
Sammons, Wilie to Martha F. Wilkes 10-4-1850 (10-10-1850)
Sanderlin, Wilson S. to Louisa C. Comer 8-29-1842 (9-1-1842)
Sanders, Andy to Matilda Ann Farr 6-26-1844
Sanders, David to C. E. Simpson 9-30-1858
Sanders, Gilliad A. to Martha W. Burt 8-19-1840
Sanders, James to Isabella Meeks(Merks?) 2-22-1838
Sanders, John Wesley to Elizabeth Taylor 3-25-1841
Sanders, Lary A. to Elizabeth J. Crawford 1-16-1849 (1-18-1849)
Sanders, Stephen to Amy Moore 10-25-1853 (10-27-1853)
Sanders, Stephen to Heisey H. Simmons 1-8-1838
Sanders, Thomas to Sarah Emily Whitehorn 4-18-1842 (4-22-1842)
Sanford, Richard to Jane Elizabeth Alexander 5-17-1851
Sarrett, William to Abigail Dougherty 10-22-1837
Sasser, Joel S. to Epsey J. Casey 11-24-1857 (11-26-1857)
Sasser, John to Mary Ann Chisum 6-10-1834 (6-20-1834)
Sasser, William to Charlotte Rhodes 1-15-1842 (1-16-1842)
Sasser, William to Litilia? Lambeth 10-11-1850 (10-13-1850)
Saterfield, James H. to Mary L. Reynolds 7-19-1836 (7-20-1836)
Sauls, Burril to Jane Matthews 8-5-1829 (8-11-1829)
Sauls, Joseph D. to Elya(Diya) Ann Jones 9-10-1856 (9-11-1856)
Sauls, William to Elizabeth C. Bunting 10-18-1849 (10-22-1849)
Saunders, Hardy to Elizabeth Wilkes 7-6-1836 (8-7-1836)
Saunders, William to Mary Israil 12-30-1830
Savage, Hamilton to Amanda Wiloughby 9-3-1849 (9-6-1849)
Savage, Hamilton to Rebecca Parr 2-17-1857 (2-18-1857)
Savage, Henry M. to Frances Mills 1-21-1858 (1-22-1858)
Savage, James M. to Mary Jane Westbrook 7-21-1858 (7-24-1858)
Savage, James M. to N. A. Bingham 8-10-1853
Savage, Jefferson C. to Lucy Dean 1-10-1843 (1-13-1843)
Savage, Levin to Rebecca Rainey 8-4-1829
Savage, W. B. to Julia A. F. Phillips 9-22-1860 (9-23-1860)
Savage, Wiseman to N. Glidwell 1-26-1848
Scaggs, William to Mary Dunn 10-15-1830
Scarbrough, George S. to Margaret Jane G. White 11-10-1840 (11-12-1840)
Scarbrough, John Y.(Z?) to Pamelia A. Jackson 1-11-1854 (1-12-1854)
Scarbrough, Joseph H. to Louisa Jane Riggins 9-21-1856
Schrimsher, G. R. to Mary Williams 6-2-1858 (6-6-1858)
Scoggins, James W. to Creesy Clouse 8-20-1836
Scoggins, James to Sarah A. C. Young 6-30-1855 (7-4-1855)
Scoggins, John to Lydia Taylor 3-20-1837 (3-22-1837)
Scoggins, Stephen to Alsy M. McClanahan 6-28-1836 (not executed?) *

Scoggins, Stephen to Martha Welch 2-6-1837 (2-7-1837)
Scoggins, William to Margaret E. Weir 4-5-1859 (4-6-1859)
Scott, Hiram to Nancy R. Vaughan 4-8-1831
Scott, Hubbard P. to Nancy Carter 6-16-1842
Scott, J. Madison to Lucey Blackwood 11-12-1831
Scott, James L. to Eliza Land 7-5-1827
Scott, James to Martha McDaniel 2-12-1839
Scott, Jessee to Edna F. Vandegrift 10-30-1861 (10-31-1861)
Scott, John W. to Margarett Ann Lake 12-30-1851 (1-3-1852)
Scott, John to Martha Ann Vandergrifft 7-25-1861 (7-15?-1861)
Scott, Lunsford W. to Sarah D. Bridges 1-14-1843 (1-25-1843)
Scott, Lycurgus to Abbey Pendleton 1-29-1838 (1-30-1838)
Scott, M. G. to Jackey Ann Willoughby 9-10-1857
Scott, Nathaniel to Elizabeth Reynolds 11-15-1835 (11-19-1835)
Scott, Nathaniel to Mary Ham 11-13-1838 (11-22-1838)
Scott, Newton C. to Harrett Mills 7-7-1841 (7-8-1841)
Scott, Reubin S. to Eliza Jane Perry 5-20-1850 (5-23-1850)
Scott, Samuel C. to Martha S. Ingram 2-9-1849 (4-10-1849)
Scott, Sandy to Alice Mills 2-5-1835 (2-6-1835)
Scott, William to Evalina Day 3-20-1861 (3-21-1861)
Scott, William to Sarah Allen 12-12-1859 (12-15-1859)
Scroggins, Giles to Nancy J. A. Shopher 1-19-1858 (1-20-1858)
Scroggins, Jesse to Lissa Yarbrough 3-6-1835 (3-11-1835)
Scroggins, Jesse to Nancy Hamilton 7-17-1830 (7-20-1830)
Seaton, Hiram to Eliza Huddleston 6-24-1846 (6-25-1846)
Seaton, Hiram to Rhoda Read 12-10-1840
Seaton, William B. to Elizabeth Herrell? 1-4-1851 (1-5-1851)
Seddens, Marshall to Frances Simpson 11-24-1828
Seddens, William H. to Assennith Lamberth 12-20-1853
Seivers, John D. to Hannah A. Haynes 12-5-1848 (12-7-1848)
Sellars, Isaac to Rebecca Guise 8-27-1857 (8-28-1857)
Sellars, Joseph to Susan McKinnie 3-3-1840 (3-4-1840)
Sexton, Allen to Fanny Hammonds 3-2-1859 (3-3-1859)
Sexton, J. R. to Mary J. Justice 9-17-1857 (9-24-1857)
Sexton, Richd. A. to Nancy A. Hogan 3-7-1861 (3-10-1861)
Sexton, Thomas to Rachael Mashburn 7-4-1855 (7-24-1855)
Shackelford, Wm. W. to Celia Hays 4-8-1837 (4-9-1837)
Shannon, Moses to Milly M. Lytle 11-11-1839 (11-14-1839)
Shaply, Wm. T. to Elizabeth M. Beard 4-20-1846 (4-28-1846)
Sharon, Albert to Arabella Shearon 8-8-1851 (8-10-1851)
Sharpe, C. C. P. to Mary Buckner 3-26-1857
Shaw, Hugh to Nancy Cornelius 9-26-1827 (9-28-1827)
Shaw, John M. to Angeline McGill 2-22-1845 (2-25-1845)
Shaw, John W. to Agness E. Hunter 11-1-1838
Shaw, Theophilus to Rebecca Harris 5-5-1835
Shaw, Theopulus to Elizabeth Randolph 6-5-1850 (6-6-1850)
Shearin, Belfield S. to Rebecca Rogers 11-24-1854
Shearin, Jesse B. to Jane C. Webster 2-16-1857 (2-18-1857)
Shearon, B. S. to Amanda Cox 7-11-1860 (7-15-1860)
Sheets, Geo. W. to Sarah J. Hines 12-18-1859
Sheets, Jacob F. to Anne Hines 1-20-1838 (1-23-1838)
Sheffield, John A. to Sarah A. McClellan 2-3-1857 (2-19-1857)
Shell, A. D. to Louisa Baker 6-12-1832 (6-?-1832)
Shell, Martin to Matilda Norris 2-24-1834
Shelly, John to Nancy Biebers 12-29-1852 (12-30-1852)
Shelton, George A. to Mary Wolverton 10-27-1835
Shelton, Robert W. to Sarah Jane Rivers 1-24-1829
Shelton, Sheppard to Sarah Ann Mashburn 1-23-1849 (1-26-1849)
Shepherd, Frederick to Matilda Ann Luttrell 5-18-1844 (5-21-1844)
Shepherd, Thomas J. to Harriet Anderson 1-10-1833
Sheppard, James H. to Rebecca Johnson 10-15-1828
Sheppard, John to Martha Beton 4-29-1845
Shepperd, John C. to Amanda Hines 2-6-1849 (2-13-1849)
Shepperd, Robt. H. to Laura H. Wood 12-29-1858 (12-30-1858)
Sherron, B. J. to Amanda Cox 1-7-1859
Sherron, G. W. to Sarah Becca Harrison 11-4-1859
Shilling, William A. to Sarah Rutherford 3-2-1836 (3-10-1836)
Shinault, Isaac to Lucindia Ragan 12-16-1833 (12-17-1833)
Shinault, Isaac to Octavia Morris 12-18-1860 (12-19-1860)
Shinault, John J. to Mary M. Puckett 9-19-1861 (9-21-1861)
Shinault, John W. to Caroline Pullum 1-13-1840 (1-14-1840)
Shinault, John W. to Martha Cook 3-7-1856 (3-9-1856)
Shinault, Walter M. to Nancy Harriss 2-26-1853 (3-2-1853)
Shinault, Walter to Mary Woods 6-19-1849 (6-27-1849)
Shinpeck, William to Martha Carroll 12-23-1826
Shipman, Samuel to Betsy Pully 11-21-1828 (11-23-1828)
Shoefer, Arma to Sally Henson 2-17-1830 (2-18-1830)
Shofer, Calvin to Mary M. Mitchell 2-6-1854 (2-10-1854)
Shofer, Frederick to Delila Weaver 11-4-1825 (11-6-1825)
Shofer, John to Nancy t. Clines 8-16-1859 (8-17-1859)
Short, Elijah to Mary Ann King 3-11-1843 (3-7?-1843)
Short, Hiram C. to Mary H. Gambell 6-26-1847 (6-29-1847)
Short, Jacob H. to Cela Long 5-8-1849
Short, Joseph to Oliva Jones 11-13-1834
Short, R. L. to Adaline Wilkison 10-15-1849 (11-25-1849)
Short, Thomas F. to Sarah F. Taylaor 11-2-1853
Shott, Charles to Mary Kennady 5-5-1851 (5-8-1851)
Shott, Hugh to Louisa McBride 2-1-1843 (2-3-1843)
Shultz, Joseph H. to Eliza Duff 1-30-1833 (1-31-1833)
Siler, Peter P. to H. F. Joyner 6-27-1853
Sills, Isham to Milly Harris 3-1-1833
Sills, William T. to Nancy J. Taylor 8-16-1856 (8-17-1856)
Simmons, Benjamin A. to Martha O. Harriss 1-21-1861 (1-24-1861)
Simmons, Caswell to Cynthia E. Barker 1-29-1859
Simmons, John H. to Olivia F. Harriss 1-13-1858
Simmons, Samuel D. to Jennie O. Howell 3-16-1858 (3-?-1858)
Simmons, W. D. to Rebecca Higgs 6-30-1846
Simmons, Willoby D. to Ann Hervey 3-29-1843
Simpson, G. B. to Malvira Grantham 9-7-1835
Simpson, Needham K. to ____ ____ 12-20-1853
Simpson, Samuel to Harriet Mitchell 12-11-1838 (12-12-1838)
Simpson, Samuel to Rebecca McKaughn 2-1-1833
Simpson, William to Mariah Ingram 1-22-1831
Simpson, Wm. to Frances Harper 8-15-1844 (8-20?-1844)
Sinclair, Daniel to Margrett M. Reynolds 3-22-1847 (3-25-1847)
Sipes, Alfred to Mary F. Lowry 2-6-1860
Sipes, Samuel R. to Elizabeth A. Lowery 12-15-1859 (12-16-1859)
Sissom, Andrew to Elizabeth Childress 7-5-1846 (7-6-1846)
Skinner, E. P. to Elizabeth Murrell 11-18-1857 (11-19-1857)
Skinner, John to Elizabeth Jones 3-10-1825
Skinner, Martin to Nancy J. Hinson 12-28-1850 (12-31-1850)
Skipper, Needham to Sarah Cartwright 3-14-1832 (3-?-1832)
Slaughter, Thomas S. to Sarah Jane Crisp 5-26-1850
Slaughter, Wm. P. to P. E. Green? 5-6-1844 (5-8-1844)
Sloan, Alexander to Helan M. Duncan 5-16-1853 (5-18-1853)
Smith, A. J. to Francisia Davis 12-18-1858 (12-22-1858)
Smith, Adam to Hannah Mitchell 11-24-1834
Smith, Anthony to Wineford Lee 5-25-1835
Smith, Cannon to Martha J. Higgs 12-27-1857 (1-5-1858)
Smith, Cannon to Nancy C. Usher 12-22-1848 (12-20?-1848)
Smith, Charles D. to Ann L. Burnett 12-11-1829
Smith, Claiborn to Sarah E. Stinson 2-7-1843
Smith, D. T. to C. A. M. Willoughby 10-4-1857
Smith, Eli to Dolly H. Moffitt 12-12-1831 (12-15-1831)
Smith, Elias to Alsey Elkins 11-16-1846 (5-23-1847)
Smith, G. F. to A. J. Smith 1-17-1843
Smith, G. Washington to Esther Lee 7-10-1841 (7-11-1841)
Smith, Harvey P. to Margaret E. Walker 10-6-1842
Smith, Haywood to Jane Wilson 6-24-1861 (6-25-1861)
Smith, Isaac to Ellen Norris 12-5-1835
Smith, Isham N. to America A. Thompson 10-29-1838
Smith, Isham N. to Clemant A. Mallory 11-23-1846 (11-26-1846)
Smith, J. W. C. to Martha L. Taylor 1-19-1861
Smith, James B. to Edny Jane Gore 8-25-1855 (8-28-1855)
Smith, James E. to Rebecca Pankey 11-6-1848 (11-8-1848)
Smith, James F. to Nancy Ann Bell 6-4-1860 (6-6-1860)
Smith, James R. to Celia Atts(Alts) 8-18-1830 (8-19-1830)
Smith, James to Nancy Marsh 9-9-1851
Smith, Jas. B. to Eliza J. Lokey 8-18-1859
Smith, Jasper N. to Mary E. Miller 6-30-1855 (7-1-1855)
Smith, John D. to Nancy C. Reagan 12-1-1854 (12-3-1854)
Smith, John F. to Ava Holly 3-18-1844 (3-19-1844)
Smith, John J. to Emily E. Hogue 8-12-1850 (8-13-1850)
Smith, John P. to Martha Jane Hodge 10-31-1848
Smith, Joseph to Harriet Lea 10-23-1839 (10-24-1839)
Smith, Joseph to Lidia Eaton 10-14-1852 (1-10-1854)
Smith, Killis McDonald to Eliza Jane Walker 6-13-1853 (6-14-1853)
Smith, Levi to Sarah Norris 1-22-1839 (1-25-1839)
Smith, M. H. to Lucy B. Wilson 3-7-1859 (3-9-1859)
Smith, Madison D. to Elvira C. Ellington 1-26-1841 (2-2-1841)

Smith, Milton to Nancy C. Crums(Crews?) 3-27-1845
Smith, Milton to Susan C. Gray 3-4-1831
Smith, Neil to Elizabeth Pingleton 5-20-1861 (5-26-1861)
Smith, Philip N. to Mary Parker 4-28-1842
Smith, Robert E. to Fannie Statler 1-27-1858
Smith, Sidney to E. P. Smith 6-11-1831
Smith, T. Lewis to Meloria S. Burrow 6-11-1856 (7-3-1856)
Smith, Thomas R. to Catharine Miller 4-28-1853
Smith, Thomas to Mary Pirtle 8-6-1827 (8-7-1827)
Smith, William C. to Amelia Overton 7-17-1851
Smith, William K. to Delilah M. Caviness 12-26-1853
Smith, William to Elizabeth Webb 9-24-1846
Smith, William to Louisa Marsh 1-29-1856 (1-31-1856)
Smith, William to Mary Moffitt 10-29-1838 (10-30-1838)
Smith, Wm. A. J. to Manerva James? 12-28-1846 (12-31-1846)
Smith, Wm. to Mary Williams 4-1-1844
Smithey, John to Elizabeth Sharp 1-9-1825
Smyth, Larkin T. to Jane Wire(Wise?) 11-2-1825
Sneed, Jno. L. T. to Mary A. Shephard 8-26-1848 (8-27-1848)
Sneed, John to Elizabeth Hodges 6-8-1843 (7-?-1843)
Snellgroves, Saml. to Jane Stone 2-16-1856 (2-17-1856)
Snow, J. W. to Nancy E. Thomas 9-28-1859 (9-29-1859)
Snow, Rufus S. to Lucretia Justice 5-17-1855
Somervell, Willis L. to Mary Ann Martin 1-11-1834 (1-16-1834)
Sommerville, Thomas to Mary A. Siler 4-26-1838
Southall, A. L. to Julia A. Buffaloe 4-3-1857 (4-5-1857)
Southern, James H. to Lorenda Doxey 12-24-1832
Spain, Littleberry to Debby Rossin? 9-30-1850
Spain, Littleberry to Mary McBride 7-28-1858
Spain, William to Mary J. Dyson 12-1-1854 (12-2-1854)
Sparks, Jefferson to Penelope Futrel 9-4-1833 (9-5-1833)
Sparks, Minas to Sarah Shinn 1-27-1851
Sparks, Solomon C. to Martha C. Smith 3-23-1841
Spears, James F. to Sarah J. Covington 12-30-1843 (1-4-1844)
Spencer, J.E. to Celestia A. Nutall 9-21-1859
Spencer, James M. to Tennessee Davis 8-26-1858 (8-29-1858)
Sperlin, Elias to Susan R. Binkley 1-25-1858
Sperling, Benj. to Milly Hamilton 9-25-1833
Sperling, John to Sarah Mayfield 1-31-1833 (2-5-1833)
Spight, James W.(M?) to Mary E. D. Rucker 12-31-1840
Spine, Alexander to Catherine Whitlock 4-29-1830
Spinks, John C. to Sarah Jane Lake 12-26-1848
Spinks, Windsor J. to Cynthia C. Laks? 10-31-1860
Spivy, John H. to Martha Howard 10-31-1845 (11-2-1845)
Spivy, W. D. to Jane Simmons 10-22-1857 (10-26-1857)
Springfield, John to Mary Ann Gray 7-7-1856 (7-8-1856)
Spurlin, A. C. to Elizabeth Hamlin? 11-30-1849 (11-31?-1849)
Spurlin, Berry to Milly Marler 7-21-1837
Spurling, Geo. W. to Minervia J. Crews 3-1-1858
Spurling, Levi to Lavina(Lavivian) Cooper 6-22-1827 (6-23-1827)
Stacy, Will A. to Mary Ann Knight 10-3-1827
Stafford, John L. to Judah Malone 4-19-1837 (4-20-1837)
Stafford, John to Sally Hatley? 2-6-1837
Stafford, Joseph A. to Cynthia Montgomery 12-24-1834 (12-25-1834)
Stafford, Uriah to Elizabeth Hanks 11-76-1825 (11-8-1825)
Stainback, Littleberry to Rebecca B. Cross 3-6-1844 (3-7-1844)
Stallings, Kemp to Harrett Bates 12-19-1845 (12-23-1845)
Stallions, Kemp to Keziah Brown 5-23-1829 (5-24-1829)
Standfield, Harvey D. to Hester Ann Griggs 3-13-1840 (3-15-1840)
Standley, William to Gatsey Caraway 12-30-1851 (1-1-1852)
Standly, Major to Cassa Johnson 11-10-1835 (11-12-1835)
Stanly, Hillery H. to Mary Z. Sasser 2-2-1847
Starkey, Elijah to Valenia Johnson 9-5-1859 (9-6-1859)
Staton, Everet to Kissiah Berry(Beny) 7-26-1828 (7-28-1828)
Steele, Geo. to Eliza Pannell 5-16-1860
Steele, Ninian to Hannah Harvey 11-2-1826
Stephens, C. H. to Louisa Bailey 11-11-1844 (11-14-1844)
Stephens, James E. to Sarah A. Little 12-14-1853 (12-15-1853)
Stephens, James to Mary Hodge 3-22-1839
Stephens, Joseph O.(C.) to Mary F. Richardson 6-21-1858 (6-23-1858)
Stephens, Lawrence to Elizabeth Brock 12-8-1840 (12-13-1840)
Stephens, Ransom to Betsy A. Sasser 11-26-1849 (12-3-1849)
Stephenson, David to Elizabeth Ammons 9-12-1843 (9-14-1843)
Stevens, Atkins to Sarah Ann Carter 12-8-1835
Stevens, Edwin to Eliza Cranford 6-26-1832
Stevens, Elliot to Elizabeth Boyte 2-13-1832
Steward, Edward H. to Mary Hale 12-18-1852 (12-19-1852)
Stewart, Able to Ann Mitchell 12-26-1853
Stewart, Alexander to Mira Tuberville 5-12-1827 (5-15-1827)
Stewart, E.B. to Lucy M. Farriss 1-26-1859 (1-27-1859)
Stewart, Edward H. to Charlotte Short 10-25-1849 (11-17-1849)
Stewart, Elisha T. to Mary E. Huddleston 7-20-1859
Stewart, Enock to Adaline O. Hancock 12-3-1851 (12-4-1851)
Stewart, H. Alexander to Elizabeth C. Cole 3-17-1853 (3-23-1853)
Stewart, James E. to Christiana E. Adams 5-9-1854
Stewart, M. A. to Sarah F. Farriss 12-26-1854 (12-27-1854)
Stewart, S.(L?) P. to Mahuldah Carr 2-19-1847 (2-21-1847)
Stewart, Samuel D. to Mourning Ingram 4-5-1852 (4-6-1852)
Stewart, W. F. to A. A. Neighbors 2-9-1856
Stewart, William to Cela Ann Bailey 2-12-1849 (2-17-1849)
Stinson, J.C. to Mary F. Prewett 9-26-1860 (10-24-1860)
Stockton, Daniel L. to Nancy Ann Jones 8-26-1833 (9-5-1833)
Stockton, John C. to Rhoda Young 8-3-1826
Stockton, Wm. to Elizabeth Barkley 1-22-1837
Stokes, W. B.(Green B.) to Masie McBee 3-30-1827 (3-31-1827)
Stone, Benjamin to Harriet Cross 5-26-1855 (5-28?-1855)
Stone, Hendley to C. J. Bass 9-4-1858 (9-5-1858)
Stone, Hendley to Emily F. Rankin 9-7-1843 (9-14-1843)
Stone, Joel M. to Lilphia Butler 8-23-1826
Stone, Reubin to Martha Bailey 4-13-1835
Stone, Wm. to Margaret Love 2-14-1834 (2-16-1834)
Stout, Elihu to Sarah J. Moore 5-11-1855 (5-13?-1855)
Stout, James M. to Mary Gray 7-14-1848
Stovall, Wm. B. to Sarah Brantley 6-13-1840 (6-14-1840)
Street, John W. to Nancy A. C. Harrison 8-31-1848 (9-7-1848)
Street, T. J. to Cynthia A. McCommon 12-15-1860 (1-1-1861)
Strickland, Cullen to Eliza Porter 6-6-1849 (6-7-1849)
Strickland, John S. to Mary Jane Allison 12-20-1841 (12-29-1841)
Stricklin, J. W. to Martha E. Jones 4-23-1861 (4-24-1861)
Stricklin, Job to F. J. Simpson 10-2-1861 (10-3-1861)
Stricklin, John to Elizabeth Ray 1-27-1857
Stricklin, Nathaniel to Mary Miller 10-14-1840 (10-15-1840)
Stricklin, Wm. P. to Mary E. Reece 12-6-1851 (12-11-1851)
Strongham, Lorenza D. to Frances Ellison 7-23-1832 (7-24-1832)
Strothers, Solomon G. to Lidia Kilgore 7-13-1830
Sturdivant, Wm. J. to Amelia Smith 9-4-1855 (9-5-1855)
Sulenger, Roger T. to Elizabeth Hill 8-25-1828 (8-27-1828)
Sullender, Samuel to Elizabeth Goodman 8-5-1834
Sullivan, Albert G. to Mary F. Crisp 5-4-1843
Sullivan, John to Polly Harrison 8-11-1855 (8-15-1855)
Sullivant, Jeremiah to Martha Gray 1-3-1842
Summons(Summers?), lJohn G. to Eliza Lakey 7-17-1838
Sumners, James A. to Ellen A. Vernon 2-23-1852 (2-24-1852)
Sutton, Benjamin to Frances Robertson 2-10-1845 (2-13-1845)
Sutton, George W. to Amanda C. Simpson 10-26-1853 (11-12-1853)
Sutton, Lewis R. to Sydney Harriss 12-16-1850 (12-17-1850)
Swain, Chas. to M. A. Mathews 4-25-1851 (4-26-1851)
Sweeton, A. E. to Mariah J. Lambert 10-24-1854 (10-25-1854)
Sweeton, Dutton M. to Serena Anderson 7-19-1836
Sweeton, Dutton to Lucy Davis 10-4-1841 (10-10-1841)
Sweeton, Jarvis to Betsy Yarbroy? 2-2-1836
Sweeton, W. B. W. to Nancy H. Lambert 1-18-1860
Swindle, Holloway to Rebecca Adamson 7-17-1838
Swindle, Jas. M. to Susan Mathews 12-17-1857
Swindle, John to Permilia Roberts 7-26-1836
Swindle, Joseph A. to Mary Tune 3-15-1837 (3-16-1837)
Swindle, R. D. to Elizabeth Lambert 3-30-1849 (4-1-1849)
Sykes, H. O. to Nancy Cooper 7-3-1861 (7-4-1861)
Taber, John to Safronia Armstrong 8-28-1832
Taber, William H. to Louisa T. Hullum 11-25-1831 (12-1-1831)
Tabor, Jno. S. to Mary J. Harris 9-26-1859 (9-28-1859)
Tackett, Geo. to Mary Hunter 7-3-1860
Tackett, George to Sarah Hodges 7-31-1834 (8-5-1834)
Tackett, Manin to Lethe Shelton 5-17-1858 (5-18-1858)
Tackett, Wm. to Susan Fortner 3-1-1859 (3-2-1859)
Tagart, William R. to Nancy E. Prewitt 7-10-1852 (7-13-1852)
Taggart, John P. to Elizabeth Prewitt 4-3-1848 (4-4-1848)
Taggart, William to CAtherine McBee 2-26-1827
Tannehill, B. N. D. to Sallie Lynch 11-4-1857 (11-5-1857)
Tanner, L. to Sarah A. Prewitt 4-9-1856 (4-23-1856)

Tanner, Lafayette to Minerva Robertson 4-7-1854 (4-13-1854)
Tanner, Wm. A. to Virginia A. Crowder 9-13-1851 (9-17-1851)
Tate, George W. to Eliza Cooper 3-11-1835
Tate, George W. to Sarah Whitford 8-13-1836
Tate, Magnis to Elizabeth Roberts 11-12-1848
Tate, T. S. to Ann Eliza Jones 12-11-1860 (12-12-1860)
Tate, Thomas W. to Mary J. Mooney 12-3-1859
Taylor, Abner to Laura Manley 3-30-1832 (3-31-1832)
Taylor, Andrew to Clarissa Polk 6-7-1824 (6-11-1824)
Taylor, Augustus to Marmu? Ferrell 7-18-1855
Taylor, George W. to Massa Parker 9-10-1828 (9-12-1828)
Taylor, Giles to Sarah Crouse 11-17-1842
Taylor, John Henry to Rachel Northcross 12-27-1851 (1-1-1852)
Taylor, Joseph to Jane Green 7-6-1826 (7-19-1826)
Taylor, Josiah to Elizabeth Biddy 10-19-1831 (10-20-1831)
Taylor, Josiah to Tempe Webster 2-27-1832 (3-1-1832)
Taylor, Rev. R. V. to Sarah L. Chunn 7-21-1853
Taylor, W. W. to Elizabeth Punch 4-6-1848
Taylor, William to Elizabeth Jane Gibson 1-6?-1847 (1-7-1847)
Taylor, William to Elizabeth McIlroy 7-6-1824 (7-8-1824)
Taylor, William to Lucinda Gage 12-15-1827
Taylor, William to Lucinda Gage 12-15-1829 (12-24-1829)
Taylor, Willis V. to Sarah K. Vincent 1-14-1840
Taylor, Willis to Louisa Hart 4-9-1829 (5-11-1829)
Teadford, John J. to Phoebe N. Rosson 2-14-1850 (2-19-1850)
Teague, Henry M. to Frances Daniel 1-27-1851
Teague, Joseph B. to Elizabeth Comer 1-1-1844
Teague, Joshua M. to Catharine A. Dean 1-16-1856
Teague, Josiah to Mary Ann Upton 10-19-1852 (10-20-1852)
Teague, William G. to Molly Thomas 10-14-1831
Tedford, John J. to Ailsy Warren 12-5-1859 (12-15-1859)
Terry, Hiram to Elizabeth Cooksey 11-3-1843 (11-5-1843)
Terry, John to Susannah Rogers 1-15-1838 (1-16-1838)
Terry, Joseph B. to Joanna Parker 11-26-1856
Thebold, Augustus to Sarah Piles 11-14-1860 (11-15-1860)
Thomas, B. F. to Zady F. Hammonds 8-27-1856
Thomas, Bedford to Elizabeth J. Hendricks 1-10-1849 (1-12-1849)
Thomas, Francis M. to Mary A. Hammond 8-20-1852 (8-22-1852)
Thomas, Henry P. to Eliza Roberts 4-10-1841 (4-15-1841)
Thomas, J. J. to Nancy E. Hendrick 2-17-1847
Thomas, James to Sarah Wilson 11-22-1852 (11-23-1852)
Thomas, Jesse to Penelope McClellan 5-6-1828
Thomas, Lewis to Nancy Carr 9-13-1828
Thomas, Wm. to Nancy Pearson 12-20-1831 (12-22-1831)
Thompson, Allen M. to Mary A. H. Pipkin 9-17-1855 (9-18-1855)
Thompson, D. C. to M. J. Burnes 8-5-1859
Thompson, D. W. to C. Andrews 3-3-1847
Thompson, E. G. to Frances Crain 11-16-1833 (11-?-1833)
Thompson, E. T. to Susan J. Hammons 11-8-1855 (11-9-1855)
Thompson, George B. to Tabita Saunders 3-10-1831 (3-11-1831)
Thompson, George W. to Sarah Ann McCommon 1-1-1851 (1-2-1851)
Thompson, Hiram to Margrett Calahan 12-29-1846
Thompson, Isaac N. to Mary J. Ayers 3-9-1840 (3-12-1840)
Thompson, James to Mary Philpot 6-1-1833 (6-4-1833)
Thompson, John J. to Polly Ann Clifft 3-14-1846 (3-24(14?)-1846
Thompson, John M. to Clarissa Norris 12-23-1847 (12-26-1847)
Thompson, John to Cloe Cadwell 1-28-1824 (2-5-1824)
Thompson, John to Nancy Gee 3-10-1857? (3-10-1858)
Thompson, John to Polly Cross 2-16-1828 (2-17-1828)
Thompson, Joseph S. to Ann C. Allen 3-9-1847 (3-10-1847)
Thompson, Josiah H. D. to Eliza Ann Rainey 10-8-1855 (10-16-1855)
Thompson, Keeble T. to Sarah A. Hammons 9-30-1846 (10-1-1846)
Thompson, LaFayette to Hanley Crocker 3-24-1834 (3-30-1834)
Thompson, Lee to Emily M. Derribery 3-21-1853
Thompson, P. H. to Nancy C. Mashburn 2-3-1858 (2-4-1858)
Thompson, Robert L. to Elizabeth J. McCarter 9-21-1835 (10-1-1835)
Thompson, Robert to Emily Norris 6-17-1835 (6-26-1835)
Thompson, Robert to Polly(Mary) Rogers 11-24-1834
Thompson, Saml. to Julia Ann Anthony 7-25-1841
Thompson, T. G. to Sally M. Rose 11-1-1841 (11-6-1841)
Thompson, Thomas A. to Kerah H. Sellers 7-29-1834 (7-31-1834)
Thompson, Thomas C. to Margaret A. Simmons 1-1-1861 (1-3-1861)
Thompson, W. W. to Clarissa Ammons 12-23-1852
Thompson, William B. to Susan E. Stevens 11-7-1849 (11-8-1849)
Thompson, William W. to Jerutia Rose 8-12-1837 (8-17-1837)
Thompson, William to Emily Hays 10-26-1847
Thompson, Willouby L. to Elizabeth Ann Crawford 10-23-1837
Thompson, Wm. to Nancy E. Higgs 10-24-1859
Thornton, Josiah to Elizabeth Vaught 8-27-1833 (9-3-1833)
Thornton, Theopilus to Delilah Deen 11-17-1827 (12-3-1827)
Thorpe, J. H. to Celia A. Rogers 8-6-1860
Thrailkill, Morgan to Rhoda C. Barrett 6-5-1861 (6-9-1861)
Thrasher, Franklin to Fatha Lock 12-1-1825
Thrasher, Jesse A. to Caroline Pankey 8-12-1858
Threlkeld, John to Delilah Highfield 3-28-1828 (3-30-1828)
Thron, David to Mary A. Toone 6-8-1857
Thurman, Meridith M. to Martha J. Lowe 5-17-1851 (5-20-1851)
Thurmond, M. M. to S. A. Low 10-8-1860 (10-9-1860)
Tilley, James H. to Delila McMicken 12-30-1861 (1-1-1862)
Tillman, James to Mary Cannon 4-20-1839 (4-25-1839)
Tilmon, Joseph to Frances Childress 9-29-1838
Tilton, J. C. to Jane Elizabeth Smally 2-2-1848 (2-3-1848)
Timberlake, John W. to Elizabeth A. Howard 1-6-1840 (1-7-1840)
Tims, E. D. L. to Louisa M. King 7-10-1861
Tims, J. C. to Lyda Hammers 3-2-1854 (3-3-1854)
Tims, John C. to Cynthia Ann Savage 9-23-1830
Tims, John H. to Tamer Richardson 7-31-1861 (8-1-1861)
Tipler, George to Sillah?(Lillah?) Cox 3-24-1841 (3-25-1841)
Tipler, John H. to Mary Conly 1-9-1851 (1-15-1851)
Tipler, John to Lucinda Harrison 11-7-1843 (11-9-1843)
Tipler, Thomas J. to Militha Tedford 1-22-1842 (2-3-1842)
Tipler, W. F. to Matilda L. Burke 3-7-1856 (3-8-1856)
Tipler, William F. to Sarah Bishop 1-6-1838
Tisdale, James H. to Betsy P. Smith 1-16-1832 (1-17-1832)
Tisdale, William H. to Mary Willey 3-21-1825 (3-24-1825)
Todd, William to Emily Rawlings 11-27-1832
Toller, Thomas E. to Narcissa Rhodes 9-6-1845 (9-14-1845)
Tomson, George W. to Mary Ann Brown 12-16-1848 (12-23-1848)
Tomson, Thos. G. N. to Martha E. F. Brewer 9-29-1848 (with 1858)
Toombes, H. B. to F. G. Puckett 2-21-1857 (3-1-1857)
Toone, James jr. to Ruth Harriss 1-16-1861 (1-17-1861)
Towler?(Lowler?), W. M. to Frances Bowers 9-13-1850 (9-18-1850)
Tozier, Samuel to Ophelia Ann Scott 7-18-1861
Traylor, Pascall G. to Catherine B. C. Gaylor? 11-16-1836
Treadwell, Timmon S. to Elizabeth E. Haynie 10-1-1850
Treece, James G. to Susan A. Box 8-10-1858 (8-12-1858)
Treese, Boyd to Jane Goad 3-7-1852 (3-18-1852)
Trousdale, Allen to Ann Burgner(Burger) 9-7-1827
Trousdale, Leonidas to Virginia F. Joy 12-21-1853
Tucker, Benj. F. to K. C. Pope 10-13-1857 (9?-18-1857)
Tucker, Jesse C. to Mary Jane Murrell 3-14-1850
Tudor, Jesse G. to Eliza Cutberth 6-20-1833 (7-19-1833)
Tudor, Kenny L. to Emily Davis 7-7-1833 (8-8-1833)
Tull, John H. to Tabitha J. McCarver 8-22-1859
Tull, T. J> to Marinda Drennon 1-5-1857 (1-9-1857)
Tull, Thomas J. to Miranda McCarver 3-14-1854
Turner, Andrew to Levina Chisham 1-1-1827
Turner, Benjamin to Sarah Johnson 11-21-1831
Turner, George to Mary Anderson 6-28-1839
Turner, Jackson to Dicey Goforth 4-13-1855 (4-14-1855)
Turner, John to Eliza Hale 1-30-1861
Turner, John to Elizabeth Johnson 12-20-1834
Turner, John to Elizabeth Savage 12-20-1860
Turner, John to Peggy Reed 7-8-1833 (7-9-1833)
Turner, Pleasant G. to Sarah F. Fowler 11-29-1854 (12-10-1854)
Turner, Thos to Elizabeth A. Shepherd 3-4-1843
Tuttle, Nathan W. to Elizabeth Ann Riddle 2-2-1826
Unthank, James H. to Mary Bell Neely 7-24-1855
Usher, William to N. C. Hankins 1-17-1835 (1-22-1835)
Ussery, Noah R. to Martha Jane Beavers 12-20-1852 (1-4-1853)
Ussery, Persan to Alsa Pullam 2-7-1840
Ussy(Ussery?), John D. to Elizabeth Bailey 2-8-1848 (2-17-1848)
Vail, Travis P. to Nancy Jane Damson-Damron-Dawson 12-11-1848 (12-26-1848)
Vails, Samuel jr. to Eliza Jane Roberts 3-28-1844
Vails, William to Sarah Blunt 1-18-1842 (1-23-1842)
Vantrease, Valentine to Rebecca B. Baskwell 1-13-1851
Vantresse, John to Tebitha D. Pool 12-25-1840
Vaughan, George to Delila Norman 1-15-1842 (1-16-1842)
Vaughan, J. L. to M. H. Steward 12-15-1856 (12-17-1856)

Vaughan, James to Melissa P. Wlkinson 11-9-1860 (11-11-1860)
Vaughan, John to Jane Cooksey 3-2-1844
Vaughan, William to Didama Cook 1-22-1828 (1-24-1828)
Vaughn, Benjamin to Giney Hamilton 4-16-1831
Vaughn, James to Sarah Burnett 4-26-1855
Vaughn, John to Rebecca Jane Lester 7-22-1837 (7-23-1837)
Vaughn, Walton H. to Frances Richardson 9-10-1832 (9-15-1832)
Vault, Stephen to Martha Gates 5-4-1846 (5-6-1846)
Vernon, A. P. to Martha Lethers 6-29-1844 (7-4-1844)
Vernon, Pryor L. to Sarah Robinson 9-27-1852
Vernon, Tho. to Easther Kelly 3-19-1837 (3-26?-1837)
Vicker, John to Martha Brantley 12-16-1842 (12-22-1842)
Vickers, James to Jane Avant 12-23-1846 (12-24-1846)
Vincent, Geo. W. to Jane Hughes 7-14-1858
Vincent, Willis to Sarah Davis 10-4-1855
Wade, Edmond to Manna E. Ayers 7-30-1829?
Wade, Edward to Rebecca Lacy 7-29-1829
Wade, Edwin to Manna Ayers 7-30-1832 (8-8-1832)
Wade, James to Frances C. McKaughan 5-13-1846
Waggener(Wagner), Solomon to Mary Wilson 4-14-1834
Wair, Wm. W. to Frances E. Fort 2-15-1841 (2-17-1841)
Walden, George I. to Louisa A. C. Rutherford 12-29-1830 (1-2-1831)
Walden, Isaac to Laura Holcombe 10-29-1857
Walker, Alford M. to Nancy Duff 1-24-1829 (1-27-1829)
Walker, David to Sally M. Blake 3-7-1831 (3-8-1831)
Walker, John B. to Mrs. Harriett Mcguire 8-14-1858 (8-17-1858)
Walker, Thomas W. to Rebecca Reynolds 3-29-1858
Walker, Thomas to Martha Willoughby 3-1-1841
Walker, Thomas to Mary L. McFall(McFarlin) 11-14-1833 (11-27-1833)
Walker, Valentine to Elizabeth White 3-14-1853 (3-15-1853)
Walker, William to Mary Ann Fowler 8-3-1833 (8-?-1833)
Wall, Ezekiel to Maria H. Hatly 1-6-1834 (1-4?-1834)
Wallace, Henderson C. to Mary C. Gahagan 5-25-1841
Wallace, J. B. to Celia Richardson 12-8-1856
Wallace, Thomas W.(M?) to Malissa Price 2-24-1840 (2-25-1840)
Wallace, Will W. to Elizabeth L. Mathews 1-4-1848 (1-6-1848)
Waller, Albert to Tina King 12-14-1853 (12-15-1853)
Waller, John to Mary Scott 10-11-1849
Waller, John to Susan Jonagan 9-2-1854 (9-3-1854)
Waller, Thomas to Altamyra Roberts 8-9-1842 (8-11-1842)
Wallis(Wilson), Jesse W. to Elizabeth W. Hubard 12-13-1845 (12-18-1845)
Walls, James B. to Harriet A. Harvey 12-13-1836 (12-21-1836)
Walton, James M. to Catharine Teague 11-24-1847 (11-25-1847)
Walton, John J. to Elizabeth Teague 12-27-1838
Walton, Joseph G. to Elizabeth Jane Flynn 10-2-1851
Walton, Robert H. to Sarah Kearney 1-8-1842 (1-9-1842)
Walton, William to Emily McIver 11-23-1836
Wamble, John to Elizabeth Sasser 1-5-1852 (1-8-1852)
Ward, James to Mary Blair 2-13-1836
Ward, James to Nancy Nabers 6-12-1830 (6-13-1830)
Ward, King W. to Martha Jane White 4-15-1851 (5-1-1851)
Ward, W. D. to Nancy I. Simpson 12-22-1853
Ware, Wm. P. to Nancy E. Gibson 4-17-1858
Warford, Jas. H. to Eliza J. Galloway 11-27-1856
Warren, Abner to Marcilla? Glenn 8-17-1846 (8-20-1846)
Warren, Alvin to Ruthey Wellman 12-24-1834 (12-28-1834)
Warren, Asbury to Eliza Anne Williams 7-23-1847 (8-4?-1847)
Warren, Daniel E. to Sarah A. Williams 4-6-1853
Warren, Elijah F. to Louisa J. Riggs 8-12-1854 (8-17-1854)
Warren, Elijah F. to Sarah Dawson 6-20-1845 (6-22-1845)
Warren, George to Mary Jane Harriss 10-15-1859 (10-16-1859)
Warren, Jefferson to Elizabeth Owen 12-21-1831 (1-5-1832)
Warren, John C. to Sarah Murphy 9-10-1828 (9-11-1828)
Warren, John M. to Sophronia Clarke 11-15-1834
Warren, John to Cora Johnson 1-11-1834 (1-16-1834)
Warren, John to Emily S. PSankey 1-29-1855 (1-30-1855)
Warren, Joseph to Lucinda Clift 11-7-1840 (11-26-1840)
Warren, Robert to Amanda Ann Mace 12-17-1840 (12-22-1840)
Warren, Thomas R. to Elizabeth E. T. Kerr 9-19-1860 (9-20-1860)
Warren, William Thomas to Emiline G. Crowder 11-19-1840 (12-2-1850)
Washington, George to Sally A. Staten? 1-13-1843
Washington, Samuel to Elizabeth Poole 3-22-1830
Watkins, Isaiah to Olivia C. Crews 12-24-1849
Watkins, Israel to Elizabeth McKinnen 6-6-1836
Watson, James to Elizabeth Floyd 12-6-1836
Watson, Joseph to Sarah Davenport 12-23-1835
Weaver, Lafayette to Elizabeth I. Parker 9-11-1852
Webb, Andrew C. to Winefred C. Corburn 5-25-1847
Webb, J. M. to Docia E. Ferrell 10-24-1853 (10-28-1853)
Webb, Jacob M. to Elizabeth J. Rogers 11-23-1843
Webb, John to Caroline Box 12-4-1854 (12-6-1854)
Webb, Joseph to Joycy Peeler 9-20-1854
Webb, M. C. to Mary J. Hogan 11-21-1856 (11-23-1856)
Webb, Mansil to Frances Rogers 1-25-1853 (1-27-1853)
Webb, McDaniel to Mary E. McKinnie 12-3-1849 (12-5-1849)
Webb, Prior to Mary Mashburn 10-10-1849 (10-11-1849)
Webb, Robert to Eliza Ann Taylor 8-26-1854 (8-26-1854)
Webb, Thos. H. to Emma H. Hamer 5-27-1858
Webb, Watson to Franky Jane Field 1-19-1847 (1-21-1847)
Webster, Henry to Hannah Shinault 12-6-1827
Webster, James to Jane Dillingham 9-8-1827
Webster, Jas. M. to Adaline Ayers 8-8-1832 (9-11-1832)
Webster, Jesse to Sarah Casey 12-12-1835 (12-17-1835)
Webster, John H. to Matilda F. Ussery 7-15-1861 (7-18-1861)
Webster, Samuel to Martha Ragan 2-6-1827
Welch, F. M. to Emily S. Gee 10-4-1858 (10-7-1858)
Welch, F. M. to Hannah J. Mayfield 5-3-1850 (5-9-1850)
Welch, George to Polly Ward 1-6-1844 (1-7-1844)
Welch, John to Nancy I. Vaugan 12-27-1852 (12-28-1852)
Wellions, Henry C. to Lenora M. F. Guy 12-11-1851
Wellions, Henry to Susan Ann Rainer 3-13-1843 (3-13?-1843)
Wellons, Charles M. to Cela M. Crawford 11-28-1850
Wellons, Henry C. to Martha C. Boston 4-12-1859 (4-14-1859)
Wellons, Larkin M. to Nancy T. Hannis 9-25-1841 (9-30-1841)
Wells, Daniel I. to Mary E. Suggett? 11-24-1836
Wells, J. C. to M. A. Ferguson 3-28-1859 (3-29-1859)
Wells, John L. to Polly M. McBride 1-13-1831
Wells, Joseph M. to Sally Burns 1-2-1830 (1-9-1830)
Wells, Lewis to Margaret H. Guthrie 10-29-1850
Wells, Pleasant B. to Emily Little 1-14-1832
Wells, Thomas S. to Sarah Rogers 8-18-1830
Wells, W. T. to Martha Davis 7-11-1859 (7-14-1859)
Wells, William H. to Nancy Rogers 6-18-1827
Wells, Wm. T. to Zelia A. Hullum 9-24-1859 (9-25-1859)
Welty, Elbert to Amanda E. Riley 7-3-1861 (7-4-1861)
Wesson, E. A. F. to Martha A. Grace 2-3-1857
West, Peter to Elizabeth McKnight 3-2-1827 (3-4-1827)
West, William to Joanna Mangrum 7-17-1850 (7-18-1850)
West, William to Susan McCarver 5-2-1837 (5-7-1837)
Westbrook, James R. to Frances Watson 8-31-1853
Westbrook, John R. to Martha A. Williams 9-3-1850
Westbrook, M. F. to Manervia Huddleston 7-19-1858
Whaley, John N. to Susan Jane Taylor 1-17-1842 (1-20-1842)
Wheeler, Jno. P. to Sarah R. Webster 7-29-1849
Wheeler, Solomon P. to Nancy Choate 10-6-1828
Whitaker, Eli to Emiline Davenport 4-9-1835
Whitaker, John C. to Nancy Riddle 1-14-1833 (1-15-1833)
Whitaker, Lusnford to Sarah Teague 7-8-1835
White, Alexander to Mary Eliza Simmons 2-22-1847 (2-23-1847)
White, George W. to Louisa Shelby 7-11-1836
White, James D. to Mary Jane Hubbard 8-8-1837
White, Josiah S. to Rebecca W. Minter 4-20-1849 (4-24-1849)
White, Ro L. to Mary C. Bright 3-21-1855 (3-22-1855)
White, Samuel to Rebecca H. Scott 6-28-1842 (6-29-1842)
White, Thomas S. to Sally Gullet 10-2-1832 (10-8-1832)
White, Thos. E. to Sophia B. Fitzhugh 4-2-1834 (4-3-1834)
White, William C. to Frances Attwood 6-22-1838 (6-24-1838)
White, Wm. C. to Octavia Harris 11-20-1859 (11-21-1859)
Whitehorn, Nicholas H. to Elizabeth I. Glass 11-26-1849 (11-29-1849)
Whitehorn, Thomas to Elizabeth Farr 7-9-1844 (7-10-1844)
Whitfield, Geo. W. to Mrs. Elizabeth Wilson 9-7-1850 (9-10-1850)
Whitford, David to Sarah Brooks 9-26-1837
Whitford, Jessee to Elizabeth Brooks 5-5-1838 (5-6-1838)
Whitlock, Thos. to Elizabeth A. ______ 7-28-1832
Whitmore, Geo. L. to Rebecca A. Usher 11-10-1845 (11-12-1845)
Whitmore, R. A. to Cornelia A. Brown 6-30-1851
Whitten, J. M. to Mary A. J. Hopkins 3-9-1857

Whitten, William E. to Susan Lovell 2-23-1850 (2-24-1850)
Wiggins, Harris to Betsy Mitchell 12-31-1827
Wiggins, James R. to Elizabeth S. Jones 6-27-1859 (6-30-1859)
Wiggins, James T. to Jane Kurby 6-15-1832
Wiggins, West W. to Mary Ann Smith 6-1-1839 (6-5-1839)
Wiggins, Wm. W. to Sophia H. Miller 11-16-1859
Wilbanks, J. S. to Mary A. Wilbanks 5-11-1860 (5-20-1860)
Wiley, A. S. to Martha E. Meek 9-9-1859
Wiley, James to Elizabeth Taylor 2-8-1836
Wiley, Nelson to Sarah L. Conner 2-4-1842 (2-6-1842)
Wilhight, Julius to Polly Friar 3-2-1837
Wilhite, Matthew to Nancy Moss 9-5-1833
Wilkerson, Benjamin to Cavell F. Birdsong 8-17-1839 (8-21-1839)
Wilkerson, George W. to Sarah B. Wood 10-20-1843
Wilkerson, Jackson to Mary Suttles 3-28-1859
Wilkes, Benjamin to Mary McMahon 2-27-1834
Wilkes, James to Laura F. Doyle 8-21-1854 (8-23-1854)
Wilkes, John W. to E. J. Mitchell 3-13-1858 (3-17-1859?)
Wilkes, Joseph to Naoma M. Barnett 3-12-1829
Wilkes, Perry C. to A. E. J. Wilkes 11-12-1856 (11-13-1856)
Wilkins, Geo. W. to Telissa Ann Kirk 11-9-1854 (11-8?-1854)
Wilkins, Wm. E. to Mary R. Adair 11-27-1854 (11-29-1854)
Wilkinson, John to Seletha Gage 5-8-1830
Wilkison, James G. to Lucinda Hannis 7-4-1827 (7-5-1827)
Willi, G. W. to Priscilla Hodge 9-6-1852
Willi, George W. to Serena Atkinson 1-5-1847 (1-6-1847)
Williams, Alvin to Sarah Ann Crawford 9-3-1837
Williams, Andrew to Emiline Boo 3-1-1858
Williams, Benjamin F. to Mary A. Minter 3-22-1842
Williams, Benjamin J. to Martha V. Chandler 6-20-1853
Williams, Benjamin to Caroline Wood 1-13-1847 (1-14-1847)
Williams, Benjamin to Martha A. R. Harly 10-26-1853 (3-13-1854)
Williams, C. H. to Mary A. Birdsong 10-29-1851 (10-31-1851)
Williams, Calvin to Eliza H. Rankin 2-13-1835
Williams, Cokely P. to Lety Tally 2-17-1831
Williams, Dan to Pricilla Carlin 2-17-1827 (2-18-1827)
Williams, David to Elizabeth V. Seaton 9-26-1834
Williams, David to Mary McKangham 9-27-1828
Williams, Emery E. to Dorcas Jones 11-25-1834
Williams, George M. to E. C. Glraham 12-5-1853 (12-7-1853)
Williams, Hamblin L. to Lucina Moore 1-12-1832 (1-17-1832)
Williams, Hiram to Polly Grant 12-27-1824 (1-13-1825)
Williams, J. G. to A. W. Clark 12-9-1850 (12-11-1850)
Williams, J. W. to Joan Harrison Duncan 4-28-1860 (4-29-1860)
Williams, James F. to Susanna Johnson 2-8-1858 (2-11-1858)
Williams, James T. to Eliza Jane Grove 9-28-1841 (9-29-1841)
Williams, James T. to Harriet R. Harris 1-29-1850 (1-31-1850)
Williams, James to Ann S. Lane 12-26-1860 (12-27-1860)
Williams, James to Susan Menley 11-23-1833
Williams, Jno. G. to Sarah A. Knight 5-6-1858 (5-7-1858)
Williams, John C. to Nancy A. Terry 10-5-1849
Williams, John to Mary L. Humphrey 12-2-1858
Williams, John to Mary Rayner 9-8-1827 (9-13-1827)
Williams, Joseph C. to Mary Lake 9-19-1840
Williams, Lewis M. to Virginia D. Harrison 10-19-1857
Williams, Mabry D. to Anvalina Belote 6-30-1856 (7-3-1856)
Williams, Moses H. to Priscilla Ward 5-27-1838 (5-30-1838)
Williams, Po A. to Deborah Gilmon(Gilmore?) 3-16-1847 (3-23-1847)
Williams, Samuel to Sarah Low 5-29-1861 (5-30-1861)
Williams, Sterling E. to Elizabeth D. Flint 2-14-1834 (2-18-1834)
Williams, Thomas to Mary Ann Craft 1-30-1860 (2-1-1860)
Williams, Thos. to Lucindia Reed 10-12-1830
Williams, W. L. C. to Julianna E. Craft 12-9-1850 (12-12-1850)
Williamson, Thomas to Eliza Jane Prewitt 11-16-1850 (11-28-1850)
Williamson, William to Prudence Richardson 9-8-1856 (9-10-1856)
Willie, Joseph to Leaner Jackson 2-1-1847 (2-2?-1847)
Willoughby, Ashly G. to Mary Jane Taylor 7-3-1841 (7-5-1841)
Willoughby, Edward to Elizabeth J. Yarbrough 6-15-1854 (6-22-1854)
Willoughby, Ewing to Emily Taylor 1-13-1836
Willoughby, Hiram B. to Catharine M. Cooper 2-3-1830
Willoughby, James to Fanny Marsh 8-25-1857
Willoughby, James to Harriet Marsh 12-17-1851 (12-16?-1851)
Willoughby, John to Nancy Lenorah Hunter 1-12-1848 (1-13-1848)
Willoughby, Thos. B. to Eliza Ann Thompson 6-15-1854 (6-29-1854)
Wills, H.S. to Frances M. High 5-4-1845
Wilson, Allen King to Amie Hicks 11-10-1829 (11-9?-1829)
Wilson, Anders to Gaberila A. McCan 10-21-1845 (10-30-1845)
Wilson, Claiburn to Martha Hunnell 3-28-1842 (3-29-1842)
Wilson, Geo. to Mary C. Smith 2-2-1846 (2-5-1846)
Wilson, Hugh to Aggy Snidy?(Sniedy?) 6-5-1828
Wilson, Ingram to Louisa Hullum(Hull?) 9-2-1840 (9-6-1840)
Wilson, Isaac to Jane M. Burden 9-28-1855 (9-30-1855)
Wilson, James to Amelia Vincent 5-21-1832
Wilson, Jason to Emily Hicks 2-28-1848 (3-2-1848)
Wilson, Jason to Lucinda Hamilton 2-2-1833 (2-5-1833)
Wilson, Jesse to Temperance Fish 9-23-1851 (9-25-1851)
Wilson, John G. to Mary Davis 12-7-1843
Wilson, Maxfield to Rachael S. Glass 1-25-1856 (1-30-1856)
Wilson, Miles to Liddy McCord 3-23-1839
Wilson, Miles to Margrett Anderson 2-25-1847
Wilson, Munford to Martha T. Pegran 6-8-1835
Wilson, Squire to Elizabeth McCan 3-16-1840
Wilson, Stephen to Martha Whitess 9-11-1837
Wilson, Thomas C. to Margaret Bond 10-2-1827
Wilson, Walker B. to Jane Owen 6-8-1838 (6-11-1838)
Wilson, William jr. to Sarah Ann King 12-15-1848 (12-17-1848)
Wilson, William to Cynthia Still? 11-17-1829 (11-25-1829)
Wimberley, James S. to Eliza Irby 12-24-1861
Wise, Burrell to Martha Yancey 12-27-1831 (12-25?-1831)
Wise, James C. to Martha Ann Mullins 7-4-1846
Wise, Wm. P. to Elizabeth L. Hill 4-20-1861 (4-21-1861)
Woford, William R. to Louisa J. Hullum 3-12-1849 (3-21-1849)
Wolfe, Jesse to Temperance Sloan 6-29-1850 (6-30-1850)
Wolverton, Bird to Ann Jane Tucker 10-27-1835
Wolverton, William A. to Martha A. Justice 1-17-1851 (1-23-1851)
Womack, Henry to Mary Bookers(Brookran) 9-22-1835
Wood, George to Eliza Haskins 2-13-1835
Wood, J. T. to Susanah Warren 6-6-1851 (6-7-1851)
Wood, Jas.R. to Sarah Buffalo 12-11-1856
Wood, Jno. L. to Elizabeth Warren 1-3-1848 (1-4-1848)
Wood, John R. to Pauline E. Guy 9-21-1859
Wood, John T. to T. B. McDowell 2-7-1852 (2-8-1852)
Wood, Robert H. to Mary Carolin Bills 1-12-1847
Wood, Robert L. to Sarah B. Norman 3-2-1835
Woodell, Isaac to Elizabeth E. Roach 4-9-1859
Woodfin, C. to Mary J. Crawford 4-27-1843
Woodfin, John to Frances Edgarton 4-23-1841
Woods, William H. to Benigna Polk 7-12-1834
Woodson, George A. to Mary L. Smith 8-4-1851
Woodson, Henry L. to Elizabeth C. Johnson 7-16-1854 (7-15?-1854)
Woodson, Josh R. to Mary N. McCrory 2-2-1856
Woolverton, D. W. M. to Sarah Jane Farris 1-12-1861 (1-15-1861)
Woolverton, R. T. to A. C. Jernagin 5-11-1861 (5-22-1861)
Worrell, Amus to Mary Barron 1-13-1840
Worrell, William B. to Mary A. Hudson 9-14-1849 (9-20-1849)
Worrell, Wm. B. to Martha Hamilton 12-21-1857 (12-23-1857)
Wortham, Johnson W. to Clarissa McBee 8-30-1837
Wrey, Joseph to Satey Bray 7-31-1848
Wright, Doctor Henry to Elizabeth W. Cody 9-1-1827 (9-6-1827)
Wright, F. D. H. to Sarah Ann Carper 12-4-1850 (12-11-1850)
Wright, James A. to Cornelia B. Adams 9-29-1860
Wright, James to Urshula Crocker 11-8-1847 (11-10-1847)
Wright, Joshua D. to Matilda L. Stephenson 1-10-1844
Wright, Joshua to Mary Cockeram 2-13-1824
Wright, L. L. to Mary A. Porch 5-18-1859 (5-22-1859)
Wright, Malcome A. to Susan Carper 4-29-1853 (4-21?-1853)
Wright, Newton to Frances A. Hamer 12-15-1851 (12-17-1851)
Wright, Raiford to Peggy Martindale 3-28-1832
Wright, Robert to Nancy Gage(Ross) 7-4-1827
Wyatt, James G. to Frances A. Harrison(Hardison?) 2-12-1847
Wyatts, G. H. to Mary Crawford 5-17-1856 (5-20-1856)
Wynn, Robert W. to Abigil P. Harriss 8-25-1858 (8-27-1858)
Yarbrough, James D. to Martha C. Carly 3-10-1859
Yarbrough, James to Nancy Pankey 3-10-1852 (3-11-1852)
Yarbrough, Jeptha to Nancy Binkly 7-6-1846 (7-9-1846)
Yarbrough, John to Gemima Jane Edwards 12-29-1851 (12-30-1851)
Yarbrough, Joseph H. to Mary E. Jackson 6-7-1854 (6-8-1854)
Yarbrough, Joshua J. to Elizabeth L. Willoughby 3-9-1859 (3-10-1859)
Yarbrough, Lewis to Narcissa Clark 3-11-1839 (3-26-1839)
Yarbrough, William H. to Catharine Davis 7-24-1854 (7-27-1854)

Yates, Rice B. to Polly Daniel 3-24-1835
Yeary, Benedict to Kesiah Raynor 11-1-1827 (11-2-1827)
Yeats, Terry to Nancy Ann Taylor 2-18-1837 (2-20-1837)
Yopp, G. W. to Mary C. Yokum 12-2-1859
Yopp, John W. to Rebecca Reprogle 8-6-1855
Yopp, William T. to Elizabeth Coleman 8-30-1844
Young, Geo. W. to Elizabeth Bonds 12-28-1859
Young, James B. to Sarah J. Reagan 11-4-1858
Young, James L. to Clementine Elizabeth Laughlin 7-14-1835
Young, James to Martha A. A. Cearley 11-23-1854
Young, John to Margrett C. Belote 12-15-1846 (12-17-1846)
Young, Jonathan J. to Nancy Sanders 8-17-1843
Young, Joseph to W. A. T. McKinza 3-21-1846 (3-22-1846)
Young, M. C. to Pheriby Stevens 9-28-1853 (9-29-1853)
Young, M. C. to Rachael Trezevant 5-8-1861 (5-9-1861)
Young, Martin to Elizabeth Erwin 7-27-1841 (7-29-1841)
Young, Milton C. to Holly S. Thompson 1-2-1854 (2-1-1854)
Young, Nathaniel M. to Tempy M. Darnell 3-1-1850 (3-3-1850)
Young, Peter to Nancy Carley 10-30-1854
Young, Samuel to Lutitia Jones 4-28-1855 (4-30-1855)
Young, Thomas to Elizabeth Smith 9-10-1849
Young, Thomas to Mareny Eleonor Goodman 1-11-1836
Youngblood, Jonathan to Margaret Kendrick 2-1-1836

Abernatha, Mary R. to Hiram G. Devinport? 11-23-1846 (11-26-1846)
Ables, Mary A. to Jacob Davis 2-21-1859 (2-23-1859)
Abraham, Rhoda to Robert Park 3-13-1843 (4-2-1843)
Absent, Martha W. to Robt. R. Rogers 11-9-1859
Adair, Mary R. to Wm. E. Wilkins 11-27-1854 (11-29-1854)
Adams, Ann to Wm. H. Jones 10-26-1842 (11-3-1842)
Adams, Christiana E. to James E. Stewart 5-9-1854
Adams, Cornelia B. to James A. Wright 9-29-1860
Adams, Elizabeth to George E. Grave 10-25-1829 (11-5-1829)
Adams, Elizabeth to Jason Cloud 1-2-1830
Adams, Elizabeth to Nathl. D. Ellis 12-3-1833 (12-5-1833)
Adams, Georgiana to Berryman Lax 12-27-1852
Adams, Harrett to George W. Browning 10-16-1840 (11-17-1840)
Adams, Isabella to James H. Harriss 10-28-1847
Adams, Isabella to James W. Black 9-3-1847
Adams, Mary to Peter R. Crews 8-30-1854
Adams, Sarah E. to Eleazar Gaugh 6-25-1861
Adams, Sarah R. to Cris R. Harrison 4-22-1845
Adams, Sarah to William H. Cole 11-4-1861
Adams, Susan F. to F. J. G. Eddlemon 3-3-1856 (3-6-1856)
Adamson, Rebecca to Holloway Swindle 7-17-1838
Addington, Elvira E. to James H. Lakey 9-8-1860
Aitkin, Mary A. L. to Ezekiel E. Low 9-3-1847 (9-5-1847)
Aldridge, Amanda E. to W. P. Mangrum 1-27-1857 (1-29-1857)
Alexander, Eliza R. to John W. Matthews 1-23-1839
Alexander, Ella M. to Saml. T. Avant 1-13-1860
Alexander, Jane Elizabeth to Richard Sanford 5-17-1851
Alexander, Jane to George L. Brotherton 1-2-1830
Alexander, Laura H. to Joseph E. Lake 11-7-1860 (11-8-1860)
Alexander, Margaret to Ezekiel Richmond 2-16-1832
Alexander, Mary C. to Abner S. Matthews 5-10-1842 (5-19-1842)
Alexander, Mary M. to Robert W. Barnett 12-4-1827 (12-6-1827)
Alexander, Mary to John Philpot 3-14-1831 (3-15-1831)
Alexander, Roberta D. to Thomas Henry 3-3-1859
Alford, Mary L. Mede to Manian Patrick 6-21-1838 (6-26-1838)
Alford, Nancy to Isaac Futrel 3-23-1843 (3-30-1843)
Allen, Ann C. to Joseph S. Thompson 3-9-1847 (3-10-1847)
Allen, Annice to Granville Nixon 1-17-1853 (2-8-1853)
Allen, Annisy to Wm. J. Fortenberry 8-10-1842 (8-11-1842)
Allen, Elizabeth to Stephen Childress 2-29-1840 (3-3-1840)
Allen, Jane to Andrew Jackson 7-6-1850 (7-10-1850)
Allen, Julia Ann to Samuel D. Jones 1-5-1843
Allen, Louisa J. to Green B. Curtis 8-23-1841
Allen, Lydia to James Hansard 6-23-1849 (6-24-1849)
Allen, Margaret to Isrial Mayfield 10-20-1835 (10-22-1835)
Allen, Martha R. to George W. Minter 11-28-1853
Allen, Mary A. to John H. Bowers 2-16-1848 (2-17-1848)
Allen, Mary T. to Benjamin Hollad 12-1-1831
Allen, Mary to Caswell Coates 12-27-1841 (12-30-1841)
Allen, Sarah to William Scott 12-12-1859 (12-15-1859)
Allison, Mary Jane to John S. Strickland 12-20-1841 (12-29-1841)
Allsup, Alsey to Barnet Clifft 1-23-1828 (1-24-1828)
Alsop, Cary to George W. Hazlegrove 12-18-1847 (12-23-1847)
Alsop, Matilda to John Easom 8-20-1851 (8-24-1851)
Alsup, Elizabeth to Isaac P. Russell 8-22-1828 (9-24-1828)
Alvorde, Harriet to J.(P?) kD. Nietschke(Dietrike?) 2-4-1851
Ames, Mary Jane to William S. Leggett 11-27-1845
Ammons, Clarissa Ann to Henry M. Roberts 5-16-1846 (5-17-1846)
Ammons, Clarissa to W. W. Thompson 12-23-1852
Ammons, Elizabeth Ann to Wm. H. Ammons 2-21-1837 (2-26-1837)
Ammons, Elizabeth to David Stephenson 9-12-1843 (9-14-1843)
Ammons, Telitha to Solomon Forehana 11-29-1837
Ammons, Winney E. to Jonathan Hodges 1-4-1851 (1-16-1851)
Anders, Sarah to Samuel Martin McKinie 9-4-1855 (9-6-1855)
Anderson, Adline M. to Andrew Moore 3-9-1846 (3-10-1846)
Anderson, Agnes P. A. to M. M. Deaton 10-1-1851
Anderson, Agness to Johnathan Polk 8-4-1851
Anderson, Allis to Charles Freeman 11-15-1845 (11-18-1845)
Anderson, Dycy? to Turner J. Martin 12-31-1839
Anderson, Eliza Jane to J. C. Armstrong 12-20-1847
Anderson, Eliza to Tho. J. Bailey 3-18-1835 (3-24-1835)
Anderson, Elmira J. to Thos. H. Hancock 2-24-1859
Anderson, Emily E. to Robert P. Alexander 7-31-1837
Anderson, Harriet to Thomas J. Shepherd 1-10-1833
Anderson, Jane to Lewis Moore 8-5-1839 (8-7-1839)
Anderson, Judah to Robert H. Hester 9-30-1846
Anderson, Julia Ann to Isaac Booe 1-13-1842
Anderson, Margrett to Miles Wilson 2-25-1847
Anderson, Martha to James M. Jacobs 12-13-1843 (12-14-1843)
Anderson, Mary Ann to Abner Moore 6-21-1842 (6-22-1842)
Anderson, Mary to George Turner 6-28-1839
Anderson, Minerva to Robert D. McMillan 10-13-1836
Anderson, Minirva to John N. Neely 1-28-1833
Anderson, Octavia D. to Hugh Moore 8-11-1859 (8-14-1859)
Anderson, Sarah E. to Archibald Overton 8-16-1859 (8-17-1859)
Anderson, Serena to Dutton M. Sweeton 7-19-1836
Anderson, Susan to Brice L. Garner 12-16-1840
Andrews, C. to D. W. Thompson 3-3-1847
Andrews, Georgia to J. A. Lay 11-30-1859 (12-2-1859)
Anthony, Julia Ann to Saml. Thompson 7-25-1841
Anthony, Martha Elizabeth to George W. Fortner 12-22-1852 (12-23-1852)
Anthony, Mary Jane to William C. Duncan 12-17-1849
Anthony, Sarah L. to Hugh Brady 9-7-1857 (9-30-1857)
Armor, Margaret to Alexander Rhodes 7-17-1835
Armstead, Julia V. to Richard G. Day 12-19-1856
Armstrong, Julia to John Casson 12-2-1833
Armstrong, Safronia to John Taber 8-28-1832
Ashby, Angelin R. to Alex G. Campbell 9-14-1852 (9-15-1852)
Atkins, Elizabeth Ann to James Leslie 8-18-1832 (8-19-1832)
Atkins, Mary to Joseph L. Rosson 6-9-1858 (6-29-1858)
Atkinson, Elizabeth to Wm. S. Daugherty 1-9-1846 (1-11-1846)
Atkinson, Martha to Clem Pulliam 12-30-1852
Atkinson, Mary E. to Jno. E. Mastin 10-20-1848 (10-26-1848)
Atkinson, Nancy J. to A. H. Green 1-15-1855 (1-18-1855)
Atkinson, Serena to George W. Willi 1-5-1847 (1-6-1847)
Atts(Alts), Celia to James R. Smith 8-18-1830 (8-19-1830)
Attwood, Frances to William C. White 6-22-1838 (6-24-1838)
Atwell, Nancy to James D. Cook 1-8-1850 (1-9-1850)
Aulford, Phebe A. to Jesse P. Dugger 5-14-1845 (5-15-1845)
Aulton, Rebecca to William Baty 4-8-1843 (4-9-1843)
Autry, Thiaza to James Grisham 5-8-1830 (5-15-1830)
Avann, Rebecca to Alexander McDonald 9-8-1837 (9-14-1837)
Avant, Anna D. to Wm. L. R. Johnson 8-22-1861
Avant, Jane to James Vickers 12-23-1846 (12-24-1846)
Avant, Mary to N. B. Sallier 12-18-1844 (12-19-1844)
Avant, Sarah J. to James H. Marshall 11-6-1854 (11-15-1854)
Avent, Eliza M. C. to John H. Gates 11-23-1852 (11-25-1852)
Avent, Mary to William McClend(McLeod?) 3-21-1847
Averett, Delila to R. W. Robinson 8-22-1833
Averett, Martha to Thomas J. Martindale 7-8-1833
Ayers, Adaline to Jas. M. Webster 8-8-1832 (9-11-1832)
Ayers, Amanda M. to William G. Fulps 2-21-1854
Ayers, Elizabeth C. to Wm. R. Holyfield 7-8-1839
Ayers, Louisa I. to Patrick F. Robinson 11-29-1850 (11-30-1850)
Ayers, Lucinda E. to Charles S. Robertson 5-12-1852 (6-12-1852)
Ayers, Manna E. to Edmond Wade 7-30-1829?
Ayers, Manna to Edwin Wade 7-30-1832 (8-8-1832)
Ayers, Mary J. to Isaac N. Thompson 3-9-1840 (3-12-1840)
Ayres, Martha to John Y. Reed 2-18-1840
Babb, Margaret E. to Andrew T. Henson 1-28-1850 (1-29-1850)
Bagley, Emily G. to Robt. A. Boyd 11-8-1858 (11-11-1858)
Bagley, Fred E. to H. J. Forbers 8-31-1861 (9-5-1861)
Bailey, Cela Ann to William Stewart 2-12-1849 (2-17-1849)
Bailey, Cornelia to Bryant Cox 10-17-1851 (10-23-1851)
Bailey, E. J. to J. L. Ferguson 11-29-1850
Bailey, Eliza Jane to Daniel H. Caviness 12-23-1851 (1-1-1852)
Bailey, Elizabeth to John D. Ussy(Ussery?) 2-8-1848 (2-17-1848)
Bailey, Emily H. S. to Cyrus Black 11-20-1843
Bailey, Jane to Pleasant Colvard 6-28-1826 (6-29-1826)
Bailey, Louisa to C. H. Stephens 11-11-1844 (11-14-1844)
Bailey, Lucinda G. to Cladius C. Jones 9-1-1834
Bailey, Luvenia to A. O. Prewett 2-16-1859 (2-17-1859)
Bailey, Mahala to John T. Hodges 3-11-1836
Bailey, Martha to Reubin Stone 4-13-1835
Bailey, Mary J. to Moses H. Grantham 5-18-1860
Bailey, Mary to Robert H. Childs 1-29-1854 (1-19?-1854)
Baines, Lila to Henry May 1-7-1828
Baker, Catherine to Peter K. Norton 1-9-1839 (1-10-1839)
Baker, Cynthia to William Burton 9-12-1829

Baker, Louisa to A. D. Shell 6-12-1832 (6-?-1832)
Baker, Matilda to Cornelius Barrett 10-13-1830 (10-14-1830)
Baker, Susannah to John F. Lucky 8-16-1847 (8-26-1847)
Baldwin, Delila F. to Thomas Irion 5-6-1851
Baldwin, Mary Jane to R. H. Cartmell(Cartwell?) 3-26-1850 (3-27-1850)
Barham, Louisa to Luke Carley 4-21-1852 (4-22-1852)
Barker, Catharine to William Black 11-3-1835 (11-5-1835)
Barker, Cynthia E. to Caswell Simmons 1-29-1859
Barker, Dicy to Starling Burrow 11-4-1837 (11-5-1837)
Barker, Elizabeth to George Beck 8-19-1834
Barker, Nancy Elmiria? to William Hall 5-7-1842 (5-8-1842)
Barker, Sarah to William James 1-5-1836
Barkley, Elizabeth to Wm. Stockton 1-22-1837
Barkley, Mary Ann to Thos. J. Clift 4-4-1842 (4-7-1842)
Barkley, Sarah Knox to Wilie D. Fleet 12-24-1850 (12-25-1850)
Barkley?, Susan C. to M. G. Cagle 5-24-1836
Barne?, Harriett A. to Edward Robertson 4-4-1839
Barnes?, Mary A. E. to M. W. Hall 5-27-1858 (6-10-1858)
Barnett, Martha to Saml. Lambert 1-11-1826 (1-12-1826)
Barnett, Naoma M. to Joseph Wilkes 3-12-1829
Barrett, Elizabeth to B. F. Haltom 9-24-1856
Barrett, Rhoda C. to Morgan Thrailkill 6-5-1861 (6-9-1861)
Barron, Mary to Amus Worrell 1-13-1840
Barry, Eudora to Roger Barton 5-2-1832
Barry?, Martha Ann Eliza to William Clark Kendel 3-11-1841
Bartlett, Mary to Adli S. Morrison 10-16-1833 (10-17-1833)
Barton(Baston?), Mary M. to Eli Littrell 5-29-1846 (6-2-1846)
Baskwell, Maria S. to Stephen F. Power 9-13-1838 (SB 1839)
Baskwell, Maria S. to Stephen F. Power 9-13-1839 (9-26-1839)
Baskwell, Rebecca B. to Valentine Vantrease 1-13-1851
Baskwell, Rutha Ann to John W. Randolph 3-16-1853
Baskwell, Sophronia to Irvin Q. Rogers 12-28-1854
Bass, Arina to Camel Cesterson 12-12-1832 (12-23-1832)
Bass, Berthena to William Brooks 7-2-1832 (7-15-1832)
Bass, C. J. to Hendley Stone 9-4-1858 (9-5-1858)
Bass, M.F. to S. L. Prewett 9-29-1860 (10-24-1860)
Bass, Margaret A. to Leonidas H. Boyce 12-31-1861 (1-5-1861)
Bass, Marselia to B. F. Gay 5-21-1857 (5-24-1857)
Bass, Matilda to John Bain 8-4-1837
Bass, Sarah to William Jacobs 8-4-1824
Bates, Ann E. V. to Calvin E. McCord 3-7-1860
Bates, Ann E. V. to Turner J. Harris 4-1-1854 (4-2-1854)
Bates, Harrett to Kemp Stallings 12-19-1845 (12-23-1845)
Bates, Lucinda to John Jones 12-26-1835
Bates, Martha to Hiram C. Crisp 10-20-1842
Bates, Susannah to Wm. A. Moore 12-14-1842 (12-17-1842)
Baugh, Agnes A. B. B. to Charles W. Hutcheson 2-27-1841 (3-4-1841)
Beabers(Biebers), Sophia F. to W. J. Beavers 11-9-1858
Beaden, Mary to James Hines 12-21-1860 (1-1-1861)
Bean, Sarah J. to E. G. Parham 2-11-1862
Beard, Elizabeth M. to Wm. T. Shaply 4-20-1846 (4-28-1846)
Beard, Martha R. A. to Thomas Harley 7-2-1849 (7-11-1849)
Beaton, Hannah Matilda to James Hines 12-27-1848 (12-28-1848)
Beaty, Nancy J. to Tho. H. Long 11-17-1859 (11-18-1859)
Beaver, Elizabeth to John A. Goad 9-17-1852 (9-22-1852)
Beavers, Elizabeth to Obediah March 10-29-1850 (10-30-1850)
Beavers, Martha Jane to Noah R. Ussery 12-20-1852 (1-4-1853)
Bell, Adelia C. to Thomas Chambliss 9-7-1853 (9-8-1853)
Bell, Ann T. L. to William C. Ervin 7-12-1855 (7-15-1855)
Bell, Malinda to William Grantham 8-30-1849
Bell, Minerva S. to Joseph Lusk 7-23-1833 (7-24-1833)
Bell, Nancy Ann to James F. Smith 6-4-1860 (6-6-1860)
Belote, Anvalina to Mabry D. Williams 6-30-1856 (7-3-1856)
Belote, E. S. to W. M. Duese? 6-24-1857
Belote, Margrett C. to John Young 12-15-1846 (12-17-1846)
Belote, Victoria to R. W. Pegram 1-2-1860
Belotte, Ariminta R. to William P. Gibson 11-29-1852 (12-16-1852)
Bennet, Nancy to John Hamlin 9-8-1828 (9-9-1828)
Bennett, Almarinda to William Moore 10-7-1850
Bennett, Elizabeth S. to Duncan T. Rich 9-2-1861 (9-3-1861)
Bennett, Elizabeth to Robert Pirtle 9-19-1833
Bennett, Mary to Raiford Bizzel 1-23-1835 (1-29-1835)
Bennett, Susan to lHenry McClory 1-25-1862
Benson, Margaret to James W. Arnold 9-21-1850 (9-25-1850)
Berry(Beny), Kissiah to Everet Staton 7-26-1828 (7-28-1828)
Berry, Elizabeth W. to William W. McNeal 11-26-1844
Beton, Martha to John Sheppard 4-29-1845
Biddy, Elizabeth to Josiah Taylor 10-19-1831 (10-20-1831)
Biddy, Mary to Anderson Glidewell 4-13-1835
Biddy, Mary to James Butler 12-9-1829 (12-10-1829)
Bieber, Equilla to Benjn. H. W. Portis 6-20-1842 (6-?-1842)
Biebers, Mary to James C. Chapman 9-5-1845 (9-?-1845)
Biebers, Nancy to John Shelly 12-29-1852 (12-30-1852)
Biles, Margaret Y. to John H. Gay 12-19-1831
Bills, Evilina M. to Marshall T. Polk 1-10-1856
Bills, Mary Carolin to Robert H. Wood 1-12-1847
Bills, Ophelia J. to Horace M. Polk 6-15-1843 (6-20-1843)
Bingham, N. A. to James M. Savage 8-10-1853
Binkley, Malinda to William Carley 8-10-1839
Binkley, Matilda C. to John Murdaugh 1-1-1842 (1-2-1842)
Binkley, Susan R. to Elias Sperlin 1-25-1858
Binkly, Mary M. to Eldrige W. Dorris 1-21-1846
Binkly, Nancy to Jeptha Yarbrough 7-6-1846 (7-9-1846)
Binkly, Rosa Ann to John C. Baily 4-11-1853 (4-12-1853)
Birdsong, Altha to Joshua Johnson 10-28-1851 (11-5-1851)
Birdsong, Cavell F. to Benjamin Wilkerson 8-17-1839 (8-21-1839)
Birdsong, Eliza Jane to John Mitchell 3-23-1848
Birdsong, Elizabeth J. to Alfred M. Rainey 7-11-1855 (7-12-1855)
Birdsong, Mary A. to C. H. Williams 10-29-1851 (10-31-1851)
Bishop, Edny to Cader Cox 12-16-1835 (12-17-1835)
Bishop, Lucy A. to Wm. J. Crates 4-29-1861 (5-1-1861)
Bishop, Mary J. to G. J. Coppadge 1-7-1856 (1-10-1856)
Bishop, Sarah to Alfred Cox 9-11-1839 (9-12-1839)
Bishop, Sarah to William F. Tipler 1-6-1838
Bishop, Susan T. to William D. Cooper 1-19-1833 (1-20-1833)
Bizzell, Mary A. to Thomas R. Grantham 12-16-1857 (12-17-1857)
Black, Cena M. to George Davis 11-2-1844 (11-4-1844)
Black, Jane B. to Thomas L. McCann 8-14-1852 (8-17-1852)
Black, Rebecca to Abner Moore 1-2-1854 (1-3-1854)
Black, Sarah to Alexander Ramsey 12-?-1843 (12-22-1843)
Blackamore, Mary to Joshua Kimber 10-10-1851 (10-12-1851)
Blackwood, Lucey to J. Madison Scott 11-12-1831
Blackwood, Rachel to Thompson Brooks 8-10-1832 (8-14-1832)
Blair, Lidia to Wm. A. Naylor 12-18-1855 (12-20-1855)
Blair, Margaret C. to John W. Reynolds 12-3-1859
Blair, Mary to James Ward 2-13-1836
Blake, Sally M. to David Walker 3-7-1831 (3-8-1831)
Blalock, Emily H. to Solomon E. Cooper 12-23-1861 (12-26-1861)
Blaylock, Nancy J. to Joseph B. Kirkland 1-9-1858 (1-13-1858)
Blount, Mary to William Hutson Chandler 8-15-1839 (8-15-1839)
Blount, Susan to Levi Pearce 5-15-1844 (5-16-1844)
Blunt, Sabrinah Jane to William Morris 4-12-1858 (4-14-1858)
Blunt, Sarah to William Vails 1-18-1842 (1-23-1842)
Bogue, Sarah S. to S. M. Harehaw 9-1-1860
Bolden, Mary to Jno. M. Lawson 5-21-1856 (5-22-1856)
Boles, Elvira T. to Jackson J. Polk 2-21-1835 (2-24-1835)
Bolling, Patsy to William Cornelius 1-21-1834
Bolt, Susan to Cicero Rhodes 11-25-1850 (11-28-1850)
Bond, Catharine Whittier to Bartholomew Dunn 5-27-1834 (5-29-1834)
Bond, Dianah to John Mills 8-21-1832 (8-24-1832)
Bond, Margaret to Thomas C. Wilson 10-2-1827
Bonds, Elizabeth to Geo. W. Young 12-28-1859
Bonds, Frances K. to Loami Harris 11-13-1854 (11-14-1854)
Boney, Elizabeth C. to Malcom H. Greenwood 6-29-1838 (7-1-1838)
Boo, Emiline to Andrew Williams 3-1-1858
Bookart, Margarett to David Glen 9-4-1834
Bookers(Brookran), Mary to Henry Womack 9-22-1835
Boothe, Elizabeth to N. M. Crenshaw 1-20-1849 (1-24-1849)
Boothe, Lucy to Henderson Cane 2-3-1843 (2-2?-1843)
Boothe, Milly to John W. Carley 10-1-1840 (10-4-1840)
Bordman, Eliza V. to Louallen Jones 12-20-1844 (12-22-1844)
Bostick, Sarah to William M. McLeod 6-7-1841 (7-29-1841)
Boston, Martha C. to Henry C. Wellons 4-12-1859 (4-14-1859)
Bostwick, Nancy to Isaac R. Dishough 12-15-1841 (12-16-1841)
Bowers, Clarissa Eliza to Lemuel Rogers 9-28-1833 (10-3-1833)
Bowers, Frances to W. M. Towler?(Lowler?) 9-13-1850 (9-18-1850)
Bowers, Olivia to Bernard Bowling 2-13-1861 (2-14-1861)
Bowers, Ruth to Wilie J.? Riddle 7-29-1833 (8-8-1833)

Bowers, Sarah Ann Rebecca to Algernon S. Bowers 9-22-1840
Bowlin, Dorathy to John Murry 3-23-1846
Bowling, Adelener H. to William D. Partlow 9-4-1831 (9-29-1831)
Box, Anna to Jackson McCowan 4-11-1835 (4-16-1835)
Box, Caroline to John Webb 12-4-1854 (12-6-1854)
Box, Charlotte to Travis Paul 9-9-1834 (9-17-1834)
Box, Keziah to Simeon Bright 4-24-1828 (4-29-1828)
Box, Maranda to Enoch Henslee 1-6-1859 (5-29-1859)
Box, Narcissa to James S. Barnett 10-22-1855 (10-24-1855)
Box, Parilee to Lewis Jackson Bullington 7-4-1850 (7-11-1850)
Box, Polly to Saunders Kennedy 4-14-1827 (4-19-1827)
Box, Racheal to John Bell 5-17-1832 (5-24?-1832)
Box, Ruth to Moses Harper 2-14-1843 (2-15-1843)
Box, Sarah to Thomas Gore 1-8-1840 (1-9-1840)
Box, Susan A. to James G. Treece 8-10-1858 (8-12-1858)
Boyd, Mary E. to William F. Hughes 8-10-1844
Boyd, Nancy to Orrin Guthry 1-20-1827 (1-21-1827)
Boyd, Rebecca to Gamaliel Parker 1-28-1829 (1-29-1829)
Boydston, Cintha to Williamson N. Burt 7-19-1838
Boydston, Sally to Jacob L. Edwards 2-7-1824 (2-8-1824)
Boyle, Clarentine M. to Elias Alexander 2-9-1847 (2-11-1847)
Boyle, Hennorah to J. W. Owen 2-3-1848
Boyt, Nancy C. to Ashley Roades 5-30-1846 (5-31-1846)
Boyt, Zilpha to Jesse Cox 7-14-1832 (7-?-1832)
Boyte, Abbe to Cullen Dunn 3-8-1833
Boyte, Ailsy E. to John Kennedy 8-21-1839 (8-29-1839)
Boyte, Alsy to James B. Brint 9-13-1828
Boyte, Ann to Morris Raiford 12-12-1837 (1-4-1838)
Boyte, Barbay to William Pate 10-8-1834
Boyte, Elizabeth to Elliot Stevens 2-13-1832
Boyte, Mary H. to William H. Ammons 1-6-1844 (1-11-1844)
Bradford, Elizabeth J. to William Polk 10-24-1850
Bradford, Margaret to James L. Coburn 7-5-1855
Bradford, Martha E. to W. Jasper Dean 10-25-1859 (11-2-1859)
Bradford, Mary C. to J. W. Deming 2-3-1860
Bradford, Mary C. to Kimbro E. Hornesby 1-2-1860
Bradford, Teressa Ann to E. H. Dorris 11-10-1853
Bradley, Mollie to S. W. Augustus 3-3-1860 (3-5-1860)
Bradly, Sousin to James Boon 3-14-1848
Bradshaw, Eliza S. to Aaron Borroughs 6-22-1835 (6-23-1835)
Brady, Sarah E. to Thomas W. Polk 10-11-1838 (10-12-1838)
Brandon, Sarah J. to Peter B. Pirtle 12-22-1847 (12-23-1847)
Brantley, Betsy to John M. Graham 5-5-1826 (5-20-1826)
Brantley, Martha to John Vicker 12-16-1842 (12-22-1842)
Brantley, Nancy to Moses Bumpass 7-14-1826 (7-16-1826)
Brantley, Sarah to Wm. B. Stovall 6-13-1840 (6-14-1840)
Brantly, Frances to Perry Nabers 1-21-1826
Brantly, Mary to Mizo Casee 2-16-1839 (2-23-1839)
Bray, Mary Ann to Ephraim B. Adams 10-30-1841 (10-31?-1841)
Bray, Satey to Joseph Wrey 7-31-1848
Breeden, Catharine to Nathan Phillips 8-21-1856
Breeding, Elizabeth to James Hamilton 1-2-1830
Breeding, Elizabeth to Stephen Pruett 4-19-1827
Breedon, Julia A. to Wm. M. Phillips 8-20-1859 (8-21-1859)
Breedon, Mary C. to W. F. Price 3-21-1861
Brenard, Elizabeth to Andrew L. Murphy 12-10-1828 (12-11-1828)
Brewer, Martha E. F. to Thos. G. N. Tomson 9-29-1848 (with 1858)
Brewer, Willy to James McCann 7-27-1841 (7-28-1841)
Bridges, Sarah D. to Lunsford W. Scott 1-14-1843 (1-25-1843)
Bright, Martha to Logan B. Adams 10-14-1851
Bright, Mary C. to Ro L. White 3-21-1855 (3-22-1855)
Brigman, Sarah Jane to W. C. Ramsey 2-25-1861 (2-26-1861)
Brigman, Tabitha to G. D. Campbell 6-23-1857
Brint, Narcissa Jane to John W. Brown 12-13-1853 (12-15-1853)
Brock, Elizabeth to Lawrence Stephens 12-8-1840 (12-13-1840)
Brock, Sarah to Andrew J. Hays 9-11-1841 (10-12-1841)
Broiles, Mary to Ethan A. Murphy 2-25-1828 (4-5-1828)
Brooks(Polk?), Betsy to Isaac Jackson 10-22-1828 (10-29-1828)
Brooks, Elizabeth to Jessee Whitford 5-5-1838 (5-6-1838)
Brooks, Lavanda to James Murdaugh 6-2-1859
Brooks, Malinda to Pleasant Rhodes 2-17-1852 (2-19-1852)
Brooks, Rachel to William Nellums(Nelms) 8-1-1840 (8-4-1840)
Brooks, Sarah J. to Jno. Moss 10-13-1857 (10-14-1857)
Brooks, Sarah to David Whitford 9-26-1837
Brotherton, Margaret to John F. Duncan 10-20-1828
Brotherton, Susan to Thomas L. Duncan 6-11-1829 (6-21-1829)
Brown, Amanda to Shadrich Hail 8-2-1837 (8-3-1837)
Brown, Ann Adeline to James High 9-8-1838 (9-10-1838)
Brown, Barbara to Hardy Mashburn 1-9-1836 (1-10-1836)
Brown, Charlotte to William Murphy 11-13-1843 (11-15-1843)
Brown, Cornelia A. to R. A. Whitmore 6-30-1851
Brown, Elizabeth C. to James O. Fleming 2-3-1851 (2-4-1851)
Brown, Elizabeth to Martin V. Brooks 7-29-1856
Brown, Elizabeth to Michael Price 8-17-1837
Brown, Elizabeth to Rufus R. Howell 11-19-1850 (11-24-1850)
Brown, Emeline Z. to Thomas Rose 9-8-1856 (9-11-1856)
Brown, Evelina to Jonothan Jones 7-15-1825
Brown, Hannah to John A. McFall 8-9-1828 (8-10-1828)
Brown, Hester to John McNeely 1-17-1843
Brown, Keziah to Kemp Stallions 5-23-1829 (5-24-1829)
Brown, Kezziah to Mathew T. Buffalo 5-13-1839 (5-15-1839)
Brown, Lucy to Thos. H. Moore 2-4-1839 (2-5-1839)
Brown, Lyda to George Kinnard 2-25-1840 (2-26-1840)
Brown, Lydia Ann to William Hamlin 7-10-1847 (7-18-1847)
Brown, Malinda C. to John P. F. Prewitt 9-20-1843
Brown, Marcilla C. to Braddock Foster 2-11-1860 (2-14-1860)
Brown, Marinda M. to Josiah Bennett 9-2-1850 (9-17-1850)
Brown, Mary Ann to George W. Tomson 12-16-1848 (12-23-1848)
Brown, Mary to Nathan Berry Eskew(Askew?) 3-6-1849
Brown, Matilda to Absalem Lane 7-10-1837 (7-15-1837)
Brown, Nancy to Charles Caricker 7-28-1854 (7-30-1854)
Brown, Nancy to John Rhodes 8-13-1851
Brown, Nancy to W. R. Howell 5-19-1842
Brown, Nancy to William H. Murley 7-24-1848 (7-26-1848)
Brown, Precilla W. to Eli Cox 8-2-1848
Brown, Priscilla to Lewis Glenn 8-9-1836
Brown, Rebecca to Gabriel Ary 10-20-1842 (10-21-1842)
Brown, Sarah J. to Robt. J. Russell 8-24-1857
Brown, Sarah to James C. Dawson 1-7-1839 (1-8-1839)
Brown, Sarah to John Caraway 5-30-1835
Brown, Sary to Williams Perkins 7-10-1827 (7-12-1827)
Brown, Susan to James Antwine 3-17-1849
Brown, Tilpha A. to Gilbert Rhodes 5-2-1857
Browning, Caroline N. to Jno. S. Bradford 12-17-1855
Browning, Mary to Thomas Boyle 11-3-1846
Broyles, Mahaly to William W. Nelson 5-10-1826 (not endorsed)
Brush, Kiziah to N. K. Johnson 12-15-1849 (12-16-1849)
Bryant, Elizabeth C. to Benjamin Fortner 12-15-1847 (12-21-1847)
Bryant, Jane to William Durden 11-30-1854 (12-3-1854)
Bryant, Sarah to John Mundin 7-15-1844
Buckner, Mary to C. C. P. Sharpe 3-26-1857
Buffalo, Sarah to Jas.R. Wood 12-11-1856
Buffaloe, Julia A. to A. L. Southall 4-3-1857 (4-5-1857)
Bumpass, Elizabeth to Jonathan Crews 9-26-1827
Bunting, Caroline to A. N. Prewett 11-15-1858 (11-18-1858)
Bunting, Eliza A. to John H. Raines 12-22-1849 (12-23-1849)
Bunting, Elizabeth C. to William Sauls 10-18-1849 (10-22-1849)
Bunting, Julia A. to E. O. Humphrey 12-18-1852 (12-30-1852)
Bunting, Virginia to Wm. E. Robinson 10-14-1859 (10-18-1859)
Burden, Jane M. to Isaac Wilson 9-28-1855 (9-30-1855)
Burden, Smithy to John Clark 8-23-1853 (9-8-1853)
Burgner(Burger), Ann to Allen Trousdale 9-7-1827
Burke, Matilda L. to W. F. Tipler 3-7-1856 (3-8-1856)
Burkhead, Mary Ann to Joshua D. Nailor 1-21-1857
Burleson, Elizabeth to Jacob Burleson 12-24-1828 (1-8-1829)
Burleson, Jane to William Beachum 1-14-1833 (1-15-1833)
Burleson, Lucinda to William Ervin 7-23-1835
Burleson, Rebecca to John Baker 12-15-1831
Burleson, Sarah to Lorenso D. Baker 7-10-1834 (7-15-1834)
Burlesson, Mary to Henry W. Duncan 10-24-1827 (10-27-1827)
Burnes, Jane to Joseph Butcher 5-6-1829
Burnes, M. J. to D. C. Thompson 8-5-1859
Burnett, Ann L. to Charles D. Smith 12-11-1829
Burnett, Martha Ann to C. H. Beachum 7-6-1854
Burnett, Sarah to James Vaughn 4-26-1855
Burney, Martha to Wm. F. Chandler 7-21-1859
Burney, Nancy to James Hamilton 10-6-1856
Burns, Ann to Thomas G. Elmore 4-28-1834
Burns, Elizabeth to Shadrach Sl. Frye? 6-28-1834 (7-3-1834)
Burns, Nancy to Hiram W. Ross 7-7-1828

Burns, Rebecca to Bradford Read 12-7-1833
Burns, Sally to Joseph M. Wells 1-2-1830 (1-9-1830)
Burrow, Meloria S. to T. Lewis Smith 6-11-1856 (7-3-1856)
Burrow?, Frances to George Ray 11-7-1833
Burt, Martha W. to Gilliad A. Sanders 8-19-1840
Burt, Mary Ann to James Robinson 8-18-1832
Burton, Elizabeth to A. B. Cavens 12-22-1860 (12-24-1860)
Burton, Elizabeth to John McIntosh 12-13-1838
Butler, Ann A. to John A. Boyte 1-11-1854 (1-12-1854)
Butler, Elizabeth to Thomas King 6-12-1824
Butler, Lilphia to Joel M. Stone 8-23-1826
Cadwell, Cloe to John Thompson 1-28-1824 (2-5-1824)
Cain, Elizabeth H. to Ott Andrews 11-25-1850
Cain, Hannah to Henry Marsh 9-17-1828 (9-18-1828)
Cain, Martha to Wm. Hardridge 12-24-1831 (12-?-1831)
Cain, Polly to Jefferson Ford 6-31?-1828 (7-3-1828)
Calahan, Margrett to Hiram Thompson 12-29-1846
Caldwell, Elizabeth to Syrus Park 11-16-1838
Caldwell, Lucinda to Josiah M. Hill 3-6-1843 (3-7-1843)
Caldwell, Mary C. to Geo. E. Armstead 10-12-1860 (10-17-1860)
Caldwell, Tirzah to Samuel F. Neely 11-14-1837 (11-16-1837)
Callahan, Clarinda to Eli Parks 5-11-1859 (5-15-1859)
Callahan, Clarinda to John J. Fitch 12-28-1854
Camp, Ann Eliza to Moses Campbell 2-14-1854
Camp, F. E. to J. T. Ferguson 10-17-1861 (10-22-1861)
Campbell, Carolin E. to Alfred M. Lambeth 4-8-1835 (4-16-1835)
Campbell, Elizabeth to Enons J. Grissom 7-4-1846 (7-9-1846)
Campbell, Elizabeth to John R. Dunn 10-7-1847
Campbell, Jane to Joseph K. Newland 11-2-1846 (11-4-1846)
Campbell, Margaret to Henson G. Newland 8-21-1839 (8-22-1839)
Campbell, Mary A. to T.C. Park 3-24-1849 (4-5-1849)
Campbell, Minervia to William J. Jones 6-8-1848 (6-11-1848)
Campbell, Nancy A. to W. D. Currin 8-7-1854 (8-14-1854)
Campbell, Nancy to James M. Lillard 10-26-1841 (10-27-1841)
Campbell, Rachael C. to John Linebarger 12-19-1860 (12-25-1860)
Campbell, Sarah to Nathaniel B. Moore 7-25-1837 (7-31-1837)
Campbell, Sarah to Robt. E. Andrews 6-13-1846 (6-14-1846)
Cannon, Mary to James Tillman 4-20-1839 (4-25-1839)
Cantwell?, Barbra to James A. Jackson 11-26-1845 (11-27-1845)
Caraway, Charlotte to David S. Hannis 12-26-1849
Caraway, Clarisa? to Albert H. Lawhorn 4-5-1845 (4-24-1845)
Caraway, Gatsey to William Standley 12-30-1851 (1-1-1852)
Cariker, Elizabeth to Doke Callihan 11-29-1852 (11-30-1852)
Carley, Levanda to John G. Binkly 3-2-1850 (3-3-1850)
Carley, Martha to Joshua Estes 6-8-1838 (6-10-1838)
Carley, Mary E. to George Henson 1-24-1861
Carley, Nancy to Elvy Mills 9-11-1841 (9-12-1841)
Carley, Nancy to Peter Young 10-30-1854
Carley, Rachel to James Leggett 2-15-1844
Carley, Sarah to Robert A. Cozby 12-17-1847 (12-28-1847)
Carley, Sarah to William Carley 10-1-1840 (10-2-1840)
Carlin, Pricilla to Dan Williams 2-17-1827 (2-18-1827)
Carly, Martha C. to James D. Yarbrough 3-10-1859
Carnes, Clemintine B. to F. W. Irvine 11-16-1850 (12-18-1850)
Carnes, Eliza B. to James W. Hall 3-16-1840
Carnes, Rebecca to James Lay 2-21-1832 (2-23-1832)
Caroker, Nancy' to W. H. McCommon 12-3-1851
Carooth, Nancy to William Reaves 12-23-1850
Carper, Mary E. to M. W. Gruber 8-9-1859 (7?-14-1859)
Carper, Mary to H. M. Goforth 6-20-1859 (6-23-1859)
Carper, Sarah Ann to F. D. H. Wright 12-4-1850 (12-11-1850)
Carper, Susan C. to P. M. Deraberry 9-18-1857 (10-2-1857)
Carper, Susan to Malcome A. Wright 4-29-1853 (4-21?-1853)
Carr, A. P. to Laban Hall 12-21-1857
Carr, Mahuldah to S.(L?) P. Stewart 2-19-1847 (2-21-1847)
Carr, Nancy to Lewis Thomas 9-13-1828
Carricker, Caroline to D. P. Rainey 5-1-1848 (5-16-1848)
Carricker, Nancy S. to James Rainey 8-23-1852 (8-26-1852)
Carricker, Tabitha D. to William D. Hannis 7-15-1848 (7-20-1848)
Carroll, Caroline to Joseph M. Eastlack 2-5-1844
Carroll, Elizabeth V. to Lonis? Adams 4-13-1833 (4-16-1833)
Carroll, Martha to William Shinpeck 12-23-1826
Carruth, Sidney Jane to Thomas A. Osborne 12-22-1858
Carruth?, Unetta? E. to Jesse Jones 8-13-1847 (8-15-1847)
Carruthers, Martha B. to David C. Bates 10-9-1854 (10-10-1854)
Carter, Caroline to James W. Hines 2-23-1847
Carter, Mahina E. to Burton Bailey 6-1-1843
Carter, Mary Ann to Alvin Grantham 12-25-1849
Carter, Mary to Thomas Buding? 1-9-1838
Carter, Nancy to Hubbard P. Scott 6-16-1842
Carter, Polly to Samuel L. Owens 3-18-1829 (3-22-1829)
Carter, S. E. to T. M. Reeser 12-23-1861 (12-27-1861)
Carter, Sarah Ann to Atkins Stevens 12-8-1835
Carter, Syrena to Eppy Crews 2-9-1837
Cartwright, Jane to Thomas Harvey 5-20-1859 (5-22-1859)
Cartwright, Sarah to Needham Skipper 3-14-1832 (3-?-1832)
Carver, Anna M. to Daniel Prescott 5-18-1828
Carver?, Sarah to John Crouse 5-17-1849
Casey, Catharine B. to M. H. Paul 10-21-1850 (10-22-1850)
Casey, Elizabeth to Spier Rogers 10-27-1836
Casey, Epsey J. to Joel S. Sasser 11-24-1857 (11-26-1857)
Casey, Mary to James Marler 8-1-1838
Casey, Nancy to James Gee 12-18-1847 (12-19-1847)
Casey, Rebecca Jane to Thos. J. Hicks 12-22-1856 (12-23-1856)
Casey, Rebecca to James M. Jones 3-18-1835
Casey, Ruth G. to Thos. D. Hankins 1-7-1860 (1-8-1860)
Casey, Ruth to John H. Russell 1-7-1829 (1-9-1829)
Casey, Sarah to Jesse Webster 12-12-1835 (12-17-1835)
Casey, Susan C. to Jas. M. Carraway 11-23-1858 (11-25-1858)
Casy, Hannah to Needham Jackson 1-25-1834 (1-26-1834)
Casy, M. to John Oliver 9-10-1831
Cavinar, Mary E. to William Jones 7-12-1850 (7-14-1850)
Caviness, Cornelia A. to Stephen Cup 8-30-1850 (9-1-1850)
Caviness, Delila A. to Thomas J. Robertson 11-11-1854 (11-12-1854)
Caviness, Delilah M. to William K. Smith 12-26-1853
Caviness, Mary C. to John Moffitt 2-21-1853 (2-22-1853)
Cavnar, Sarah to J. P. Lumley 1-31-1859
Cearley, Martha A. A. to James Young 11-23-1854
Cearley, Mary J. to J. L. Eaton 2-8-1862
Cearly, Hannah to Samuel Murdaugh(Mordough) 11-30-1848
Cearly, Mary Ann to Jacob A. Cozby 2-17-1847
Cerly, Nelly to Jno. C. Davis 11-28-1849
Chambless, Jane Ann to William Y. McBride 7-25-1852 (7-29-1852)
Champ, Drucilla V. to Geo. J. Hunter 10-16-1850
Champ, Louisa J. to Joel Mayfield 11-17-1854 (11-19-1854)
Champion(Anderson), Parthena H. to James Champion 10-2-1833
Champion, Elizabeth to Enoch S. Galling(Gatling?) 9-2-1845
Champion, Mary B. to John A. Pirtle 8-19-1831 (8-24-1831)
Champion, Mary C. D. to Joseph Rudisill 12-6-1832
Chandler, Judy to Uriah Pierce 4-26-1833 (4-30-1833)
Chandler, Martha V. to Benjamin J. Williams 6-20-1853
Chandler, Sarah to Wilie Futrell 7-7-1855
Chapman, Charity to W. F. Perry 5-17-1858 (5-18-1858)
Chapman, Elizabeth J. to W. J. K. Rucker 11-23-1841
Chapman, Mary Ann to Sherrod Hines 9-9-1844 (9-?-1844)
Chapman, Susan to Able Hodges 7-12-1836
Cheairs, Mary F. to Atlas Jones 3-7-1853 (3-10-1853)
Cheairs, SophiaH. to Jos. T. Knight 12-11-1860
Chears, Margaret B. to Theophelus Higgs 1-24-1856 (1-31-1856)
Cheisher, Louisa to Wilson N. Pankey 12-16-1844 (12-17-1844)
Cherry, Jinnette C. to Kinchen L. Rose 10-20-1853 (10-27-1853)
Cherry, Zilphy to C. P. Jourdan 10-26-1847 (10-28-1847)
Chesher, Nancy to Benjamin R. Hainline 7-27-1847 (7-29-1847)
Cheshier, Alvira to James Hutson Harrison 4-1-1844 (4-2-1844)
Cheshier, Lucinda to Thomas Harris 10-17-1838 (10-18-1838)
Cheshier, Mahala to William S. Beaton 1-1-1850
Cheshier, Mary to Clinton Crisp 9-28-1854
Chessher, Emeline to Marshall Raines 4-8-1847
Childress, Ann to William Johnson 3-29-1841 (4-1-1841)
Childress, Catharine to D. W. Hall(Hale) 6-19-1837 (6-20-1837)
Childress, Elizabeth to Andrew Sissom 7-5-1846 (7-6-1846)
Childress, Frances to Joseph Tilmon 9-29-1838
Childress, Julian to John Forbis 12-5-1832
Childress, Lucinda to Braetin Nelson 8-28-1834 (9-3-1834)
Childress, Minerva to G. Glasgow 11-30-1830
Chisham, Levina to Andrew Turner 1-1-1827
Chism, Peggy to Elijah Brown 5-16-1833 (5-17-1833)
Chisolm, Eliza Ann to William Littlejohn 9-10-1833 (9-11-1833)
Chisum, Barbara to Elisha Robinson 1-5-1830 (1-7-1830)
Chisum, Belinda to Thomas G. Chisum 11-19-1829

Chisum, Elizabeth to Jonas Robertson 8-6-1828 (8-7-1828)
Chisum, Mary Ann to John Sasser 6-10-1834 (6-20-1834)
Chisum, Mary Ann to William Chisum 2-24-1828
Chisum, Mary C. to G. P. Harris 5-16-1860 (5-23-1860)
Chisum, Rachael to John F. Rhodes 7-19-1839 (7-29-1839)
Choate, Nancy to Solomon P. Wheeler 10-6-1828
Cholwell, Darcus to Eli Park 2-26-1840 (3-10-1840)
Chunn, Sarah L. to Rev. R. V. Taylor 7-21-1853
Clark, A. W. to J. G. Williams 12-9-1850 (12-11-1850)
Clark, Chrisriana to Eli M. Andrews 6-28-1843
Clark, Mary A. to Benjamin G. Johnson 8-7-1847 (9-12-1847)
Clark, Mary Jane to J. J. Carruth 5-27-1858 (8-10-1858)
Clark, Mary to Hezekiah Dyson 2-14-1860 (3-18-1860)
Clark, Narcissa to Lewis Yarbrough 3-11-1839 (3-26-1839)
Clarke, Sophronia to John M. Warren 11-15-1834
Clary, Jane to J. A. J. Parker 10-7-1858
Clayton, Susannah to Joseph J. Brantley 7-19-1835
Clement, U. L. to Wm. R. Nelms 2-9-1860
Clements, Ann E. to Johnathan Cheshier 2-15-1860 (2-16-1860)
Clifft, Martha A. to Mathew Dickens 10-31-1857 (11-3-1857)
Clifft, Polly Ann to John J. Thompson 3-14-1846 (3-24(14?)-1846
Clifft, Susannah to Thomas Morrow 11-29-1830 (11-30-1830)
Clift, Lucinda to Joseph Warren 11-7-1840 (11-26-1840)
Clift, Sarah Ann to Radford F. Blackard 7-30-1836
Clifton, Sarah A. to J. E. Puckett 12-23-1858
Clines, Nancy t. to John Shofer 8-16-1859 (8-17-1859)
Clinton, E. J. to West Harriss 10-29-1857
Cloud, Artemesia to Pleasant Oliver 11-5-1836
Clouse, Creesy to James W. Scoggins 8-20-1836
Cloyd, Margaret Milissa to Stephen Henry Rainey 8-26-1848 (8-29-1848)
Coates, Ann E. to John T. Hodges 1-9-1850 (1-11-1850)
Coates, Mary Ann to Henry Johnson 1-3-1857 (1-4-1857)
Coates, Sarah Ann to William S. Clinton 1-22-1850
Cobb, Sarah to Telemicus H. Collier 10-10-1849 (10-11-1849)
Coburn, Elvira E. to John G. Freeman 2-7-1842 (2-8-1842)
Coburn, Lucinda E. to John C. Graham 1-18-1851 (1-27-1851)
Cocke, Nancy E. to John C. Hudspeth 8-30-1834
Cockeram, Mary to Joshua Wright 2-13-1824
Cockram, Sarah to Joel J. Reynolds 11-27-1834
Cody, Elizabeth W. to Doctor Henry Wright 9-1-1827 (9-6-1827)
Cody, Nancy to Andrew Ross 6-6-1826 (6-7-1826)
Coffey, Adaline to John Coates 10-31-1846 (11-11-1846)
Colbert, Elizabeth to Alexander Ross 1-3-1826 (1-5-1826)
Colbert, Elizabeth to Charles F. Eastman 7-28-1834 (7-29-1834)
Colbert, Janie to James Cody 4-19-1826 (4-20-1826)
Colbert, Rebecca to John H. Ricks(Riggs) 5-2-1829 (5-7-1829)
Cole, Eady Ann to Pleasant B. McBride 9-14-1857 (9-15-1857)
Cole, Edy Ann to Thomas Grantham 6-23-1841
Cole, Elizabeth C. to H. Alexander Stewart 3-17-1853 (3-23-1853)
Cole, Elizabeth to E. R. McBride 12-15-1849 (12-26-1849)
Cole, Margaret to James C. Harrison 8-13-1852 (9-19-1852)
Cole, Mary Ann to Francis M. Harrison 8-13-1852 (8-14-1852)
Cole, Tebitha C. to Seth Brownlee McCommon 1-6-1841 (1-7-1841)
Coleman, Clara M. to John Brown 1-14-1832
Coleman, Elizabeth to William T. Yopp 8-30-1844
Coleman, Sarah Ann to Andrew Caps 12-1-1855 (12-6-1855)
Collins, Ann E. to Wm. H. Crittenden 1-3-1843
Collins, Mary A. to Francis M. Pylant 7-11-1849 (7-12-1849)
Colverd, Sarah to John Dunaway 7-14-1828 (7-17-1828)
Comer, Elizabeth to Joseph B. Teague 1-1-1844
Comer, Harret? to Braxton W. Kiernan 11-20-1845
Comer, Louisa C. to Wilson S. Sanderlin 8-29-1842 (9-1-1842)
Comer, Sarah to Wm. T. Jones 12-5-1855
Comwell?, Rhoda N. to Edward J. Mathews 12-6-1859
Condra, Matilda to Asa McKinza 2-17-1828
Conly, Mary to John H. Tipler 1-9-1851 (1-15-1851)
Conner, Martha to William H. Miller 7-11-1837
Conner, Polly to Spencer Birdin 8-23-1830
Conner, Sarah L. to Nelson Wiley 2-4-1842 (2-6-1842)
Coody(Cody), Eliza to John Little 10-9-1834
Cook, Didama to William Vaughan 1-22-1828 (1-24-1828)
Cook, Eliza to J. L. Lax 12-7-1859
Cook, Elizabeth to B. F. Hunt 10-29-1831 (11-3-1831)
Cook, Margaret to William Dunn 2-14-1851 (2-16-1851)
Cook, Martha to John W. Shinault 3-7-1856 (3-9-1856)
Cookburn?, Tabitha to William Reynolds 11-4-1830
Cooksey, Elizabeth to Hiram Terry 11-3-1843 (11-5-1843)
Cooksey, Jane to John Vaughan 3-2-1844
Cooksey, Mary to William Green 1-14-1847
Cooksey, Melissa to Archibald Pennington 11-16-1833 (11-17-1833)
Cooksey, Rebecca to William Henly 11-19-1834 (11-20-1834)
Coonrod, Sarah to Robert Clinton 3-8-1826 (3-9-1826)
Cooper, A. E. to J. G. Dubois 10-9-1845 (10-10-1845)
Cooper, Catharine M. to Hiram B. Willoughby 2-3-1830
Cooper, Eliza to George W. Tate 3-11-1835
Cooper, Lavina(Lavivian) to Levi Spurling 6-22-1827 (6-23-1827)
Cooper, Mary M. to Wm. F. Babb 3-26-1860 (4-3-1860)
Cooper, Nancy to H. O. Sykes 7-3-1861 (7-4-1861)
Cooper, Susan E. to Edwin J. Barham 11-8-1849
Cooper, Terissa S.? to Richard A. Barham 3-28-1848 (3-30-1848)
Coor(Coon), Caroline to Miles Elkins 7-31-1838 (8-2-1838)
Coor, Nancy to Raiford Crawford 7-1-1839 (7-15-1839)
Coor?, Zilphia to Benjamin Rose 7-20-1833
Corburn, Winefred C. to Andrew C. Webb 5-25-1847
Corburn?, Elizabeth to John Mason 12-1-1834 (12-2-1834)
Cordle, Jane to William Lakey 3-9-1856
Core, Avy to John D. Holley 4-20-1833
Core, Harriet to Clark Freeman 5-2-1843 (5-5-1843)
Core, Sarah to Joseph Fleming 9-16-1854 (9-21-1854)
Cornelius, Matilda to Win Adams 7-2-1827 (7-4-1827)
Cornelius, Nancy to Hugh Shaw 9-26-1827 (9-28-1827)
Cornelius, Sally Ann to Jessee Fletcher 11-17-1838 (11-18-1838)
Cornelius, Vina to John H. Robertson 11-4-1832 (11-6-1832)
Cosby, Margarett to Messer Norton 1-6-1829
Cosby, Sarah T. to Geo. W. Doyle 9-29-1860 (9-30-1860)
Couch, Rebecca to Tilman A. Crisp 4-8-1848 (4-9-1848)
Covington, Lucinday Ann to John S. Clark 11-2-1838 (11-4-1838)
Covington, Sarah J. to James F. Spears 12-30-1843 (1-4-1844)
Covington, Susan Jane to Kincheon L. Rose 6-5-1841 (6-10-1841)
Cox, Amanda to B. J. Sherron 1-7-1859
Cox, Amanda to B. S. Shearon 7-11-1860 (7-15-1860)
Cox, Eldiss to Isaiah Macon 3-1-1844
Cox, Eliza to John jr. Rogers 10-28-1835 (10-29-1835)
Cox, Jemima to Philip Brantly 7-9-1833 (7-11-1833)
Cox, Margaret to David Allison 5-16-1828 (5-22-1828)
Cox, Margaret to Lemmon B. Gay 12-22-1852 (12-29-1852)
Cox, Mary Jane to Alvin Bishop 10-15-1841 (10-21-1841)
Cox, Mary Jane to John J. Lambert 7-12-1858 (7-14-1858)
Cox, Mary to James H. Rhodes 3-12-1832
Cox, Mary to William Hicks 3-14-1828 (3-18-1828)
Cox, Nelly(Ellen) to William Hughes 9-28-1829 (10-2-1829)
Cox, Rebecca to William Galloway 12-20-1837 (12-21-1837)
Cox, Sarah Ann to John M. Faucett 3-26-1853 (3-29-1853)
Cox, Sarah to John A. Lanier 12-15-1856 (12-18-1856)
Cox, Sarah to William Brown 7-22-1834 (7-24-1834)
Cox, Sillah?(Lillah?) to George Tipler 3-24-1841 (3-25-1841)
Cox, Susan A. to R. M. Callahan 1-28-1860 (1-29-1860)
Cox, Susan to G. W. Hudson 12-17-1859 (12-15?-1859)
Cox, Susan to John McDonald 2-8-1836
Cox, Tabitha J. to Franklin Haley 9-4-1858 (9-5-1858)
Cox, Vashti to Moses J. Mashburn 4-7-1828 (4-10-1828)
Cozby, Elizabeth J. to H. Scruggs Hays 6-4-1856 (6-5-1856)
Cozby, Frances to Asa Robinson 12-29-1833
Cozby, Jane to Buckner Jones 2-28-1829
Cozby, Jane to William W. Glidewell 9-10-1851 (9-28-1851)
Cozby, Lotty to Samuel Henson 9-21-1849 (9-23-1849)
Cozby, Mary J. to Edwin Fish 8-13-1855
Cozby, Mary to Mathew Gillaspie 8-29-1835
Cozby, Semon to Jonathan McKennie 3-31-1836
Craft, Elizabeth to Andrew J. Nevill 2-9-1846 (2-11?-1846)
Craft, Julianna E. to W. L. C. Williams 12-9-1850 (12-12-1850)
Craft, Mary Ann to Thomas Williams 1-30-1860 (2-1-1860)
Craft, Sally Ann to William New 9-21-1846 (9-22-1846)
Craig, Mary A. to Joseph R. Robertson 6-26-1840 (7-7-1840)
Craig, Sarah Jane to L. M. Harrison 10-15-1857 (10-18-1857)
Craig, Susan to Raiford Fulghum 11-26-1836 (11-27-1836)
Crain, Dorothy to Benjamin Alsup 1-20-1830
Crain, Frances to E. G. Thompson 11-16-1833 (11-?-1833)
Crane, Margaret J. to Ephraim McGlothlin 3-12-1857

Cranford, Eliza to Edwin Stevens 6-26-1832
Craton, Polly to Buckner Candell 2-18-1828
Craton?, Margaret to John H. Parker 5-28-1833 (6-9?-1833)
Craven, Eliza Caroline to John Wesley Little 9-2-1854 (9-3-1854)
Craven, Lavina J. to William J. Foster 12-27-1854 (12-28-1854)
Craven, Samira C. to John C. Foster 12-22-1854 (12-24-1854)
Crawford, Adelia to Alfred Myrick 5-18-1844 (5-19-1844)
Crawford, Cela M. to Charles M. Wellons 11-28-1850
Crawford, Cholley to Abraham Baker 11-16-1858 (11-18-1858)
Crawford, Eliza C. to William K. Dowdy 10-31-1855 (11-1-1855)
Crawford, Elizabeth Ann to Willouby L. Thompson 10-23-1837
Crawford, Elizabeth J. to Lary A. Sanders 1-16-1849 (1-18-1849)
Crawford, M. F. to James A. Park 1-3-1856
Crawford, Margaret to George W. Hensley 6-7-1843 (6-13-1843)
Crawford, Mary J. to C. Woodfin 4-27-1843
Crawford, Mary Jane to David K. Edwards 4-30-1853 (5-1-1853)
Crawford, Mary to G. H. Wyatts 5-17-1856 (5-20-1856)
Crawford, Merinda to Benjamin R. Fulghum 6-22-1840 (6-25-1840)
Crawford, Olive to Solomon Jacobs 1-30-1838 (2-1-1838)
Crawford, Sarah Ann to Alvin Williams 9-3-1837
Crawford, Sarah Ann to Enoch Eskew? 4-22-1847 (4-18?-1847)
Crawford, Sarah F. to Wm. P. McKinnie 12-1-1832 (12-5-1832)
Crawford, Sarah to Doctor Ammons 12-13-1854 (12-14-1854)
Crawford, Susan F. to John R. McKinnie 2-11-1830 (2-16-1830)
Crawford, Temperance to Wm. Faison 2-2-1846 (2-5-1846)
Crews, E. F. to A. E. Lewis 7-16-1856
Crews, Eliza T. to James A. Rose 3-10-1852 (3-11-1852)
Crews, Fannie N. to John W. Holford 3-14-1859 (3-15-1859)
Crews, Martha C. to Saml. H. Lambert 4-14-1858 (4-15-1858)
Crews, Mary Ann to Richard C. Hill 11-27-1849 (11-29-1849)
Crews, Mary H. to Timothy Lax 12-17-1852 (12-19-1852)
Crews, Mary Jane to Jonathan Joyner 4-14-1858 (4-20-1858)
Crews, Milly to Willson B. McElroy 10-15-1838
Crews, Minervia J. to Geo. W. Spurling 3-1-1858
Crews, Nancy Ann to Green B. Carter 1-3-1839
Crews, Olivia C. to Isaiah Watkins 12-24-1849
Crews, Ophelia J. to Wm. Dodson 3-19-1857 (3-17?-1857)
Crews?, Martha R.(P?) to Thomas Oliver 1-14-1840
Crisp, Cynthia to E. H. Osborne 6-24-1850
Crisp, Elizabeth J. to Shelton Oliver 6-26-1850 (6-25?-1850)
Crisp, Elizabeth to Greenberry Bright 1-28-1830
Crisp, Lucy J. to Thos. J> Gardner 6-14-1843
Crisp, Lydia to Wm. Reaves 5-14-1844
Crisp, Mary F. to Albert G. Sullivan 5-4-1843
Crisp, Melvina to James Johnson 8-22-1829 (8-23-1829)
Crisp, Nancy to Charles A. Crisp 4-7-1842
Crisp, Sarah Jane to Thomas S. Slaughter 5-26-1850
Crocker, Deborah to James Rosson 1-23-1841 (1-26-1841)
Crocker, Hanley to LaFayette Thompson 3-24-1834 (3-30-1834)
Crocker, Sarah S. to Joseph K. Newland 10-28-1858 (11-10-1858)
Crocker, Urshula to James Wright 11-8-1847 (11-10-1847)
Croose, Sarah to John Polk 1-16-1830 (1-17-1830)
Croslin, Elizabeth to William Hamblin 7-23-1824
Cross, Frances J. to James M. Fortner 2-5-1850 (2-10-1850)
Cross, Harriet to Benjamin Stone 5-26-1855 (5-28?-1855)
Cross, Harriet to M. D. Pankey 2-20-1860
Cross, Louisa E. to John W. Ross 10-8-1859 (10-12-1859)
Cross, Louisa to M. D. L. Anderson 7-25-1856 (8-5-1856)
Cross, Lucy Ann to John A. Gatlin 9-26-1849 (9-27-1849)
Cross, Polly to John Thompson 2-16-1828 (2-17-1828)
Cross, Rebecca B. to Littleberry Stainback 3-6-1844 (3-7-1844)
Cross, Virginia A. to G. C. Evans 2-7-1857 (2-12-1857)
Crouse, Lioty(Sioty?) to Vinson King 7-5-1847
Crouse, Sarah to Giles Taylor 11-17-1842
Crowder, Emiline G. to William Thomas Warren 11-19-1840 (12-2-1850)
Crowder, Sarah A. to Wm. T. Cross 9-15-1855
Crowder, Virginia A. to Wm. A. Tanner 9-13-1851 (9-17-1851)
Crumply, Sarah to Thomas D. Moore 2-9-1852 (2-10-1852)
Crums(Crews?), Nancy C. to Milton Smith 3-27-1845
Cummings, Emily to Hampton C. Misenheimer 3-4-1848 (3-9-1848)
Cunningham, Eunisa to Isaac Pirtle 12-13-1828
Cup, Mary Ann Elizabeth to James Brim 7-27-183 (7-28-1833)
Cupp, Adaline to Thomas B. Clifton 1-1-1855 (1-5-1855)
Curley(Carley?), Elizabeth to Jacob N. Norton 12-22-1838 (12-25-1838)
Curley?, Elizabeth to John McLain 12-13-1837
Cutberth, Eliza to Jesse G. Tudor 6-20-1833 (7-19-1833)
Damson-Damron-Dawson, Nancy Jane to Travis P. Vail 12-11-1848 (12-26-1848)
Dandridge, Agnes Neilson to Joseph Brooks 2-22-1847 (2-25-1847)
Dandrige, Mildred S. to Benjamin Cash 7-23-1838 (8-1-1838)
Daniel, Frances to Henry M. Teague 1-27-1851
Daniel, Lucy E. to Henry M. Comer 10-25-1842
Daniel, Mary Jane to George Donnell 2-24-1851
Daniel, Nancy A. to Wm. Bizzle 12-22-1856 (12-23-1856)
Daniel, Polly to Rice B. Yates 3-24-1835
Darnall, Ann E. to Saml. N. Abraham 2-27-1860 (3-15-1860)
Darnell, Jane to J. C. H. Fowler 11-1-1850
Darnell, Jane to J. C. H. Fowler 7-14-1853
Darnell, Salina to James T. Pugh 9-28-1853 (9-29-1853)
Darnell, Sophia to James L. Miller 3-2-1854
Darnell, Tempy M. to Nathaniel M. Young 3-1-1850 (3-3-1850)
Darnell?, Sarah G. to John E. Hopkins 9-7-1847 (9-9-1847)
Davenport, Emiline to Eli Whitaker 4-9-1835
Davenport, Sarah to Joseph Watson 12-23-1835
David, Ellen to James Coleman 1-4-1853 (1-5-1853)
David, Margaret R. to Prestly H. Roberts 9-14-1853
David, Mary A. to G. M. Dugan 2-2-1857
Davidson, Eliza A. to Eliphlet G. Fulton 7-21-1845
Davie, Sarah to Jeptha Mathews 4-20-1830
Davis, Catharine to William H. Yarbrough 7-24-1854 (7-27-1854)
Davis, Delelah to James P. Panky 11-29-1845 (11-30-1845)
Davis, Eliza to Orin Guthrie 1-23-1829
Davis, Elizabeth to John Carley 1-27-1849 (2-4-1849)
Davis, Emily to Kenny L. Tudor 7-7-1833 (8-8-1833)
Davis, Frances C. to William A. McDonald 3-10-1847 (3-11-1847)
Davis, Francisia to A. J. Smith 12-18-1858 (12-22-1858)
Davis, Jane to John Reagan 9-19-1833
Davis, Jane to Stephen L. Brook 8-6-1829
Davis, Josephine to Chas. P. Brewton 4-2-1857
Davis, Louisa G. to A. W. Bryant 10-13-1847 (10-14-1847)
Davis, Lucy to Dutton Sweeton 10-4-1841 (10-10-1841)
Davis, Mahaly to Abraham Deeson? 12-18-1826
Davis, Margaret Ann to Danl. B. Hood 9-8-1857 (9-10-1857)
Davis, Martha to Jesse Cerly 1-18-1849
Davis, Martha to W. T. Wells 7-11-1859 (7-14-1859)
Davis, Martha(Maletha?) J. to Caleb jr. Cope 7-1-1856 (7-2-1856)
Davis, Mary R. to John D. Chisum 12-24-1860 (12-27-1860)
Davis, Mary to John G. Wilson 12-7-1843
Davis, Mary to Matthew A. Poterfield 10-4-1838
Davis, Mary to Wm. H. Evans 10-4-1859 (10-6-1859)
Davis, May to Alfred Mashburn 4-19-1847
Davis, Nancy L.(S.) to James H. Glass 1-18-1858 (1-21-1858)
Davis, Nancy to Daniel M. Prewett 6-6-1838 (6-12-1838)
Davis, Nancy to David Cowan 11-7-1846 (11-8-1846)
Davis, Nancy to E. S. Little 10-9-1858 (10-12-1858)
Davis, Patsy to John P. Chappell 12-14-1839 (12-15-1839)
Davis, Racheal to John C. Gullender? 1-18-1835
Davis, Rena Caroline to James Parr 11-4-1833 (11-5-1833)
Davis, Sarah Elizabeth to Robert H. Morris 6-10-1852
Davis, Sarah to Jeptha Mathews 4-20-1831 (4-21-1831)
Davis, Sarah to Willis Vincent 10-4-1855
Davis, Tennessee to James M. Spencer 8-26-1858 (8-29-1858)
Davis, Visa Ann to John B. Daniel 1-24-1852 (1-26-1852)
Davis, Williammetta to Miles N. Lockard 11-20-1860
Dawson, Mary E. to Robert R. McCall 9-16-1846 (9-20-1846)
Dawson, Mary to Barnabas Nelson 12-15-1834 (12-18-1834)
Dawson, Sarah to Elijah F. Warren 6-20-1845 (6-22-1845)
Day, Evalina to William Scott 3-20-1861 (3-21-1861)
Dean, Catharine A. to Joshua M. Teague 1-16-1856
Dean, Gilly to Randolph Casey 5-25-1828 (5-26-1828)
Dean, Lucy to Jefferson C. Savage 1-10-1843 (1-13-1843)
Dean, Malinda to John B. Hardage 11-6-1837
Dean, Matilda to Williamson B. Rainey 11-5-1841 (11-7-1841)
Dean, Rebecca to William Pare 12-12-1837
Dean, Salina to James Carter 4-27-1836
Deason?, Mary to Henry Evans 12-4-1839
Deen, Delilah to Theopilus Thornton 11-17-1827 (12-3-1827)

Delk, Louisa I.? to Reubin M. Riggs 12-18-1850 (12-24-1850)
Delk, Matilda to James M. Ray 3-12-1859 (3-13-1859)
Delk, Nancy E. to James T. Little 6-16-1857 (6-18-1857)
Dennis, Martha O. to John J. Givens 11-29-1854 (11-29-1854)
Denny, Louisa to Archibald Joyce 1-1-1838
Denton, Catharine to W. B. Cox 1-2-1860
Derribery, Emily M. to Lee Thompson 3-21-1853
Devenport, Jane E. to Levi Park 12-7-1846 (12-8-1846)
Dial, A. C. to Theophulis S. Robertson 5-24-1847 (5-30-1847)
Dial, Artimissa to William T. Myers 9-25-1850
Dial, Jane C. to Wm. R. Robertson 12-26-1844 (12-28-1844)
Dial, Jane to W. K. Dowdy 3-19-1856
Dial, Manervia Ann to John W. Harrison 7-23-1844 (7-24-1844)
Dial, Marcilla E. to W. K. Dowdy 9-3-1860 (9-4-1860)
Dial, Martha A. to Robert Dowdy 1-1-1857 (1-8[18]-1857
Dickens, Dicey Ann to W. A. Moore 1-11-1860 (1-12-1860)
Dickinson, Mary C. to R. R. Gwyn 11-1-1854 (11-9-1854)
Dickinson, Sally G. to Hugh A. Gwyn 6-7-1852 (6-9-1852)
Dill, Nancy to Benjamin Malone 4-25-1845
Dillard, Elizabeth to Poleman Martin 8-16-1836 (8-17-1836)
Dillard, Jane to Henry Jacobs 5-14-1826 (5-15-1826)
Dillard, Jane to Theophilus Ervin 1-22-1861
Dillard, Martha L. to Willis Dillard 9-3-1834
Dillard, Rebecca to John T. Garner 8-29-1832 (8-30-1832)
Dillard, Rebecca to Solomon Needham 12-3-1834 (12-4-1834)
Dillard, Sarah to Linnear Dixon 9-10-1836
Dillard, Sarah to Owen Dillard 7-13-1833 (7-14-1833)
Dillenham, Permelia to Richard D. Hutson 10-10-1828
Dillingham, Elizabeth Ann to Vann R. Chism 6-18-1836
Dillingham, Jane to James Webster 9-8-1827
Dishough, M. E. to N. J. Cox 11-12-1860
Dison, Elizabeth A. to John A. Moore 1-8-1852
Dixon, A. E. to T. J. Ferguson 9-12-1861 (10-21-1861)
Dixon, Elizabeth A. to Thomas E. McClendon 6-5-1856
Dixon, M. Pryor to James P. Holloway 8-24-1861
Dixon, Susan to Leolen Jones 12-10-1857
Dizen, Lucretia to Willis E. Lewis 3-12-1829
Dodd, Elizabeth to Alexander Nordin 2-16-1828 (2-17-1828)
Dodd, Mary W. to Lemuel M. Pledge 12-23-1826 (12-24-1826)
Dodd, Tabitha to Levi D. Miller 1-22-1858 (1-27-1858)
Dodson, Nancy to A. S. Bills 12-22-1853 (12-25-1853)
Dollar, Elizabeth to John Brooks 3-16-1853 (3-17-1853)
Donnell, Elizabeth to David Evans 2-6-1843 (2-9-1843)
Donnelson, Martha to Wm. Fulgham 3-10-1831 (3-16-1831)
Dority(Daugherty?), Orphy to Alford Eskew 3-9-1846 (3-11-1846)
Dorsey, Belinda to John Kesterson 2-1-1827 (2-?-1827)
Dotson, Mary Ann to Henry H. Brown 2-11-1835
Dougherty, Abigail to William Sarrett 10-22-1837
Dougherty, Hollen to John Davis 8-13-1836
Dougherty, Mary L. to W. H. Daniel 7-15-1860 (7-17-1860)
Doughty, Serilda to Harrison Brown 12-8-1838 (12-10-1838)
Downs, Minerva to John Parmour 11-26-1836 (11-27-1836)
Doxey, Lorenda to James H. Southern 12-24-1832
Doxey, Virginia to Wm. H. Moon(Moore?) 4-27-1846 (4-28-1846)
Doyle, Laura F. to James Wilkes 8-21-1854 (8-23-1854)
Doyle, Margaret A. to Wm. H. Coburn 3-20-1861
Doyle, Rebecca J. to Harmon Harrison 12-21-1858 (12-22-1858)
Drake, Louisa to D. H. Porter 3-7-1851 (3-9-1851)
Drake, Marcella Frances to Benjamin Hainline 6-13-1857 (6-16-1857)
Drannon, Elizabeth to Joshua McCarver 10-25-1838 (10-26-1838)
Drennon, Marinda to T. J> Tull 1-5-1857 (1-9-1857)
Drennon, Sarah C. to John R. Maxwell 1-15-1850 (1-20-1850)
Drinnon, C. J. to T. W. Chambliss 6-3-1848 (6-4-1848)
Duberry, Mahulda to Hardy Carr 2-29-1840 (3-1-1840)
Duberry, Rebecca to Williamson E. Rainey 3-21-1843
Dubois, Catharine I. to George W. Deaton 1-7-1835
Dubois, Harriett E. to Benjamin W. Pirtle 12-29-1837 (1-4-1838)
Dubois, Mary to Wilson Luckado 2-3-1835
Duboise, Martha Jane to Martin Pirtle 12-20-1833 (12-25-1833)
Duboyce, Nancy to Robert Harrison 3-1-1830 (3-2-1830)
Duff, Eliza to Joseph H. Shultz 1-30-1833 (1-31-1833)
Duff, Maria to Abner Kerkendall 12-8-1829 (9-30-1830)
Duff, Nancy to Alford M. Walker 1-24-1829 (1-27-1829)
Duff, Sophia to Winfrey Owens 2-14-1827 (2-18-1827)
Duncan, Amanda to William S. Blasingame 12-21-1857 (2-12-1858)
Duncan, Elizabeth M. to Willis Davis 8-2-1845 (8-3-1845)
Duncan, Emilia to Johnson Isbell 10-15-1827
Duncan, Freedonia to Henry H. Brooks 1-17-1855
Duncan, Helan M. to Alexander Sloan 5-16-1853 (5-18-1853)
Duncan, Joan Harrison to J. W. Williams 4-28-1860 (4-29-1860)
Duncan, Malinda to John Duncan 2-17-1830 (2-18-1830)
Duncan, Mary J. to John W. Little 12-17-1856 (12-18-1856)
Duncan, Minney(Winney) W. to Abner Harvey 2-12-1836 (1?-17?-1836)
Duncan, Winaford to James Jones 10-5-1848 (11-7-1848)
Dunn, Elizabeth to W. R. Dean 2-19-1859 (2-26-1859)
Dunn, Mary to William Scaggs 10-15-1830
Dunn, S. J. to Thomas A. Bass 4-12-1861
Durham, Ann C. to Charles Mulherron 12-12-1849 (12-13-1849)
Durner, Nancy E. to Ralph Byram 2-6-1860 (2-9-1860)
Durrett, Jane C. to John A. Jarrett 11-30-1842 (12-1-1842)
Durrett, Martha to A. D. Neilson 3-19-1851
Dyson, Mary J. to William Spain 12-1-1854 (12-2-1854)
Eaton, Ailsy to John F. Curtis 4-28-1855 (5-1-1855)
Eaton, Alsy to Jacob Harty 9-26-1845 (10-1-1845)
Eaton, Lidia to Joseph Smith 10-14-1852 (1-10-1854)
Eaton, Nancy to John M. Curtis 6-23-1855 (6-25-1855)
Eatus, Dovist? Ann to Andrew Jackson Pugh 1-22-1852
Eaver, Elizabeth to William Y. Rook 12-23-1834
Edgarton, Frances to John Woodfin 4-23-1841
Edmonson, Lavender D. to Will O. Furgason 10-12-1838 (10-14-1838)
Edwards, Elizabeth to James Edwards 11-5-1849 (11-8-1849)
Edwards, Gemima Jane to John Yarbrough 12-29-1851 (12-30-1851)
Edwards, Jane to RLobert B. Dukes 6-30-1847 (7-1-1847)
Elkins, Alsey to Elias Smith 11-16-1846 (5-23-1847)
Elkins, Exy(Elizabeth) S. to Samuel B. Harris 1-14-1834 (1-14-1834)
Elkins, Mahala to Isaac Rogers 3-18-1834
Elkins, Mary Ann to David Evans 12-24-1861 (12-26-1861)
Elkins, Winney to George R. Langston 5-21-1841 (5-26-1841)
Ellington, Elvira C. to Madison D. Smith 1-26-1841 (2-2-1841)
Ellis, Jullia to John Holland 4-1-1859
Ellison, Frances to Lorenza D. Strongham 7-23-1832 (7-24-1832)
Elmore, Nancy J. to Wm. A. Bryant 10-22-1851 (10-23-1851)
Epps, Elizabeth S. to Patrick H. Cliburn 1-11-1833 (1-13-1833)
Ervin, Olivia to Benjamin Bell 4-24-1857
Erwin, Elizabeth to Martin Young 7-27-1841 (7-29-1841)
Erwin, Susan Jane to Ralph Hawkins 9-14-1861 (9-16-1861)
Estes, Minnerva A. to Wilie Jones 9-21-1849 (9-23-1849)
Estes, Nancy L. to Wm. P. Howell 7-5-1858 (7-8-1858)
Evans, Martha A. to W. H. Prewett 10-19-1860
Ewing, Sarah to Owen Dillard 1-7-1828 (1-8-1828)
Faison, Sarah to Danl. J. McCalap 1-16-1839 (1-?-1839)
Faller, Terissa to William Mayfield 10-6-1828
Fargason, Charity? to William Morrow 1-3-1837
Farguson, Olive W. to Leroy Cook 1-22-1840
Fariss, Melvina to Davis N. Bell 11-21-1832
Farned, Sophronia W. to Thomas Cox 1-18-1858 (1-19-1858)
Farr, Elizabeth to Thomas Whitehorn 7-9-1844 (7-10-1844)
Farr, Matilda Ann to Andy Sanders 6-26-1844
Farris, Nancy to K. P. Howell 7-25-1859
Farris, Sarah Jane to D. W. M. Woolverton 1-12-1861 (1-15-1861)
Farris, Sarah to William Reeves 4-3-1835 (4-7-1835)
Farriss, Lucy M. to E.B. Stewart 1-26-1859 (1-27-1859)
Farriss, Mary Ann to J. P. Lokey 9-27-1854
Farriss, Nancy to L. M. Hargrove 11-14-1857 (11-16-1857)
Farriss, Sarah F. to M. A. Stewart 12-26-1854 (12-27-1854)
Faughton?, Louisa to Richard Gilmore 1-9-1837 (1-15-1837)
Faw?, Mary to Leroy D. Butts 8-25-1851 (8-28-1851)
Fawcett, Ruth to J. M. Grace 3-8-1859
Felts, Susan H. to William A. Justice 1-5-1854
Fenler?, Martha to James Harris 12-15-1834
Ferguson, Eliza J. to Thos. R. McCommon 4-5-1859 (6-11-1859)
Ferguson, Elizabeth J. to W. M. McCommon 12-21-1857 (12-22-1857)
Ferguson, Esther A. to Robert Hood 7-31-1849
Ferguson, Lavanda to John M. Barnett 3-20-1860
Ferguson, M. A. to J. C. Wells 3-28-1859 (3-29-1859)
Ferguson, M. N. to J. F. McAlister 10-17-1861 (10-28-1861)
Ferguson, Sarah A. to W. H. Black 12-11-1852 (12-22-1852)
Ferguson, Susan E. to John R. Hood 12-24-1855
Ferrell, Docia E. to J. M. Webb 10-24-1853 (10-28-1853)

Ferrell, Marmu? to Augustus Taylor 7-18-1855
Fewtrill, Agelina to William Cumings 1-26-1853 (1-27-1853)
Field, Franky Jane to Watson Webb 1-19-1847 (1-21-1847)
Field, Martha Ann to Cornelius Rain 4-11-1838 (4-12-1838)
Field, Susan E. to Daniel G. Kelly 4-3-1843 (4-5-1843)
Fields, Nancy to James Benton 7-11-1837
Fields, Sarah to John Hunter 5-19-1850 (6-19-1850)
Fish, America to Calvin H. Dunahoe 3-4-1856 (3-6-1856)
Fish, Elizabeth to Bryant Johnson 5-9-1849 (5-17-1849)
Fish, H. A. to Joseph Johnson 11-19-1859 (11-20-1859)
Fish, Temperance to Jesse Wilson 9-23-1851 (9-25-1851)
Fitzgerald, Margaret to Stephen jr. Jones 9-19-1832 (9-27-1832)
Fitzhugh, Anne E. to John R. Fentress 6-15-1848
Fitzhugh, Ellen M. to Charles P. Polk 10-7-1835
Fitzhugh, Mary B. to John T. Macon 7-21-1842
Fitzhugh, Sophia B. to Thos. E. White 4-2-1834 (4-3-1834)
Flake, Sophia to Hoyle Holly 5-12-1835
Fleet, Nancy to Richard Anderson 3-20-1856
Flemming, Elizabeth to G. W. Grantham 6-30-1858 (7-4-1858)
Flenn, Sarah J. to Jarman W. Davis 1-5-1858
Fletcher, Carolin to David Rogers 10-9-1845 (10-12-1845)
Fletcher, Martha A. to Turner Garrett 11-26-1860 (11-27-1860)
Flint, Elizabeth D. to Sterling E. Williams 2-14-1834 (2-18-1834)
Flint, Sarah M. to Joel Furguson 2-6-1834 (2-11-1834)
Flower, Casey Lee to Isaac Moore 7-12-1834 (7-17-1834)
Floyd, Elizabeth to James Watson 12-6-1836
Floyd, Elizabeth to William Clayton 12-28-1836
Floyd, Tabitha A. to Wm. M. Farned 11-12-1857 (11-15-1857)
Flynn, Elizabeth Jane to Joseph G. Walton 10-2-1851
Flynt, Caroline C. to Moses McKnight 6-12-1852
Flynt, Mary P. to Robert T. Dodson 12-31-1849 (1-8-1850)
Foltz, Nancy E. to Dennis M. Lyles 7-21-1840
Foot, Susan to L. H. Bradford 2-11-1856 (2-12-1856)
Forbess, Elizabeth to James T. Bailey 8-5-1856 (8-6-1856)
Forbess, Mahala to Isaac J. Lucade 12-16-1843 (12-20-1843)
Forbuss, Martha M. to Eli Harriss 2-25-1846 (2-26-1846)
Foreman, Susan L. to R. T. Chandler 1-21-1861 (1-23-1861)
Forsheath, Margaret to Elam Rogers 10-23-1844 (10-25-1844)
Forsyth, Elizabeth to David Harrison 10-1-1840 (10-4-1840)
Forsythe, Milley to Wm. R. Harrison 4-29-1840 (4-30-1840)
Fort, Elizabeth to John Mott 3-7-1827
Fort, Frances E. to Wm. W. Wair 2-15-1841 (2-17-1841)
Fort, Priscilla to Alfred Castellaw 7-8-1833
Fort, Sarah to Thos. L. Collins 6-15-1847
Forte, Sylvester to B. T. Richards 10-3-1836 (10-4-1836)
Fortner, Caroline to Will H. Cole 9-16-1846 (9-20-1846)
Fortner, Martha L. to Lewis Grantham 10-11-1853
Fortner, Susan to Wm. Tackett 3-1-1859 (3-2-1859)
Fortune, Amanda S. to James E. Bryant 9-1-1858 (9-2-1858)
Fortune, Jinnetta A. to William R. Jacobs 12-10-1855 (12-13-1855)
Fortune, Martha Ann to Bailey Macon 11-25-1846 (11-26-1846)
Fortune, Mary to Henry Jacobs 10-11-1854 (10-12-1854)
Fortune, Nancy C. to John Cheshier 11-28-1849 (11-29-1849)
Foster, Amanda to Zadoc Casey 3-6-1841
Foster, Elizabeth to Jesse H. Irwin 7-20-1861 (7-22-1861)
Foster, Louisa to John McKee 12-22-1856 (12-23-1856)
Foster, Prudence to Enoch Ross(Rass-Russ) 1-14-1829
Foster, Prudence to Robert Nabers 11-21-1829
Foster, Sarah A. to John B. Parks 2-2-1856 (2-5-1856)
Foster, Sarah to S. R. Davis 1-28-1862 (1-29-1862)
Foster, Susan to Hansford Hank 1-7-1829 (1-11-1829)
Foster, Winsey to Thomas Morrow 9-16-1838 (9-22-1838)
Fowler, Ann H. to Peyton Powell 6-23-1835
Fowler, Drucilla to William Crain 5-24-1830
Fowler, Martha Ann M. to Wm. B. Matthis 6-3-1834
Fowler, Mary A. to Henry W. Brown 7-4-1831 (7-7-1831)
Fowler, Mary Ann to William Walker 8-3-1833 (8-?-1833)
Fowler, Mary to G. B. McAfee 3-24-1860
Fowler, Sarah F. to Pleasant G. Turner 11-29-1854 (12-10-1854)
Fox, Polly to Benjamin Bell 12-5-1834
Freels, Nancy J. to Wm. Eaton 9-21-1860 (9-23-1860)
Freeman, Cary Ann to Francis M. Claxton 2-24-1857
Freeman, Elizabeth to Wm. H. Rose 8-20-1860 (8-23-1860)
Freeman, Margaret to Hezekiah Morris 2-21-1843
Freeman, Unity to Abner McDaniel 5-19-1847
Friar, Polly to Julius Wilhight 3-2-1837
Fulgham, Charlotte N. to Robert D. Hooks 3-16-1828 (3-18-1828)
Fulgham, Polly to Stephen Rogers 12-8-1829 (12-10-1829)
Fulgham, Susan to John N. Jenkins 9-5-1826
Fulgham, Winefred to R. W. Howell 2-15-1835 (2-26-1835)
Fulgum, Caroline to Giles B. Crain 2-15-1832 (2-16-1832)
Fulgum, Sarah to John B. Donaldson 3-21-1833
Futill, Eliz R. to Lindsey Haney 8-12-1839 (8-13-1839)
Futrel, Penelope to Jefferson Sparks 9-4-1833 (9-5-1833)
Gadd, E. J. to R. H. Powell 1-10-1860 (1-11-1860)
Gaddy, Malinda to John B. Ferrell 8-28-1856
Gage(Ross), Nancy to Robert Wright 7-4-1827
Gage, Lathey to Wade H. Colbert(Colvard) 1-30-1830
Gage, Lucinda to William Taylor 12-15-1827
Gage, Lucinda to William Taylor 12-15-1829 (12-24-1829)
Gage, Seletha to John Wilkinson 5-8-1830
Gage, Susannah to Jacob Laraner 9-19-1831 (9-?-1831)
Gahagan, Mary C. to Henderson C. Wallace 5-25-1841
Galloway, Eliza J. to Jas. H. Warford 11-27-1856
Galloway, Mary to Cunningham Cox 12-30-1834 (1-2-1835)
Galoway, Margaret Jane to E. S. Caldwell 12-23-1857 (12-24-1857)
Gambell, Fanny to John Jackson 4-18-1845 (4-25-1845)
Gambell, Lucy A. to William Gray 2-7-1839
Gambell, Mary H. to Hiram C. Short 6-26-1847 (6-29-1847)
Gamble, Nancy to Thomas D. Gray 12-23-1848
Gamble, Susan to Alfred W. Gray 8-26-1851 (8-27-1851)
Gambriel, Lucy Ann to Martin G. Adams 8-1-1840
Gardner, Lydia to Henry Gardner 11-11-1843 (11-16-1843)
Gardner, Mary J. to Martin V. Miller 4-17-1860
Garner, Susannah to Berry Beany(Beny) 10-23-1841 (10-24-1841)
Garrett, Hulda Ann to Elijah H. Bomer 8-28-1856
Garrett, Malinda to Joseph Nabors 8-2-1838
Garrett, Martha J. to Elihu S. Pannell 8-24-1859
Garrett, Mary to William B. Henry? 4-7-1847
Garrett, Nancy J. to Eli Halton 11-10-1856 (11-12-1856)
Garrett?, C. to A. Alloway 9-7-1846
Garrison, Tinsey to Adam Chronister 1-5-1826
Gately, Lavinia to Gabrial Cannon 6-11-1841 (6-12-1841)
Gately, Nancy to Marshall W. Cox 11-21-1840 (11-26-1840)
Gates, Elizabeth to Nathan Nooner 8-28-1828
Gates, Jane H. to Thos. F. Anderson 12-5-1834 (12-9-1834)
Gates, Martha to Stephen Vault 5-4-1846 (5-6-1846)
Gates, Nancy V. to Benjamin Lax 3-2-1846 (3-5-1846)
Gates, Susan to Drewry Avent 3-29-1845 (4-3-1845)
Gatewood, Amanda J. to Geo. L. Burnet 2-6-1858 (2-7-1858)
Gatewood, Caroline to William P. Burnett 12-26-1860
Gay, Lydia Ann to Thomas J. Clifft 2-11-1860 (2-13-1860)
Gay, Mary to Richard E. Powell 10-15-1836 (10-20-1836)
Gay, Mary to Thomas Hester 9-30-1850
Gayler, Joana B. to Daniel S. Cannon 1-13-1857
Gaylor?, Catherine B. C. to Pascall G. Traylor 11-16-1836
Gee, Emily S. to F. M. Welch 10-4-1858 (10-7-1858)
Gee, Mary to Archibald Mayfield 11-1-1852 (11-2-1852)
Gee, Nancy to John Thompson 3-10-1857? (3-10-1858)
Gee, Willey to James Lambert 9-15-1859
George, Nancy W. to William Lawrence 4-11-1826 (4-12-1862)
George, Sarah to James F. Ross 4-27-1841
German, Amanda P. to Luther Ables 4-10-1858 (4-13-1858)
German, Elizabeth to William R. Alexander 11-3-1829 (11-4-1829)
Gibson, Elizabeth Jane to William Taylor 1-6?-1847 (1-7-1847)
Gibson, Mary to James R. Black 10-1-1857
Gibson, Nancy E. to Wm. P. Ware 4-17-1858
Gibson, Sarah Catharine to Joseph A. Black 3-17-1859
Gillespie, Cynthia to Felix Houston 6-6-1832
Gillespie, Melinda C. to Saml. R. Morrow 1-24-1842 (1-27-1842)
Gilmon(Gilmore?), Deborah to Po A. Williams 3-16-1847 (3-23-1847)
Gilmore, Eleonor to Jeremiah Hooper 12-30-1841
Gilmore, Jane to Anderson King 1-4-1849 (1-7-1849)
Glasgow, Ann Eliza to Thomas Peters 6-15-1837 (6-22-1837)
Glass, Elizabeth I. to Nicholas H. Whitehorn 11-26-1849 (11-29-1849)
Glass, Jan M. to Wm. Bryant 9-1-1845 (9-16-1845)
Glass, Margaret Ann to George R. McCommon 10-1-1852 (10-3-1852)
Glass, Mary A. to Daniel Gray 1-29-1848 (2-1-1848)
Glass, Nancy A. to William J. Brantly 12-31-1844 (1-2-1845)
Glass, Rachael S. to Maxfield Wilson 1-25-1856 (1-30-1856)

Glass, Rachel S. to George W. Belote 6-2-1838
Glass, Rebecca Ann to Mathew Thomas Prewitt 4-10-1848 (4-11-1848)
Glass, Rebecca T. to John K. Neely 11-29-1858 (11-30-1858)
Glen, Mary to William Lamkin 4-4-1840
Glenn, Marcilla? to Abner Warren 8-17-1846 (8-20-1846)
Glenn, Susannah to Green? B. Elerson 11-18-1845 (11-20-1845)
Glidwell, Mary M. to James M. Jackson 5-5-1856 (5-13-1856)
Glidwell, N. to Wiseman Savage 1-26-1848
Glraham, E. C. to George M. Williams 12-5-1853 (12-7-1853)
Goad, Emily E. to Richd. Grantham 12-5-1844 (12-12-1844)
Goad, Jane to Boyd Treese 3-7-1852 (3-18-1852)
Gocher, Tempa to Saml. Middleton 2-8-1860
Godlin, Nancy to Alexander Chapman 6-5-1846 (6-6-1846)
Goff, Fanny to William Maddox 11-2-1846 (11-4-1846)
Goforth, Dicey to Jackson Turner 4-13-1855 (4-14-1855)
Goforth, Margaret to William Carper 2-2-1861 (2-5-1861)
Goforth, Sarah F. to Robt. J. Rankin 4-11-1859 (4-17-1859)
Golden, Lotty to John McMahan 7-7-1851 (7-10-1851)
Goode, Mary A. to J. J. H. Greer 7-9-1860
Goodman, Elizabeth to Nathan New 1-1-1838
Goodman, Elizabeth to Samuel Sullender 8-5-1834
Goodman, Mareny Eleonor to Thomas Young 1-11-1836
Goodwin, Anna to Everett Ritter 5-15-1828 (5-20-1828)
Goodwin, Diana C. to John McKee 9-20-1832
Goodwin, Haley to Josiah Pierce 11-5-1836 (11-7-1836)
Gore, Edny Jane to James B. Smith 8-25-1855 (8-28-1855)
Gossett, Clemintine M. to Wm. McD. Rains 12-9-1840 (12-10-1840)
Gossett, Mary M. to Joseph F. Fenner 8-31-1852 (8-30?-1852)
Grace, Ardenia F. to Wm. E. Fawcett 7-26-1859
Grace, Martha A. to E. A. F. Wesson 2-3-1857
Grace, Mary Jane to Benj. W. Davis 2-24-1847
Grace, Polina M. to John R. Rutherford 4-29-1851 (4-30-1851)
Graham, Angeline A. to John S. Gilmore 8-28-1860
Granby, Louisa to William Combs 3-22-1847 (3-25-1847)
Grant, Clarky to Sion Grantham 8-31-1833 (9-1-1833)
Grant, Polly to Hiram Williams 12-27-1824 (1-13-1825)
Grant, Virtuous? C. to Eli Cox 8-2-1836
Grantham, Abegill to Chalkley Grantham 5-29-1841 (5-31-1841)
Grantham, Elizabeth to Robt. J. Fortner 8-6-1856 (8-7-1856)
Grantham, Levisa to John Robinson 8-28-1826 (8-28-1826)
Grantham, Louisa to David Bishop 10-1-1856 (10-2-1856)
Grantham, Lydia M. to Wm. J. Brown 8-1-1857 (8-4-1857)
Grantham, Malvira to G. B. Simpson 9-7-1835
Grantham, Mary to James M. Gray 9-5-1850 (9-8-1850)
Grantham, Nancy to John Hamilton 9-24-1842 (9-25-1842)
Grantham, Rachel to Anson Brown 2-12-1831 (2-14-1831)
Graves, Mary J. to Geo. M.(W.?) Nolen 8-3-1859
Graves, Sarah A. to D. W. Rosson 3-14-1853 (3-16-1853)
Gray, Bettie T. to L. L. Asburry 11-4-1858
Gray, Cathanne(Catharine) to Saml. Enis 2-18-1858
Gray, Elizabeth to George M. Carricker 8-7-1852
Gray, Martha I.? to Thomas H. Feagan 11-14-1843 (11-15-1843)
Gray, Martha to Jeremiah Sullivant 1-3-1842
Gray, Mary Ann to John Springfield 7-7-1856 (7-8-1856)
Gray, Mary to James M. Stout 7-14-1848
Gray, Matilda to Albartis Chapman 11-20-1828
Gray, Nancy Jane to James B. Patterson 8?-22-1859 (8-23-1859)
Gray, Nancy to John Holder 1-30-1854 (2-2-1854)
Gray, Susan C. to Milton Smith 3-4-1831
Gray, Temperance to Robert Box 1-4-1841 (1-7-1841)
Gray, Winaford to Ephraim B. Gamble 12-6-1853
Green, Ann to Christopher Chappel 12-31-1838 (1-1-1839)
Green, Jane to Joseph Taylor 7-6-1826 (7-19-1826)
Green, Lucy K. to Hamden McClanahan 1-27-1851 (2-4-1851)
Green, Mary Pricilla to George F. Nappier 11-29-1849
Green, Nancy to Joseph Baker 7-25-1837
Green, Sophia to John L. Parker 9-10-1833
Green?, P. E. to Wm. P. Slaughter 5-6-1844 (5-8-1844)
Greenleaf, Martha to Joseph I. Dew? 7-23-1831 (7-24-1831)
Greenlee, Zilpha to Joseph S. Rainer 12-18-1851 (12-19-1851)
Greenwood, Nancy Ann to James W. Hunt 4-19-1843 (4-20-1843)
Greer, Susan Ann Elizabeth to Reubin F. Garland 7-25-1853 (7-26-1853)
Gregory, Elizabeth to Jesse Parker 1-30-1841
Gregory, Lucy to William Roach(Roark?) 7-17-1844
Gregory, Martha to Joel Booth 10-2-1851
Griffith, Nancy to John F. Burton 10-14-1850 (10-17-1850)
Griggs, Hester Ann to Harvey D. Standfield 3-13-1840 (3-15-1840)
Grooms, Wilmurth to Thomas Butler 10-28-1824
Grove, Eliza Jane to James T. Williams 9-28-1841 (9-29-1841)
Grove, Sarah Ann to J. C. Parmer 9-29-1847
Guin?, D. M. to Daniel D. Berry 4-12-1831
Guise, Caroline to S. B. Holyfield 2-6-1861 (1?-10-1861)
Guise, Elvira E. to Daniel Campbell 12-21-1857 (12-23-1857)
Guise, Rebecca to Isaac Sellars 8-27-1857 (8-28-1857)
Gullet, Sally to Thomas S. White 10-2-1832 (10-8-1832)
Gunter, Mahala to Jas. H. Brown 6-28-1832
Gunter, Martha to Robert L. Criner 12-28-1835
Gunter, Mary to John Hurley 12-28-1835
Gurly, Elizabeth to W. H. Goforth 12-8-1854
Guthrie, Margaret H. to Lewis Wells 10-29-1850
Guthrie, Mary C. to John W. Riggs 11-8-1856 (11-9-1856)
Guy, Fanny S. to Wm. C. Oates 10-11-1859 (10-12-1859)
Guy, Lenora M. F. to Henry C. Wellions 12-11-1851
Guy, Louisa C. to Gilbert D. T. Malone 10-17-1848 (10-25-1848)
Guy, Pauline E. to John R. Wood 9-21-1859
Guynn, Cynthia G. to Jackson M. Clay 12-14-1839 (12-15-1839)
Hadden, Nancy T. to M. W. Hall 4-27-1861 (4-29-1861)
Hail, Sarah to William C. Maxwell 8-22-1832
Haily, Martha E. to Hugh A. Gray 10-26-1857
Hainline, Sarah Ann to George A. Booe 7-4-1839
Hale, Arimencia to John C. Blackwell 8-23-1830 (9-3-1830)
Hale, Eliza to John Turner 1-30-1861
Hale, Mary to Edward H. Steward 12-18-1852 (12-19-1852)
Hale, Matilda to Abraham Jones 10-4-1834 (10-7-1834)
Hale, Phafama Elizabeth to Richd. T.k Lyon 12-21-1854 (12-27-1854)
Hale, Sarah Jane to James Grantham 4-17-1850 (4-24-1850)
Hale, Sydney M. to lHiram Casey 6-4-1861 (6-6-1861)
Hall, Mary to Robert W. Robinson 5-10-1831
Hall, Olive to John Deason 10-30-1828
Hall, Sallie J. to M. C. Humphrey 3-15-1858 (3-17-1858)
Hallaburton, Martha to C. F. Moliter 3-6-1857 (3-8-1857)
Haltom, Ann E. to Thomas D. Harris 12-15-1860
Ham, Caroline to Wm. C. Fleet 12-15-1842
Ham, Emblem to James C. Pruete 9-23-1839 (9-26-1839)
Ham, Lucinda to Franklin Minter 1-19-1847
Ham, Mary to Nathaniel Scott 11-13-1838 (11-22-1838)
Ham?, Susan S. to Andrew J. Howard 7-23-1850 (7-24-1850)
Hamblin, Sarah to Robert Cartwright 4-7-1828
Hamer, Emma H. to Thos. H. Webb 5-27-1858
Hamer, Frances A. to Newton Wright 12-15-1851 (12-17-1851)
Hamilton, Giney to Benjamin Vaughn 4-16-1831
Hamilton, Lucinda to Jason Wilson 2-2-1833 (2-5-1833)
Hamilton, Martha to Wm. B. Worrell 12-21-1857 (12-23-1857)
Hamilton, Milly to Benj. Sperling 9-25-1833
Hamilton, Nancy to Jesse Scroggins 7-17-1830 (7-20-1830)
Hamlet, Frances to Joseph J. Boguss 9-24-1845 (9-27-1845)
Hamlett, Mary A. to Jesse S. Harvey 8-14-1855 (8-15-1855)
Hamlin?, Elizabeth to A. C. Spurlin 11-30-1849 (11-31?-1849)
Hamm, Elizabeth to R. H. Isbell 4-24-1841 (4-29-1841)
Hammers, Lyda to J. C. Tims 3-2-1854 (3-3-1854)
Hammond, Mary A. to Francis M. Thomas 8-20-1852 (8-22-1852)
Hammonds, Fanny to Allen Sexton 3-2-1859 (3-3-1859)
Hammonds, Zady F. to B. F. Thomas 8-27-1856
Hammons, Billa E. to William W. McKinnie 12-18-1855 (12-26-1855)
Hammons, Martha J. S. to Giles G. Hudson 7-1-1853 (7-3-1853)
Hammons, Sarah A. to Keeble T. Thompson 9-30-1846 (10-1-1846)
Hammons, Susan J. to E. T. Thompson 11-8-1855 (11-9-1855)
Hampton, Mathena C. to William Blackburn 2-14-1831
Hancock, Adaline O. to Enock Stewart 12-3-1851 (12-4-1851)
Hancock, Mary Jane to Abram Maury 8-22-1859
Hanis(Harris?), Mary A. to James W. Prewett 1-21-1848 (1-25-1848)
Hankins, N. C. to William Usher 1-17-1835 (1-22-1835)
Hankley, Philadelphia Ann to Gilbert B. Boucher 12-1-1858
Hankly, Dohorty J. to Robert K. Ruddle 1-23-1849 (1-29-1849)
Hanks, Elizabeth to Uriah Stafford 11-76-1825 (11-8-1825)
Hanks, Joisey to Wm. R. Rogers 9-8-1827
Hanks, Kesiah to Wilie Caldwell 7-11-1827
Hanley, Lucretia to Calvin Philley 7-18-1827 (7-22-1827)

Hannis, Lucinda to James G. Wilkison 7-4-1827 (7-5-1827)
Hannis, Nancy T. to Larkin M. Wellons 9-25-1841 (9-30-1841)
Hannis, Rebecca E. to James W. Phillips 6-9-1849 (6-10-1849)
Hannis, Sinah P. to James Duncan 7-7-1831
Hannis?, R. E. to Robert J. Marrs 3-9-1848
Hanniss, Martha Ann to Wm. B. Ragan 11-10-1838 (11-15-1838)
Hansen, Henrietta to A. J. Norman 5-19-1852
Hansford, Deliah L. to Jno. W. Rogers 10-25-1858 (10-28-1858)
Hanson, Jane to James Boling 7-13-1830 (7-15-1830)
Harbin, Ellen V. to A. M. Davis 5-14-1861 (5-21-1861)
Harbin, Ellen V. to B. A. McDaniel 4-28-1858 (5-11-1858)
Hardeman, Mary to John M. Hardeman 5-13-1828
Hardin, Sarah R. to James Aston 2-14-1837
Hardison, Laura J. to A. M. Hamer 11-29-1858
Hardwick, Pritena to Bryant Hunphreys 4-16-1839 (5-1-1839)
Hardy, Martha E. to Jos. H. Neilson 5-26-1859
Hardy?, Elizabeth Ann to Isaac M. Daniels 4-3-1852 (4-4-1852)
Hargrove, Amanda to George Cowan 12-16-1853
Harland, Manerva Ann to James P. Kinnard 8-10-1832 (8-13-1832)
Harly, Martha A. R. to Benjamin Williams 10-26-1853 (3-13-1854)
Harmon(Hannon), Charlotte to Saml. Kelly 12-16-1833
Harper, Betsy to Richard Dabb 6-22-1826
Harper, Elizabeth to Stephen Box 1-28-1835
Harper, Frances to Wm. Simpson 8-15-1844 (8-20?-1844)
Harper, Nancy Ann to Lindsey G. Nixon 8-22-1845 (8-28-1845)
Harrell(Howell?), Nancy to Robert Michell 8-5-1828 (4?-6-1828)
Harrell?, Malinda to Absalom Overton 1-18-1845 (1-23-1845)
Harris(Hanis?), Mary R. to Benj. Owens 5-29-1839 (6-1-1839)
Harris, Ailsy O. to John J. Lambert 7-19-1848
Harris, Annis to James Bogard 7-14-1837 (7-27-1837)
Harris, Clemintine to John C. Hubbard 10-24-1837
Harris, Elizabeth to David E. Putney 9-25-1831 (9-27-1831)
Harris, Harriet R. to James T. Williams 1-29-1850 (1-31-1850)
Harris, Jane H. to James H. Grove 1-29-1850 (1-31-1850)
Harris, Jane to James G. Casey 9-30-1861 (10-6-1861)
Harris, Lucretia to Edward M. Myrick 10-14-1840 (10-15-1840)
Harris, Mary Ann to John Caldwell 10-12-1827
Harris, Mary E. to T. N. Prewett 1-4-1860 (1-5-1860)
Harris, Mary J. to Jno. S. Tabor 9-26-1859 (9-28-1859)
Harris, Mary S. to William O. Bryan 12-16-1833 (12-18-1833)
Harris, Mary to Addison McMillin 5-18-1830
Harris, Mary to Dyes Cain 12-15-1832 (12-27-1832)
Harris, Milly to Isham Sills 3-1-1833
Harris, Nancy to Asa Cox 12-21-1835 (12-22-1835)
Harris, Octavia to Wm. C. White 11-20-1859 (11-21-1859)
Harris, Parmelia to James M. Jacobs 12-2-1858 (12-8-1858)
Harris, Rebecca to Theophilus Shaw 5-5-1835
Harris?, Marry A. to Josiah Grantham 11-3-1859
Harrison(Hardison?), Frances A. to James G. Wyatt 2-12-1847
Harrison, Hannah T. to Nathan M. Burns 1-13-1840
Harrison, Lucinda to John Tipler 11-7-1843 (11-9-1843)
Harrison, Martha L. to J. L. McBride 3-19-1855 (3-21-1855)
Harrison, Mary E. to James A. McBride 2-28-1845 (3-6-1845)
Harrison, Nancy A. C. to John W. Street 8-31-1848 (9-7-1848)
Harrison, Polly to John Sullivan 8-11-1855 (8-15-1855)
Harrison, Sarah Becca to G. W. Sherron 11-4-1859
Harrison, Virginia D. to Lewis M. Williams 10-19-1857
Harriss, Abigil P. to Robert W. Wynn 8-25-1858 (8-27-1858)
Harriss, Charlotte to Isaac Brewer 3-13-1843 (3-14-1843)
Harriss, Elizabeth S. to John P. Moore 12-23-1843
Harriss, Helen C. to Martin L. Hardin 6-22-1846 (6-25-1846)
Harriss, Martha O. to Benjamin A. Simmons 1-21-1861 (1-24-1861)
Harriss, Mary Jane to George Warren 10-15-1859 (10-16-1859)
Harriss, Nancy to Walter M. Shinault 2-26-1853 (3-2-1853)
Harriss, Olivia F. to John H. Simmons 1-13-1858
Harriss, Ruth to James jr. Toone 1-16-1861 (1-17-1861)
Harriss, Sydney to Lewis R. Sutton 12-16-1850 (12-17-1850)
Hart, Bathis to Jesse G. Grice 11-14-1827
Hart, Eliza to Robert Hays 6-4-1827 (6-7-1827)
Hart, Louisa to Willis Taylor 4-9-1829 (5-11-1829)
Hartsfield, Sallie F. to Charles Fox Fennel 11-22-1859 (11-23-1859)
Harty, Louisa Jane to Joseph Herryman 11-10-1842
Harty, Parrylee Ellen to Stephen Harriman 9-6-1858 (9-12-1858)
Harvey, Elizabeth to Crawford A. Duncan 4-11-1838
Harvey, Emily to Charles Murphy 12-29-1828 (1-1-1829)
Harvey, Hannah to Ninian Steele 11-2-1826
Harvey, Harriet A. to James B. Walls 12-13-1836 (12-21-1836)
Harvey, Mary A. to Thomas D. Gray 7-13-1838
Harvey, Newoma to Smith H. Hill 1-13-1844
Harvill, Elizabeth to Samuel J. Cabell 6-1-1827 (6-3-1827)
Haskins, Eliza to George Wood 2-13-1835
Hateley, Susan to Gabril Bumpass 9-22-1844
Hatfield, Mary Jane to William S. Devenport 11-27-1848 (11-28-1848)
Hatley, Frances C. to John Gossett 1-15-1840
Hatley, Mary N.? to V. D. Gossett 3-21-1825 (3-24-1825)
Hatley, Sarah to Joseph W. Matthews 1-1-1829
Hatley?, Sally to John Stafford 2-6-1837
Hatly, Maria H. to Ezekiel Wall 1-6-1834 (1-4?-1834)
Hawkins, Sarah C. to W. L. Low 2-23-1850 (2-26-1850)
Hay(May), Polly to John Bosberne 9-9-1829
Haynes, Hannah A. to John D. Seivers 12-5-1848 (12-7-1848)
Haynes, Nancy J. to Robert Alexander Jones 7-31-1856
Haynie, Elizabeth E. to Timmon S. Treadwell 10-1-1850
Hays, Celia to Wm. W. Shackelford 4-8-1837 (4-9-1837)
Hays, Emily to William Thompson 10-26-1847
Hays, Jane to John Cortner 7-5-1824 (7-7-1824)
Hays, Lodoriska to Asa Parker 2-14-1834 (2-15-1834)
Hays, Lucinda to Gabriel Malone 1-11-1839 (1-6?-1839)
Hays, Pernisia to John Neil 11-26-1832
Hays, Rachel to Abram Castell 8-2-1826
Hays, Rebecca H. to Silas Brook 1-6-1832 (1-5?-1832)
Hendly, Malissa to Gillard King 2-3-1836
Hendrick, Nancy E. to J. J. Thomas 2-17-1847
Hendricks, Elizabeth J. to Bedford Thomas 1-10-1849 (1-12-1849)
Hendricks, Martha E. F. to Samuel J. Goforth 10-31-1853
Hendricks, Mary to Benj. Lux(Sax?) 3-13-1860 (3-14-1860)
Hendricks, Polly to Wm. H. DeBerry 6-23-1828 (6-24-1828)
Henry, Bethenia to Sample Mills 11-24-1851 (11-27-1851)
Henry, Isabel to John Crow 9-22-1829
Henry, Nancy M. to William H. Kindrick 2-17-1853? (2-21-1855)
Hensly, Mary E. to L. W. Brown 12-23-1858
Henson, Elizabeth to James M. Mitchell 11-17-1858 (11-20-1858)
Henson, Lucy to Wm. H. Bass 9-20-1859
Henson, Margaret to Hiram Elkins 12-24-1850 (12-29-1850)
Henson, Martha J. to N. P. Haltom 10-10-1861 (10-13-1861)
Henson, Mary to Stephen Gibson 11-1-1836
Henson, Minny E. to John Dill 3-7-1856 (3-9-1856)
Henson, Nancy to George S. Gibson 1-27-1828 (1-29-1828)
Henson, Nancy to Wm. G. Hays 3-7-1833
Henson, Sally to Arma Shoefer 2-17-1830 (2-18-1830)
Henson, Sarah C. to John Baker 3-1-1850 (3-7-1850)
Henson, Sarah to Hiel Gibson 12-23-1846 (12-24-1846)
Herendon, Mary Jane to J. R. Parish 3-18-1858
Herne?, Elizabeth to Jacob Cox 2-27-1834
Herrell?, Elizabeth to William B. Seaton 1-4-1851 (1-5-1851)
Herryman, Sarah to James C. Irvin 2-4-1836
Hervell?, Sarah L. to David A? Gates 11-9-1850
Hervey, Ann to Willoby D. Simmons 3-29-1843
Hervey, Elizabeth to James Murphy 10-31-1843 (11-2-1843)
Hervey, Lovenia to John A. Long 12-20-1848
Hester, Ann Eliza to William High 8-8-1837
Hester, Judah to Edward L. Peters 6-7-1848
Hester, Lucinda to Claiborne Campbell 1-25-1836 (1?-7-1836)
Hicks, Ally to Nathaniel S. Isbell 11-4-1846 (11-9-1846)
Hicks, Amie to Allen King Wilson 11-10-1829 (11-9?-1829)
Hicks, Centhia to John Fish 9-24-1844 (9-26-1844)
Hicks, Eliza Ann to Solomon C. Casey 9-8-1856 (9-11-1856)
Hicks, Elizabeth to Caleb Cox 8-4-1832 (8-9-1832)
Hicks, Emily to Jason Wilson 2-28-1848 (3-2-1848)
Hicks, Mary L. to Jesse Bryant 9-30-1856 (10-2-1856)
Hicks, Nancy to H. S. Owen 3-21-1846
Hicks, Sally to Green B. Hicks 3-26-1844 (3-28-1844)
Higgs, Louvenia to Elija Cannon 5-25-1850 (5-26-1850)
Higgs, Martha J. to Cannon Smith 12-27-1857 (1-5-1858)
Higgs, Mary M. to Dempsey E. Curl 12-4-1858 (12-5-1858)
Higgs, Nancy E. to Wm. Thompson 10-24-1859
Higgs, Rebecca to W. D. Simmons 6-30-1846
High, Frances M. to H.S. Wills 5-4-1845
High, Mary A. to James Bagley 4-12-1836 (4-14-1836)
Highfield, Cela A. to Stephen Gibson 5-28-1856 (5-29-1856)

Highfield, Delilah to John Threlkeld 3-28-1828 (3-30-1828)
Highfield, Nancy to James W. Norton 1-26-1853 (2-2-1853)
Highfill, Malenda to Henry J. Rogers 12-6-1845
Hight, Christiana to Jesse Blount 9-7-1840
Hill, Elizabeth L. to Wm. P. Wise 4-20-1861 (4-21-1861)
Hill, Elizabeth to Roger T. Sulenger 8-25-1828 (8-27-1828)
Hill, Martha E. to J. H. Prewett 12-18-1858 (12-22-1858)
Hill, Nancy to John Jackson 8-11-1851
Hill, Racheal to Asa Arnold 9-22-1828
Hill, Rebecca to Walter Robertson 6-15-1824 (6-17-1824)
Hillhouse, Martha C. to L. B. Murdaugh 12-1-1853
Hines, Amanda to John C. Shepperd 2-6-1849 (2-13-1849)
Hines, Anne to Jacob F. Sheets 1-20-1838 (1-23-1838)
Hines, Cytha to Joseph Minton 5-19-1836
Hines, Hester A. to Pearce Fulgham 3-3-1832 (3-6-1832)
Hines, Mary to Charles C. Gregg 2-12-1838
Hines, Sarah J. to Geo. W. Sheets 12-18-1859
Hinson, Martha J. to Tilman P. Pulliam 12-20-1854
Hinson, Nancy J. to Martin Skinner 12-28-1850 (12-31-1850)
Hitchcock, P. to Wm. T. Cheairs 9-6-1847
Hitchcok, Parthenia to James S. Nunnelly 8-6-1852 (8-15-1852)
Hobbs, Eliza Ann to William Cross 10-23-1837 (10-24-1837)
Hobbs, Mary Ann to William Brim 4-8-1834
Hodge, Martha Jane to John P. Smith 10-31-1848
Hodge, Mary Henry to Peter Perkins 1-20-1841
Hodge, Mary to Charley Holland 8-30-1838
Hodge, Mary to James Stephens 3-22-1839
Hodge, Priscilla to G. W. Willi 9-6-1852
Hodge, Sary to Jonas Baker 10-30-1828
Hodges, Elizabeth to John Sneed 6-8-1843 (7-?-1843)
Hodges, Hetty to Linzy J. Rutherford 9-28-1830 (10-7-1830)
Hodges, Martha to John D. Adams 3-4-1847
Hodges, Rebecca to Alston Grant 1-7?-1834
Hodges, Rebecca to Amasa Rice 4-23-1836
Hodges, Rebecca to Robert D. Chapman 10-6-1836
Hodges, Sarah to George Tackett 7-31-1834 (8-5-1834)
Hogan, Margaret Jane to Robert Park 10-6-1841 (10-7-1841)
Hogan, Mary J. to M. C. Webb 11-21-1856 (11-23-1856)
Hogan, Nancy A. to Richd. A. Sexton 3-7-1861 (3-10-1861)
Hogue, Emily E. to John J. Smith 8-12-1850 (8-13-1850)
Hoke, Rebecca to Jesse Pence 6-22-1839 (6-23-1839)
Holbut?, Lucretia to Abner Rosson 8-26-1836 (8-25?-1836)
Holcombe, Laura to Isaac Walden 10-29-1857
Holder, Martha to William Gamble 3-10-1851 (3-13-1851)
Holiday, Arlamesa to Abijah Baker 5-18-1830
Holiday, Penelope to John Perry 12-23-1852 (12-24-1852)
Holland, E. C. H. to Wm. Campbell 10-7-1845
Holliday, Mary Ann to Louis Beauchamp 12-18-1827
Holliday, Sarah Jane to William B. Elks 7-16-1850 (7-21-1850)
Holliday, Sarah to Wilie Jones 12-26-1837
Holliway, Emily to Thomas Robertson 4-25-1855 (4-28-1855)
Holloway, Mary A. to Michael Johnson 3-30-1857
Holloway, S. J. to S. W. Casey 10-18-1861
Holly, Ava to John F. Smith 3-18-1844 (3-19-1844)
Holly, Sarah J. to James L. Brown 9-11-1854 (9-12-1854)
Holman, Marry to Hartwell Howard 5-17-1829
Holyfield, Frances E. to Thomas D. Isbell 11-10-1838 (11-13-1838)
Honel, Margaret to James A. Casey 5-5-1829
Hood, Elizabeth M. to Lawson W. Brown 9-19-1843
Hood, Telitha C. to James L. Ferguson 11-28-1855 (11-29-1855)
Hooper, Amanda M. to Wm. H. Howell 11-29-1861
Hooper, Elizabeth to Alex Morris 2-22-1858 (2-24-1858)
Hooper, Elizabeth to Stephen Marler 4-6-1839
Hooper, Frances to Henry Killman 6-20-1846 (6-21-1846)
Hooper, Serbnny? to Jno. W. Blunt 12-25-1844 (12-26-1844)
Hopkikns, Sarah to James Coly 12-20-1834
Hopkins, Julia Ann to Ruebin Heatcock 5-22-1838
Hopkins, Lugina to Finiss Reed 7-28-1831 (8-4-1831)
Hopkins, Mary A. J. to J. M. Whitten 3-9-1857
Hopper, Jemina to Clinton Fitzgerald 3-9-1833 (3-19-1833)
Hopper, Sally to Thomas Crain 8-31-1829
Hopton, Anna to J. J. Marshall 9-12-1859
Horn, Charlotte to Charles J. Cox 4-24-1844 (4-25-1844)
Horn, Sarah to Thomas Floyd 9-11-1838 (9-13-1838)
Horne, Martha to John Allen Cox 12-13-1847 (12-17-1847)
Hornesby, Olivia Ann to Jno. M. Mitchell 2-25-1857 (2-26-1857)
House, Charlotte to John Myers 12-5-1848 (12-6-1848)
House, Jane to David House 12-22-1843
House, Merseny to James M. Brazell 9-8-1838
House, Nancy to J. D. Clifton 9-1-1851 (9-4-1851)
Houston, Margaret to Humphrey Mills 12-29-1832 (12-30-1832)
Howard(Howell?), Martha to Wrigdon Jernigan 1-28-1848
Howard, Delilah to James Allison 8?-31-1829 (8-6-1829)
Howard, Elizabeth A. to John W. Timberlake 1-6-1840 (1-7-1840)
Howard, Jane to Joseph H. Lacey 6-25-1833 (6-26-1833)
Howard, Mariah V. to Geo. R. Bridges 11-6-1844 (11-8-1844)
Howard, Martha to John H. Spivy 10-31-1845 (11-2-1845)
Howell(Harrell), Mary to Benj. M. Hill 8-9-1833 (8-15-1833)
Howell, Jennie O. to Samuel D. Simmons 3-16-1858 (3-?-1858)
Howell, Margaret A. to James Jernigan 2-27-1854 (3-2-1854)
Howell, Marietta to Will F. Ferguson 11-27-1854 (11-29-1854)
Howell, Minney Jane to William Brown 5-14-1857
Howell?, Elizabeth E. to Thomas C. Harrell(Howell?) 10-13-1846
Hubard, Elizabeth W. to Jesse W. Wallis(Wilson) 12-13-1845 (12-18-1845)
Hubbard, Mary Jane to James D. White 8-8-1837
Hubbard, Mary M. to R. P. Moore 10-25-1831 (10-27-1831)
Hubbard, Nancy B. to Wm. F. Palmer 6-9-1840
Hubbard, Samantha E. to John C. Hughes 3-3-1857
Hubbard, Sarah M. to Thomas Moore 12-13-1848
Huckaby, Martha to Joseph E. Bailey 1-6-1844 (1-8-1844)
Huddleston, Ann to W. F. Ayers 7-27-1848
Huddleston, Biddy to Grove Rook 7-26-1845 (7-29-1845)
Huddleston, Catharine to David M. Huddleston 11-26-1855
Huddleston, Eliza to Hiram Seaton 6-24-1846 (6-25-1846)
Huddleston, Emily to Alexander Hamilton 10-16-1852 (10-17-1852)
Huddleston, Mahala to William H. Huddleston 3-27-1850
Huddleston, Malinda to Josiah T. Faucett 5-13-1853 (5-17-1853)
Huddleston, Manervia to M. F. Westbrook 7-19-1858
Huddleston, Martha to William Arms 11-14-1839
Huddleston, Mary E. to Elisha T. Stewart 7-20-1859
Huddleston, Mincy Jane to Jehu Lambert 9-15-1854 (9-18-1854)
Hudson, Amarintha to Henry C. Jobe 2-22-1858 (2-24-1858)
Hudson, Caroline to S. James Rogers 3-22-1858 (3-25-1858)
Hudson, Elizabeth to John Corley 12-29-1834 (12-30-1834)
Hudson, Elvira to Elijah V. Brown 6-12-1843 (6-13-1843)
Hudson, Frances S. to James M. Box 10-7-1846
Hudson, Margret to Peter P. Crawford 8-22-1845
Hudson, Martha A. to Chas. T. Newland 3-24-1860 (4-3-1860)
Hudson, Martha A. to John A. Baker 8-20-1857 (8-26-1857)
Hudson, Martha to John Davis 7-17-1846
Hudson, Mary A. to William B. Worrell 9-14-1849 (9-20-1849)
Hudspeth, Frances A. A. to Alexander Bogards 2-13-1861 (2-14-1861)
Hudspeth, Lillie Ann to Allen Cox 3-11-1833
Hudspeth, Rebecca to John Bolen 5-27-1837 (5-30-1837)
Huffman, Mary to Alexander Carper 5-19-1857 (5-22-1857)
Hughes, Angelina to John G. Allen 8-9-1837 (8-24-1837)
Hughes, Anna to A. J. Henry(Heniny) 9-28-1829
Hughes, Catharine to John E. Meek(Merk) 5-7-1838 (5-10-1838)
Hughes, Jane to Geo. W. Vincent 7-14-1858
Hughes, Nancy O. to John Elgin 3-24-1839 (3-25-1839)
Hull, Mary to R. J. Neely 4-2-1851
Hullum(Hull?), Louisa to Ingram Wilson 9-2-1840 (9-6-1840)
Hullum, Harriet A. to Jerimiah S. Claunch? 4-24-1835 (4-27-1835)
Hullum, Louisa J. to William R. Woford 3-12-1849 (3-21-1849)
Hullum, Louisa T. to William H. Taber 11-25-1831 (12-1-1831)
Hullum, Mary to William Brown 6-19-1829 (6-25-1829)
Hullum, Miss Martha M. to Reuben W. Biggs 12-24-1845
Hullum, Zelia A. to Wm. T. Wells 9-24-1859 (9-25-1859)
Humphrey, Julia A. to M. C. Pearce 9-29-1860
Humphrey, Lucy E. to Wm. C. Hudson 3-31-1845
Humphrey, Mary E. to Jno. H. McCleland 11-4-1858 (11-10-1858)
Humphrey, Mary L. to John Williams 12-2-1858
Hundley, Elizabeth V. to H. M. Anderson 12-16-1858 (12-18-1858)
Hunnell, Cinderralla to Harmon O. Jackson 11-30-1833 (12-4-1833)
Hunnell, Martha to Claiburn Wilson 3-28-1842 (3-29-1842)
Hunnell, Polly to Henry Rogers 3-3-1831
Hunt, Ann E. to Nathaniel Atkinson 10-27-1837 (10-29-1837)
Hunt, Clarissa to Jno. M. Neely 7-9-1833 (7-23-1833)
Hunt, Eugenia D. V. to Beverly L. Holcomb 6-25-1829 (7-2-1829)

Hunt, Mary S. to Jno. R. Dickins 2-21-1842 (2-22-1842)
Hunt, Melvina to William Rosser 5-29-1833
Hunt, S. S. to C. H. Dabbs 12-5-1834
Hunt, Susannah E. to James S. Boney 6-7-1838 (6-10-1838)
Hunt, Virginia to Samuel Dickins 2-21-1842 (2-22-1842)
Hunter, Agness E. to John W. Shaw 11-1-1838
Hunter, Diena M. L. to Jefferson M. Fields 1-8-1851 (1-9-1851)
Hunter, Mary to Geo. Tackett 7-3-1860
Hunter, Nancy Lenorah to John Willoughby 1-12-1848 (1-13-1848)
Hunter, Sarah Ann to John A. Mashburn 3-13-1854 (3-16-1854)
Hurt, Mary to Abel Pennington 3-14-1841
Hutson, Jane to Mathew Cozby 6-12-1833 (6-15-1833)
Hynnell, Permelia to William Ragan 12-9-1837
Ingram, Luch sH. to C. H. Hicks 10-6-1848
Ingram, Mariah to William Simpson 1-22-1831
Ingram, Martha S. to Samuel C. Scott 2-9-1849 (4-10-1849)
Ingram, Mourning to Samuel D. Stewart 4-5-1852 (4-6-1852)
Ingram, Rebecca W. to James E. Dodson 4-7-1851 (4-9-1851)
Ingram, Sarah E. T. to Boling Branch 7-22-1840 (7-23-1840)
Ingram, Virginia C. to N. A. D. Bryant 5-27-1856
Inman, Mary Ann to Matthew Doyle 12-9-1843 (12-17-1843)
Irby, Eliza to James S. Wimberley 12-24-1861
Irions, Ann Eliza to James M. McCalla 1-29-1842 (2-1-1842)
Irions, Sarah Jane to Thomas Peters 10-28-1846
Irons, Mary C. to Thomas C. Jones 5-17-1837
Irvin, Jinnetta to William Pate 6-23-1836
Irvin, Polly to Wm. Harrison 2-18-1830
Irwin, Martha E. to Elijah W. Cross 11-9-1842 (11-10-1842)
Isaacs, Harnett N. to Hiram Andlerson 3-14-1842
Isam, Elizabeth to Giles Parker 10-29-1828
Isam, Tempie to Benjamin Parker 1-6-1827 (1-7-1827)
Israil, Mary to William Saunders 12-30-1830
Isum, Annie to Isaac Parker 10-25-1827 (11-18-1827)
Jackson, Barbry to Martin Case 1-2-1845
Jackson, Clara to John Bozzle 4-29-1851 (5-4-1851)
Jackson, Cornelia to M. P. Mitchell 8-22-1861
Jackson, Ebby to John L. Ash 8-4-1835
Jackson, Edy to William Merlin 2-13-1827
Jackson, Elizabeth to Alexander Polk 6-17-1829
Jackson, Frances to Hamilton Murley 12-9-1857
Jackson, Hollis to Sampson Rogers 12-8-1830 (12-9-1830)
Jackson, Leaner to Joseph Willie 2-1-1847 (2-2?-1847)
Jackson, Lucinda C. to Wm. T. Dial 1-19-1857 (1-20-1857)
Jackson, M. A. to J. M. C. Barrett 12-16-1857 (12-17-1857)
Jackson, M. F. to J. A. Prast? 7-12-1847
Jackson, Margarett to Lewis Hill 12-16-1848 (12-17-1848)
Jackson, Martha to James Highfill 4-22-1833 (4-25-1833)
Jackson, Mary E. to Isaac M. Daniel 12-10-1857 (12-13-1857)
Jackson, Mary E. to Joseph H. Yarbrough 6-7-1854 (6-8-1854)
Jackson, Mary L. A. to Benj. F. Priest 1-31-1855 (2-1-1855)
Jackson, Mary to David Fortner 9-10-1859 (9-11-1859)
Jackson, Mary to Thomas Case 6-24-1840
Jackson, Nancy to James Howard McMillan 3-22-1842
Jackson, Pamelia A. to John Y.(Z?) Scarbrough 1-11-1854 (1-12-1854)
Jackson, Rachael to T. J. Barret 1-2-1860 (1-5-1860)
Jackson, Susannah? to Lewis Pirtle 10-8-1846 (10-13-1846)
Jacob, Elizabeth to William Rossen 12-22-1824
Jacobs, Adeline M. to Eli Moore 7-16-1839 (7-18-1839)
Jacobs, Eliza to Payton L. Parker 8-12-1840 (8-13-1840)
Jacobs, Elizabeth to Benjamin J. Boydston 11-12-1825 (11-15-1825)
Jacobs, Elizabeth to David Macon 11-20-1848 (11-23-1848)
Jacobs, Elmina to Edward Bass 7-15-1828 (not executed)
Jacobs, Elmina to Ethelana Pitman 9-27-1829
Jacobs, Mary to John W. Barnett 6-7-1834 (6-12-1834)
Jacobs, Nancy McK. to lPerry Sain 1-6-1845 (1-7-1845)
James, Eliza J. to Jas. W. Allen 12-28-1857
James, Jane to James M. Jones 12-16-1841
James, Mariah to Jefferson Macklin 10-21-1851
James, Martha Ann to James R. Griffin 8-9-1848 (8-10-1848)
James?, Manerva to Wm. A. J. Smith 12-28-1846 (12-31-1846)
Janes, S. A. to J. R. Joyner 11-5-1860 (11-8-1860)
Janes, Sarah Ann to A. M. Hamer 12-2-1854 (12-5-1854)
Jansen, Emma M. to Charles J. Miller 12-3-1851
Jarman, Elizabeth N. to Saml. J. Harrington 1-28-1846 (1-30-1846)
Jarman, Mary D. to Albert D. Duncan 8-5-1831 (8-10?-1831)
Jarman, Philpina to Thomas M. Cuthbertwson 4-1-1824 (4-3-1824)
Jarmon, Rosanna S. to Robert F. Jarmon 11-14-1845 (11-18-1845)
Jarnigan, Polly to Haliard King 11-25-1856
Jarrett, Sarah to Henry Knight 9-11-1844 (9-12-1844)
Jenkins, Martha A. to Wm. S. Carson 4-17-1860 (4-22-1860)
Jenkins, Minerva to Jesse Gray 3-20-1832
Jernagin, A. C. to R. T. Woolverton 5-11-1861 (5-22-1861)
Jernigin, Mary Ann to John Coates 9-8-1847 (9-19-1847)
Jobe, Henrietta to Logan D. Brotherton 7-8-1835
Jobe, Polly to William Rosson 4-19-1826
Johnson, Abigil to Will H. Childress 7-17-1856 (7-20-1856)
Johnson, Alphia to Andrew C. Elliott 10-18-1828 (10-19-1828)
Johnson, Amanda J. to A. J. Nelson 2-13-1856 (2-14-1856)
Johnson, Anlize to James C. Nowlin 12-22-1837 (12-24-1837)
Johnson, Ann to Jackson Hargroves 8-2-1839 (9-2-1839)
Johnson, Anna to Jesse A. Carter 9-19-1857
Johnson, Barbara B. to James O. Dawson 1-9-1839 (1-11-1839)
Johnson, Benigna to Thomas McCary 9-19-1851 (9-21-1851)
Johnson, Candia to W. C. McIntyre 2-21-1855 (2-25-1855)
Johnson, Cassa to Major Standly 11-10-1835 (11-12-1835)
Johnson, Cely to Uzzell Benson 6-16?-1833
Johnson, Charity to John M. Covington 12-17-1838 (12-20-1838)
Johnson, Cora to John Warren 1-11-1834 (1-16-1834)
Johnson, Elizabeth C. to Henry L. Woodson 7-16-1854 (7-15?-1854)
Johnson, Elizabeth to Harmon Jackson 12-28-1853 (12-29-1853)
Johnson, Elizabeth to Henry Parris 9-15-1849 (9-27-1849)
Johnson, Elizabeth to John Turner 12-20-1834
Johnson, Frances to E. F. Fortune 11-17-1855 (11-6?-1855)
Johnson, Lucinda to William Childress 8-6-1847 (8-8-1847)
Johnson, Margaret J. to Wm. M. Johnson 1-4-1862 (1-5-1862)
Johnson, Margrett to Bennett Highfield 12-29-1846 (12-31-1846)
Johnson, Martha to Hiram N. Brown 1-27-1845
Johnson, Mary Ann to W. N. Farris 10-4-1838
Johnson, Mary E. to Carrol Butler 2-2-1856 (2-5-1856)
Johnson, Mary to John Rogers 9-19-1861
Johnson, Merilla H. to John R. Howell 6-3-1840 (6-4-1840)
Johnson, Nancy C. to John Coates 2-20-1839
Johnson, Nancy H. to Richard H. McNees 9-24-1828 (9-25-1828)
Johnson, Nancy L. to James Little 11-24-1857 (11-25-1857)
Johnson, Nancy M. to W. R. B. Powell 10-23-1857 (11-5-1857)
Johnson, Nancy to John F. Robertson 7-31-1827
Johnson, Rebecca to James H. Sheppard 10-15-1828
Johnson, Ruth to Henry Cockeram 7-30-1828 (4-6-1829)
Johnson, Sarah C. to John sr. Eaton 9-13-1858 (9-14-1858)
Johnson, Sarah to Benjamin Turner 11-21-1831
Johnson, Sarah to Egbert Haywood 5-7-1828 (5-10-1828)
Johnson, Susanah R. to John Allen 8-23-1852 (8-24-1852)
Johnson, Susanna to James F. Williams 2-8-1858 (2-11-1858)
Johnson, Valenia to Elijah Starkey 9-5-1859 (9-6-1859)
Johnston, Mariah to Jacob Ross 6-19-1825 (7-19-1825)
Jonagan, Susan to John Waller 9-2-1854 (9-3-1854)
Jones, Ann Eliza to T. S. Tate 12-11-1860 (12-12-1860)
Jones, Ann Mariah to William L. Birdsong 12-17-1849 (12-20-1849)
Jones, Ann S. to Samuel B. Harper 12-27-1827 (1-1-1828)
Jones, Caroline to Munford S. Marsh 11-13-1829 (11-17-1829)
Jones, Catharine to James M. Richardson 4-4-1855 (4-10-1855)
Jones, Catherine to Benjamin Davis 9-1-1831
Jones, Clemency Jane to James W. Jones 10-2-1851
Jones, Dorcas to Emery E. Williams 11-25-1834
Jones, Elender to James M. Gunter 4-7-1828 (4-13-1828)
Jones, Eliza B. to Wyatt Hester 12-2-1823 (12-4-1823)
Jones, Eliza V. to John B. Barnes 1-22-1848 (1-23-1848)
Jones, Eliza to Sidney Cooper 3-24-1835
Jones, Eliza to William Haywood 3-27-1836
Jones, Elizabeth S. to James R. Wiggins 6-27-1859 (6-30-1859)
Jones, Elizabeth to Hughie Davis 10-7-1830 (10-14-1830)
Jones, Elizabeth to John Johnson 12-15-1826 (1-6-1827)
Jones, Elizabeth to John Skinner 3-10-1825
Jones, Elizabeth to Will Henson 2-21-1835
Jones, Elya(Diya) Ann to Joseph D. Sauls 9-10-1856 (9-11-1856)
Jones, Emily J. to Calvin C. Hundley 5-27-1861 (5-29-1861)
Jones, Harriet Ann to Wilie Deming 10-18-1853
Jones, Harriet to W. Brooks Ruffin 3-9?-1833
Jones, Harriett G. to Samuel G. Pegram 7-25-1836 (7-27-1836)
Jones, Jane to Allen Carroll 2-2-1826 (2-4-1826)

Jones, Janella? to Kinard Norman 7-1-1845
Jones, Louisa F. to Sylvester G. Parker 9-10-1851 (9-11-1851)
Jones, Lucinda to Daniel Brown 12-29-1843 (12-31-1843)
Jones, Lucinda to Thomas R. Hervey(Harvey?) 5-29-1848 (6-1-1848)
Jones, Lucy Ann to Jesse B. Cobb 12-22-1847 (12-28-1847)
Jones, Lutitia to Samuel Young 4-28-1855 (4-30-1855)
Jones, Margarette to Edwin Gay 7-19-1855 (11-11-1855)
Jones, Martha A. F. to John M. Davis 11-27-1824
Jones, Martha E. to J. W. Stricklin 4-23-1861 (4-24-1861)
Jones, Mary A. E. to James Cooper 4-5-1855
Jones, Mary D. to Danl. Harper 10-14-1825
Jones, Mary J. to James Y. Reed 3-23-1861
Jones, Mary T. S. to Thomas M. Ingram 10-30-1850 (11-14-1850)
Jones, Mary to Martin Johnson 6-15-1828 (6-19-1828)
Jones, Milinda to Lemuel W. Cruise 10-1-1833
Jones, Nancy Ann to Daniel L. Stockton 8-26-1833 (9-5-1833)
Jones, Nancy Jane to David C. Howell 12-12-1851 (12-18-1851)
Jones, Nancy to J. W. Deming 12-15-1845 (12-23-1845)
Jones, Nancy? to James Mills 12-7-1836 (12-8-1836)
Jones, Octavia R. to Edwin Polk 7-29-1846 (7-30-1846)
Jones, Oliva to Joseph Short 11-13-1834
Jones, Rozy Ann to Robert Carter 9-5-1844
Jones, Sarah A. W. to Barzillai Hopper 5-24-1859 (5-25-1859)
Jones, Sarah Ann to John W. Kirkland 1-1-1855 (1-4-1855)
Jones, Sarah Jane to John S. Munn 7-26-1849
Jones, Sarah to John Killough 10-12-1830
Jones, Winniford to Calvin Clayton 1-6-1842
Jordan, Julia Ann to John J. Jacobs 12-12-1859 (12-15-1859)
Jordan, Lucindia to Tavner Lewis 1-3-1853 (1-5-1853)
Jorden, Elizabeth to dJohn Green 9-16-1838 (9-18-1838)
Jourdan, Elizabeth to Edmund Deshaze 6-19-1837 (6-20-1837)
Jourdan, Mary to Ellen F. Bryan 12-31-1829
Jourden, Jane Maria to Whitson Macon 2-7-1849 (2-8-1849)
Journagan, Jane to Jacob Hughey 8-28-1839 (8-29-1839)
Joy, Elizabeth J. to Thomas E. Moore 9-17-1846
Joy, Virginia F. to Leonidas Trousdale 12-21-1853
Joyes, Eliza to Jno. Brooks 1-10-1845 (1-12-1845)
Joyner jr., Louisa to William Hughes 5-18-1854
Joyner, Cynthia G. to R. D. Casey 12-31-1857 (1-5-1858)
Joyner, H. F. to Peter P. Siler 6-27-1853
Joyner, Martha G. to Albert G. Harvey 5-16-1848
Joyner, Mary C. to William L. Jones 12-7-1843
Joyner, Sarah J. to Thos. G. Patrick 8-1-1844 (8-8-1844)
Justice, Louisa Ann to William A. McSwain 9-24-1852 (9-26-1852)
Justice, Lucretia to Rufus S. Snow 5-17-1855
Justice, Martha A. to William A. Wolverton 1-17-1851 (1-23-1851)
Justice, Mary J. to J. R. Sexton 9-17-1857 (9-24-1857)
Kearley, Chatarine to Orrin Lambert 3-13-1832
Kearley, Martha to Amon Y. Rook 1-15-1840 (1-22-1840)
Kearney, Sarah to Robert H. Walton 1-8-1842 (1-9-1842)
Keer, Nancy J. to M. J. G. Pevahouse 6-24-1856 (6-25-1856)
Keith, Martha to Andrew F. Janes 5-15-1861 (5-16-1861)
Keller, Eunice to John McGlothlin 11-2-1826 (11-4-1826)
Kelley, Easter to George Beck 7-27-1833
Kelly, Easther to Tho. Vernon 3-19-1837 (3-26?-1837)
Kelly, Martha J. to Pitser R. Rainer 12-10-1850 (12-19-1850)
Kelly, Racheal to Joseph Rhea 8-15-1835 (8-16-1835)
Kelly, Sarah to Zephaniah Hines 2-10-1841 (2-11-1841)
Kemp, Elmira to Lemuel L. Ray 5-4-1834
Kendrick, Margaret to Jonathan Youngblood 2-1-1836
Kenedy, Fainy to Elias Crum 2-15-1831
Kennady, Mary to Charles Shott 5-5-1851 (5-8-1851)
Kenneday, Lydia Ann to Henry M. Jones 8-30-1843 (9-2-1843)
Kennedy, Eliza to Isaac Hays 11-19-1832 (11-22-1832)
Kennedy, Lucy to Wesley C. Brown 10-28-1836
Kennedy, Mary E. to J. R. McKinne 2-18-1856 (2-21-1856)
Kennedy, Priscilla to Jesse Davis 6-5-1828 (6-14?-1828)
Kerby, Sally to Leonard Lambert 2-5-1829
Kerly, Mary Ann to Wm. McGee 1-21-1833
Kernay?, Giley to Larkin Hays 12-17-1829
Kerr, Elizabeth E. T. to Thomas R. Warren 9-19-1860 (9-20-1860)
Kerr, Margaret to Silas Marler 7-4-1842
Kerr, Nancy L. to Jo L. Graham 11-6-1860 (11-27-1860)
Kesterson, Lucinda to Zachiriah Richardson 10-6-1832 (10-?-1832)
Kesterson?, Rebecca to William Blackwood 1-11-1826
Kilgore, Lidia to Solomon G. Strothers 7-13-1830
Kilpatrick, Harriet to James Cox 5-19-1855
Kilpatrick, Tebitha H. to Richard B. Jarmon 12-19-1829 (12-24-1829)
Kinard, Lydia Ann to William Hamlin 12-7-1846
Kindrick, Nancy R. to George W. Henry 2-17-1855 (2-21-1855)
Kindrick, Polly to Aaron Freeman 8-23-1853 (8-24-1853)
King, Armasa to Thomas J. Collins 1-11-1841 (1-13-1841)]
King, Arsena to William Oliver 10-21-1846 (10-22-1846)
King, Catharine to Jerimiah Harris 3-22-1836
King, Eliza Jane to Robt. Glidewell 8-5-1845 (8-10-1845)
King, Elizabeth to Isaac Hammon 11-2-1830
King, Louisa M. to E. D. L. Tims 7-10-1861
King, M. J. to Stephen H. Dawson(Damson) 1-20-1845
King, Mary A. M. to N. M. Ozment 2-1-1860 (2-2-1860)
King, Mary Ann to Elijah Short 3-11-1843 (3-7?-1843)
King, Mary F. to Isaac Baker 8-1-1853 (8-2-1853)
King, Mary to James Hassal 8-31-1840
King, Melinda to Robert D. Jackson 10-5-1835
King, Polly to Jesse Glidewell 11-7-1842 (11-8-1842)
King, Sarah Ann to Henry M. Mills 7-25-1849
King, Sarah Ann to William jr. Wilson 12-15-1848 (12-17-1848)
King, Sarah to Bray Hawkins 4-16-1840
King, Susan to Saml. Henson 10-17-1838 (10-18-1838)
King, Tina to Albert Waller 12-14-1853 (12-15-1853)
Kirk, Catharine to Robert Knox 11-30-1823 (11-31?-1823)
Kirk, Martha J. to A. R. Neely 1-5-1853
Kirk, Matilda W. to Wicke H. Pace 10-26-1836
Kirk, Telissa Ann to Geo. W. Wilkins 11-9-1854 (11-8?-1854)
Kirkland, Fanny M. to William E. Jones 9-3-185 (9-6-1855)
Kirkland, Virginia to J. J. Cooper 12-22-1857 (1-7-1858)
Kirkman, Rachael C. to Thomas Fleming 2-12-1859 (2-19-1858?)
Knight, Mary Ann to Will A. Stacy 10-3-1827
Knight, Sarah A. to Jno. G. Williams 5-6-1858 (5-7-1858)
Koffman, Narcissa to Andrew M. McKalip 5-23-1854 (5-24-1854)
Kremer(Creamer), Nancy to William M. Ratten 4-1-1835 (4-5-1835)
Kurby, Jane to James T. Wiggins 6-15-1832
Kyle, Ellin to Dangerfreld? Carpenter 3-7-1835 (3-8-1835)
Lackey, Elizabeth to Timothy Ellison 7-18-1839
Lacy, Jane G. to Thomas James 11-1-1836
Lacy, Mary V. to William S. Midlebrooks 12-25-1849
Lacy, Rebecca to Edward Wade 7-29-1829
Ladd, Minerva A. to David B. Jones 10-27-1860 (10-28-1860)
Lake, Margarett Ann to John W. Scott 12-30-1851 (1-3-1852)
Lake, Marion to D. C. Arbuckle 12-18-1852 (1-4-1853)
Lake, Martha W. to George W. Harris 5-7-1836
Lake, Mary J. to N. H. Dunlap 1-20-1861
Lake, Mary to Joseph C. Williams 9-19-1840
Lake, Sarah Jane to John C. Spinks 12-26-1848
Lakey, Eliza to lJohn G. Summons(Summers?) 7-17-1838
Laks?, Cynthia C. to Windsor J. Spinks 10-31-1860
Lallier(Sallier?), L. J. to Joseph Hutchison 2-21-1857 (2-22-1857)
Lamar?, Isabella to Joseph A. McCommon 7-27-1835
Lamber, Martha Jane to William G. Cox 4-25-1853 (5-5-1853)
Lambert, Elizabeth to R. D. Swindle 3-30-1849 (4-1-1849)
Lambert, Jane Catharine to Mathew G. Babb 2-5-1852 (2-8-1852)
Lambert, Julian to Andrew J. Estes 1-30-1850 (1-31-1850)
Lambert, Mariah J. to A. E. Sweeton 10-24-1854 (10-25-1854)
Lambert, Martha J. to Reubin Estes 1-6-1846 (1-6-1846)
Lambert, Nancy H. to W. B. W. Sweeton 1-18-1860
Lambert, Nancy to Archibald Mayfield 10-3-1859
Lambert, Sarah to Geo. W. Gee 3-10-1852 (3-11-1852)
Lamberth, Assennith to William H. Seddens 12-20-1853
Lambeth, Jane E. to Andrew Craig 3-17-1845 (3-18-1845)
Lambeth, Litilia? to William Sasser 10-11-1850 (10-13-1850)
Lampkins, Kizziah to William Roberts 10-16-1851 (10-16-1851)
Land, Eliza to James L. Scott 7-5-1827
Land, Martha to Asa J. Hardison 3-18-1858
Land, Susan O. to William A. Bennett 11-12-1861
Lane, Ann S. to James Williams 12-26-1860 (12-27-1860)
Laney, Elizabeth to Alfred W. Gray 4-12-1854 (4-19-1854)
Laney, Mary Jane to Josiah Hall 4-22-1854 (4-23-1854)
Lankford, Mary E. to Tignell Jones 3-8-1861
Lany, Margaret C. to Geo. M. Leathers 7-24-1860
Lasiter, Nancy C. to Wm. McKehan 5-28-1860 (5-30-1860)
Latta, Mary J. to Willis G. Reeves 11-6-1854 (11-8-1854)

Laughlin, Clementine Elizabeth to James L. Young 7-14-1835
Lawhorn, Angeline B. to Moses P. Crisp 9-18-1855
Lawhorn, Sarah E. to William Benson 10-19-1858 (10-26-1858)
Lawhorn, Sarah G. to Thomas J. Gardner 5-4-1847 (5-?-1847)
Lawrence, Margaret to F. W. Ferguson 2-4-1837
Laws, Matilda Jane to Martin V. Dowdy 5-3-1859 (5-4-1859)
Lawson, Clemintine to Benjamin F. Lackey 1-4-1854 (1-5-1854)
Lawson, Nancy T. to Ephraim A. Lackey 5-13-1854 (5-14[18]-1854)
Lax, Ann to Hiram D. Casey 5-21-1847 (5-23-1847)
Lax, Tabitha to David R. Compton 8-8-1853 (8-10-1853)
Lea, Clementina to Charles W. Gazzam 11-29-1827
Lea, Elizabeth to Rufus P. Neely 5-16-1829 (5-19-1829)
Lea, Harriet to Joseph Smith 10-23-1839 (10-24-1839)
Lea, Hester to William M. H. Newton 1-4-1824
Lea, Mary(Polly) to John Needham 1-31-1835 (2-?-1835)
Lea, Rosana to Jesse Blalock 4-13-1833 (4-14-1833)
Lear?, Lucretia to James A. L. Neely 4-1-1833 (4-14-1833)
Leathers, Elizabeth to E. L. Nearin 2-21-1845 (2-23-1845)
Leathers, Mary Ann to W. H. Pace 9-16-1835
Leathers, Sarah Jane to Benjamin W. Pirtle 9-16-1839
Lee, Esther to G. Washington Smith 7-10-1841 (7-11-1841)
Lee, Harriet D. to Arthur McKinnie 3-23-1833 (3-26-1833)
Lee, Pearcy Ann to Augustin P. Ford 8-9-1849
Lee, Susan to Wm. W. Easterwood 12-30-1844 (12-31-1844)
Lee, Wineford to Anthony Smith 5-25-1835
Leea?, Frances to Alfred Boyd 6-5-1833 (6-6-1833)
Leech, Nancy L. to William Edmonson 12-2-1833
Leeton, Elizabeth to David Billingsly 12-31-1856
Leggett, Mary to John Murdaugh 2-12-1840
Leggett, Sarah to Robert Murdaugh 10-6-1840
Leming, A. A. to Ephraim Parks 5-15-1861
Lemings, Martha S to Daniel D. Foster 12-17-1860 (12-27-1860)
Lennard, Lucy to James Beck 9-27-1836
Lester, Rebecca Jane to John Vaughn 7-22-1837 (7-23-1837)
Lethers, Martha to A. P. Vernon 6-29-1844 (7-4-1844)
Lewdermilk, Racheal to William Brown 1-21-1834 (1-23-1834)
Lewis, Ann H. to George W. Blair 7-3-1848 (7-6-1848)
Lewis, Emily to R. G. Burrow 12-23-1844
Lewis, Emma J. M. E. to C. A. Black 7-2-1858
Lewis, M. A. to R. W. Robinson 3-1-1859 (3-13-1859)
Lewis, Martha to John Jacobs 12-9-1829 (12-10-1829)
Lewis, Nancy to Wm. Herrell 8-5-1857 (8-11-1857)
Liggett, Susannah to Peter K. Carley 1-26-1843
Lile, N. E. to William C. Coates 7-13-1846
Lile?, Martha Ann to James C. Mauldin 11-30-1842 (12-1-1842)
Lillard, Lucinda D. to Richard Nuckolls 3-15-1855
Lillard, Sarah to Isaac W. Crawford 8-10-1846 (8-12-1846)
Lineberry, Rebecca to Martin V. Lacefield 4-18-1861
Linsey, Melissa Ann to Joel Lee? 11-15-1837
Linsey, Sarah Alingny? to Andrew Davis 7-23-1836
Litrell, Nancy C. to William L. Hudson 7-11-1853 (7-13-1853)
Little, Emily to Pleasant B. Wells 1-14-1832
Little, Mary Ann to E. G. Duncan 6-14-1855 (6-15-1855)
Little, Sarah A. to James E. Stephens 12-14-1853 (12-15-1853)
Littrell?, Prudence to James Rose 9-27-1848 (9-28-1848)
Littrull?, Thursday Matilda to Benjamin Haney 7-14-1849 (9-7-1849)
Lock, Fatha to Franklin Thrasher 12-1-1825
Lock, Julianna to Green Parrish 11-30-1825
Lokey, Eliza J. to Jas. B. Smith 8-18-1859
Long, Cela to Jacob H. Short 5-8-1849
Long, Maria to Isaac Mills 12-8-1827
Long, Mary to Samuel Park 1-29-1834
Long, Minerva to Asa Estes 11-29-1827
Lonsberry, Rebecca to Joseph Riley 8-24-1839
Lorance, Hannah Jane to William Sadberry 9-26-1843 (10-5-1843)
Lorance, Polly to William Dranna 5-29-1838
Lorant, Nancy N. to Newton A. Ewing 12-15-1829
Lourance, Eliza M. to Zophar Lourance 4-15-1835
Love, Aura? to Joseph Campbell 1-30-1835
Love, Margaret to Wm. Stone 2-14-1834 (2-16-1834)
Love, Mary Jane to Thomas Boyle 10-19-1841 (10-21-1841)
Love, Sarah to John Ritchey 4-23-1836
Lovell, Susan to William E. Whitten 2-23-1850 (2-24-1850)
Low, Charity M. to James R. Pugh 1-20-1840 (1-24-1840)
Low, Martha to James L. Dawson 2-18-1843
Low, S. A. to M. M. Thurmond 10-8-1860 (10-9-1860)
Low, Sarah to Samuel Williams 5-29-1861 (5-30-1861)
Low?, Mary Ann to George Damson? 5-19-1836 (5-22-1836)
Lowdermilk, Peggy to Benjamin Brown 10-6-1829
Lowe, Cynthia A. to R. G. Patterson 4-11-1851 (4-15-1851)
Lowe, Frances M. to Francis M. Carroll 7-25-1838 (7-26-1838)
Lowe, Martha J. to Meridith M. Thurman 5-17-1851 (5-20-1851)
Lowe, Sarah M. to E. N. Hunt 5-22-1857 (6-4-1857)
Lowery, Elizabeth A. to Samuel R. Sipes 12-15-1859 (12-16-1859)
Lowery, Lucy Jane to T. J. Ayers 9-28-1859 (10-2-1859)
Lowrance, Maria Jane to William W. Beard 11-3-1855 (11-4-1855)
Lowry, Mary F. to Alfred Sipes 2-6-1860
Luggett, Amanda S. M. to Thompson C. Coates 12-17-1845
Lunsford, Mary to Elliote H. Nixon 5-1-1837
Lutrell, Elizabeth J. to James McCarter 12-15-1858 (12-26-1858)
Luttrell, Mary Ann to Joseph Barber 7-28-1847 (7-29-1847)
Luttrell, Matilda Ann to Frederick Shepherd 5-18-1844 (5-21-1844)
Lyle, Sarah P. to Andrew J. Clark 4-15-1843
Lynch, Lucretia to Allen Dillard 5-11-1831 (5-15-1831)
Lynch, Sallie to B. N. D. Tannehill 11-4-1857 (11-5-1857)
Lyons, Louisa to Robert Denny 11-24-1836 (11-25-1836)
Lytle, Milly M. to Moses Shannon 11-11-1839 (11-14-1839)
Mace, Amanda Ann to Robert Warren 12-17-1840 (12-22-1840)
Machaum(Michum), Frankey to Henry Dickson 7-4-1827 (7-5-1827)
Macon, Elizabeth to Johnathan Cox 10-31-1850 (11-7-1850)
Macon, Louisa to James Sain 12-19-1843 (12-21-1843)
Macon, Lucy K. to Sherwood Green 6-30-1837 (7-3-1837)
Macon, Mary Jane to Nimrod Graham 8-17-1851
Macon, Mary to Hugh B. McCarty 4-4-1846
Macon, Wincy to James S. Jourdan 1-3-1848 (1-6-1848)
Magby, Elisabeth to Moses N. Jones 3-7-1838 (3-11-1838)
Magee, Martha to William Ford 12-7-1840
Mahern(Mahan), Minerva to J.W. Crow 2-20-1832 (2-21-1832)
Malery, Mary Martha to William R. Groves 7-1-1848 (7-2-1848)
Mallay, D. Jane to John W. Bickers 8-7-1851
Mallery, Mary to William James 5-7-1844 (5-21-1844)
Mallory, Ann Mildred to Ashbey Reavis 12-21-1846 (12-24-1846)
Mallory, Clemant A. to Isham N. Smith 11-23-1846 (11-26-1846)
Malone, Judah to John L. Stafford 4-19-1837 (4-20-1837)
Malone, L. F. J. to F. D. Cassitt 12-10-1844
Mangrum, Joanna to William West 7-17-1850 (7-18-1850)
Mangum, Rebecca to Reuben Higgs 11-6-1844 (11-10-1844)
Manley, Laura to Abner Taylor 3-30-1832 (3-31-1832)
Manson, Mary T. to Geo. M. Lloyd 2-13-1860 (2-15-1860)
Marlar, C. A. to Wm. W. Hooper 2-19-1845
Marler, M. to Isham Ritter 3-3-1845
Marler, Martha to Wm. W. Hooper 8-7-1843
Marler, Milly to Berry Spurlin 7-21-1837
Maroney, Frances D. to Lunsford L. Kimball 12-28-1829 (12-29-1829)
Marsh, Catharine to Wm. B. Ferrell 11-17-1851 (11-19-1851)
Marsh, Fanny to James Willoughby 8-25-1857
Marsh, Hannah to John Mesham(Mesbow?) 12-5-1834
Marsh, Harriet to James Willoughby 12-17-1851 (12-16?-1851)
Marsh, Louisa to William Smith 1-29-1856 (1-31-1856)
Marsh, Margarett F. to John T. Morrow 9-9-1854
Marsh, Maria(Mana) to John J. Neely 7-1-1858
Marsh, Nancy A. to Thomas Evens 9-13-1848 (9-14-1848)
Marsh, Nancy to James Smith 9-9-1851
Martin, Anny to Henry H. Durrum 10-5-1826
Martin, Jane to Hiram Marsh 2-11-1839 (2-14-1839)
Martin, Jane to Saml. M. McKinnie 2-28-1848 (3-2-1848)
Martin, Judith E. A. to John E. Hopkins 6-30-1838
Martin, Louisa to William McGee 6-22-1833 (6-23-1833)
Martin, Maranda to Moses Hunnell 10-8-1838 (10-18-1838)
Martin, Margaret Y. to Wm. H. Herndon 2-20-1841
Martin, Mary Ann to Willis L. Somervell 1-11-1834 (1-16-1834)
Martin, Polly Ann to John Jones 10-26-1826
Martindale, Peggy to Raiford Wright 3-28-1832
Mashburn, Hulda E. to John W. Lee 12-22-1846 (12-23-1846)
Mashburn, Martha to John C. Reynolds 5-29-1847
Mashburn, Mary J. to Wm. Overton 9-30-1856 (10-2-1856)
Mashburn, Mary Jane to William H. Hammons 2-26-1853 (2-27-1853)
Mashburn, Mary to Prior Webb 10-10-1849 (10-11-1849)
Mashburn, Nancy C. to P. H. Thompson 2-3-1858 (2-4-1858)
Mashburn, Rachael to Thomas Sexton 7-4-1855 (7-24-1855)

Mashburn, Sarah A. to Wm. T. Rainy? 9-4-1846
Mashburn, Sarah Ann to Sheppard Shelton 1-23-1849 (1-26-1849)
Mashburn, Susan to William Rogers 1-9-1829
Mashburn, Vasty to Lewis Mashburn 2-6-1839 (2-7-1839)
Mask, Catharine M. to W. F. Hancock 9-10-1855 (9-13-1855)
Mask, Eliza to Nathaniel Cheairs 3-7-1853 (3-10-1853)
Mask, Martha to Thomas Chambers 10-23-1846 (10-28-1846)
Mask, Mary A. to S. O. Myers 8-18-1852
Mask, Mary to Thomas H. Bayliss 4-8-1848 (4-13-1848)
Mask, Sarah to John S.(L?) Roper 8-23-1838
Mask, Sarah to Thomas Hamer 11-10-1856 (11-19-1856)
Mason, Jane R. to H. E. Bickers 7-25-1853
Mathews, Elizabeth L. to Will W. Wallace 1-4-1848 (1-6-1848)
Mathews, M. A. to Chas. Swain 4-25-1851 (4-26-1851)
Mathews, Susan to Jas. M. Swindle 12-17-1857
Mathews, Virginia to Thomas T.? Ramsey 7-29?-1858 (7-30-1858)
Mathis, Elizabeth to Benjamin Bond(Vaughan) 6-26-1834
Mathis, Hannah to William Dunn 10-24-1859
Mathis, Martha L. to Washington B. Carroll 1-1-1828
Matthews, Amanda to John Holland 4-9-1861
Matthews, Isabella to David Hull 12-5-1842 (12-13-1842)
Matthews, Jane to Burril Sauls 8-5-1829 (8-11-1829)
Matthews, Jane to John Nelson 9-7-1840 (9-17-1840)
Matthews, Martha to John Darnell 7-13-1861
Matthews, Mary to Reuben Bass 12-18-1837
Matthews, Surany? to Stephen Jones 11-11-1836 (11-13-1836)
Matthis, Hannah to Sherwood Lowe 1-24-1831
Mauldin, Exes Jane to N. B. Hicks 2-29-1840 (3-12-1840)
Mauldin, Mary W. to William T. Brown 2-24-1851 (2-27-1851)
Maxwell, Cela A. to German W. Davis 4-16-1858 (4-18-1858)
Maxwell, Elizabeth to James Rose 4-30-1832 (5-3-1832)
Maxwell, Nancy J. to Danil W. Lowrance 9-29-1845 (10-11?-1845)
Maxwell, Sally to A. H,. Lorance 7-26-1848 (7-27-1848)
Maxwell, Sarah to Thomas Musgrave 2-13-1828
May, Anide to Joab Harrell(Howell) 1-11-1834 (1-13-1834)
May, Cyntha to William A. Burnes 10-28-1837 (10-31-1837)
May, Elizabeth to Josephus Meeks 8-13-1838 (8-19-1838)
May, Louise to John Crunk 5-24-1826
May, Susannah to David McClendon 8-1-1827 (8-3-1827)
Mayfield, Diannah to Nathan Gee 11-23-1853 (11-24-1853)
Mayfield, Hannah J. to F. M. Welch 5-3-1850 (5-9-1850)
Mayfield, Malinda E. to Stevin Oliver Babb 5-3-1858 (5-4-1858)
Mayfield, Sarah to John Sperling 1-31-1833 (2-5-1833)
McAlexander, Ann C. to Wm. E. Beard 4-20-1846 (4-26-1846)
McAlexander, Eliza G. to John A. Garner 5-4-1850 (5-16-1850)
McAnulty, Mary G. to John H. McClellan 5-29-1838
McAnulty, Nancy B. to Henry B. Misenheimer 3-2-1837 (3-7-1837)
McArver, Celia to Woodson Kinchey? 5-8-1828
McBee, CAtherine to William Taggart 2-26-1827
McBee, Clarissa to Johnson W. Wortham 8-30-1837
McBee, Hannah to William Copeland 1-26-1825 (2-27-1825)
McBee, Masie to W. B.(Green B.) Stokes 3-30-1827 (3-31-1827)
McBride, Elizabeth to Joshua Coleman 11-24-1855 (11-26-1855)
McBride, Elizabeth to Thomas Carnes 6-26-1835 (6-28-1835)
McBride, Elizabeth to William Bottoms 6-26-1848 (7-6-1848)
McBride, Louisa to Hugh Shott 2-1-1843 (2-3-1843)
McBride, Mary kSLusan to John Nelems 6-19-1847 (6-21-1847)
McBride, Mary to Littleberry Spain 7-28-1858
McBride, Polly M. to John L. Wells 1-13-1831
McCan, Elizabeth to Squire Wilson 3-16-1840
McCan, Gaberila A. to Anders Wilson 10-21-1845 (10-30-1845)
McCarley, Melinda to Abijah H. Boothe 2-2-1842 (2-3-1842)
McCarter, Elizabeth J. to Robert L. Thompson 9-21-1835 (10-1-1835)
McCarter, Martha A. to John W. Childress 5-15-1859 (6-16-1859)
McCarver, Lucindia to Isaac Ralph 1-6-1842
McCarver, Miranda to Thomas J. Tull 3-14-1854
McCarver, R. E. to G. W. Hansford 4-10-1856 (4-16-1856)
McCarver, Susan to William West 5-2-1837 (5-7-1837)
McCarver, Tabitha J. to John H. Tull 8-22-1859
McCearly, Sarah to Daniel Osment 12-26-1846 (12-27-1846)
McClanahan, Alsy M. to Stephen Scoggins 6-28-1836 (not executed?) *
McClarty, Sarah A. to J. H. McKinley 12-31-1851 (12-18?-1851)
McClellan, Penelope to Jesse Thomas 5-6-1828
McClellan, Sarah A. to John A. Sheffield 2-3-1857 (2-19-1857)
McClennand, Agness to James M. McCommon 1-2-1846 (1-6-1846)
McCommon, Cynthia A. to T. J. Street 12-15-1860 (1-1-1861)
McCommon, M. J. to J. C. Dixon 1-1-1861
McCommon, Martha C. to Nathan M. Mitchell 9-17-1842 (9-22-1842)
McCommon, Mary Catherine L. to Nazerith Perry 11-10-1853
McCommon, Sarah Ann to George W. Thompson 1-1-1851 (1-2-1851)
McCommon, Tabitha A. to J. F. Caldwell 2-20-1849 (2-22-1849)
McCommons, Talibhta C. to William T. Rainey 10-17-1848 (10-19-1848)
McCommun?, Elizabeth D. to B. B. Beard 12-16-1847 (12-23-1847)
McConell?, Polly to Elijah Coffey 3-22-1847
McCord, Liddy to Miles Wilson 3-23-1839
McCord, Rebecca to Amasa Gillet 1-9-1844 (1-11-1844)
McCoy, Betsey to David McClanahan 7-28-1830 (7-28-1830)
McCoy, Rebecca to John W. C. Mace 7-16-1850 (7-18-1850)
McCoyen?, Jane M. to D. M. C. Miles 9-13-1828
McCrewry, Mary A. to Andrew J. Holliday 12-30-1857
McCrory, Jane Milisse to Rufus P. Crawford 10-2-1848 (10-4-1848)
McCrory, Martha to Robert Galloway 8-7-1839 (8-8-1839)
McCrory, Mary N. to Josh R. Woodson 2-2-1856
McDaniel, Angeline to Geo. W. Moran 3-28-1860 (3-29-1860)
McDaniel, Jane to John Bryant 9-16-1850 (9-17-1850)
McDaniel, Martha to James Scott 2-12-1839
McDaniel, Mary to John Geoghegan 6-30-1856 (7-1-1856)
McDaniel, Nancy E. to John A. Gatlin 5-19-1855 (5-27-1855)
McDanile, Syrena to Leonard W. Hendley 12-10-1839
McDonald, Mary E. to Jesse J. Brewer 7-19-1838 (7-20-1838)
McDonald, Nancy to John F. Gatewood 11-3-1840 (11-15-1840)
McDowell, Eveline L. to George B. Peters 7-29-1841
McDowell, Isabela Jane to Rufus S. Hardy 9-9-1847
McDowell, T. B. to John T. Wood 2-7-1852 (2-8-1852)
McFall(McFarlin), Mary L. to Thomas Walker 11-14-1833 (11-27-1833)
McGee, Elizabeth to John B. Harrison 10-27-1842
McGee, Sarah Ann to James Mitchel 2-8-1831 (2-10-1831)
McGehee, Horpolacy? to Joseph B. Matthews 3-3-1843
McGill, Angeline to John M. Shaw 2-22-1845 (2-25-1845)
McGlaughlin, Elizabeth to Geo. McClendon 12-22-1851 (12-23-1851)
McGowan, Jane L. to William Maris 12-1-1841 (12-2-1841)
McGowan, Mary E. to J. T. Eubanks 12-20-1858 (12-24-1858)
McGuire, Mary E. to James Harlow 9-16-1848 (9-18-1848)
McIlroy, Elizabeth to William Taylor 7-6-1824 (7-8-1824)
McIver, Emily to William Walton 11-23-1836
McIver, Margaret to Josiah Ramage 9-9-1831 (9-15-1831)
McIver, Martha to Lennard Piles 10-6-1827 (10-?-1827)
McKangham, Mary to David Williams 9-27-1828
McKaughan, Frances C. to James Wade 5-13-1846
McKaughan, Nancy M. to John B. Boyte 7-6-1842 (7-7-1842)
McKaughan?, Jane to William H. McBride 8-14-1829
McKaughn, Rebecca to Samuel Simpson 2-1-1833
McKaugn, Amanda A. to Thomas J. Billingsly 2-6-1849 (2-7-1849)
McKay, Elizabeth to George McGuire 1-5-1836
McKay, Margaret to Edwin Gay 4-3-1829
McKearly, Rebecca to David Clinton 6-11-1833 (6-13-1833)
McKee, Frances A. to John Foster 1-6-1851 (1-7-1851)
McKee, Mary Margaret to Martin Bizzle 1-26-1850 (1-27-1850)
McKenzie, Mary to Ezekial Humphries 8-27-1837
McKerly, Mary Ann to T. A. Barnes 3-23-1833
McKinly, Mary A. C. to Josiah C. Bullington 11-8-1850 (11-14-1850)
McKinne, Sarah J. to Hezekiah Cheshire 10-2-1854 (10-3-1854)
McKinne, Zelphi A. E. to John McKee 12-12-1848 (12-16-1848)
McKinnen, Elizabeth to Israel Watkins 6-6-1836
McKinnie, Abacilla to Henry Carraway 3-14-1843
McKinnie, Charlotte to Edmund Reaves 2-17-1838
McKinnie, Elizabeth C. to Thos. W. Hudson 5-7-1846
McKinnie, Elizabeth J. to James M. Mask 12-29-1851 (12-31-1852)
McKinnie, Elizabeth Z. to Thomas Bowden 3-6-1843 (3-8-1843)
McKinnie, Frances Z. to James M. Field 8-11-1855 (8-12-1855)
McKinnie, Julia to Michial McKinnie 11-13-1832 (11-22-1832)
McKinnie, Mary E. to McDaniel Webb 12-3-1849 (12-5-1849)
McKinnie, Nanney to Wash D. Avent 11-17-1855 (11-19-1855)
McKinnie, Sallie E. to T. L. McGee 4-10-1858 (4-22-1858)
McKinnie, Susan N. to Eli Harris 7-22-1848 (7-27-1848)
McKinnie, Susan to Joseph Sellars 3-3-1840 (3-4-1840)
McKinnie, Susannah to William McKinnie 3-15-1826 (3-16-1826)

McKinsey, Mary to Jefferson Jerman 2-3-1826 (2-7-1826)
McKinza, Narcissa to Starling Nuckells 5-1-1832 (5-8?-1832)
McKinza, W. A. T. to Joseph Young 3-21-1846 (3-22-1846)
McKnight, Elizabeth to Peter West 3-2-1827 (3-4-1827)
McLain, Elizabeth to Jordan Oatsfall 2-5-1844
McLarty, Mary Jane to Richard Lake 12-19-1853 (12-22-1853)
McLaughlin, Rachel to Thomas McLaughlin 2-21-1824 (2-24-1824)
McLendon, Margaret to Alfred D. Philips 12-21-1853 (12-22-1853)
McMahan, Martha J. to Green B. Curtis(Carter?) 1-11-1848 (1-12-1848)
McMahon, Mary to Benjamin Wilkes 2-27-1834
McMicken, Delila to James H. Tilley 12-30-1861 (1-1-1862)
McMillan, Mary to William Anderson 1-6-1837 (1-12-1837)
McNeal, Evelina S. to Erasmus Patton McDowell 4-23-1838 (4-24-1838)
McNeal, Jane F. to David F. Brown 10-14-1829 (10-15-1829)
McNeal, Mary Jane to Austin Miller 10-22-1849 (10-23-1849)
McNeely, Nelly to John C. Floyd 12-29-1839 (1-2-1840)
McNeese, Narcissus C. to William McCain 1-31-1853 (2-2-1853)
McVay, Nancy to Patrick Boyte 8-3-1853 (8-4-1853)
McVey, Florida to John Lackey 11-22-1853 (11-23-1853)
McWhirter, Paulina L. to James B. McWhirter 2-15-1832
Mcguire, Mrs. Harriett to John B. Walker 8-14-1858 (8-17-1858)
Meachum, Caroline to George R. Philips 7-19-1850 (7-25-1850)
Medford, Mary Ann to George W. Rogers 2-3-1840 (2-4-1840)
Meek, Martha E. to A. S. Wiley 9-9-1859
Meeks(Merks?), Isabella to James Sanders 2-22-1838
Meeks, Margaret E. to William B. Cavenor 5-25-1853 (5-26-1853)
Meeks, Martha to James S. Gilman 4-10-1857 (4-16-1857)
Meeks, Roena M. to W. H. Jenkins 5-2-1853 (5-10-1853)
Menley, Susan to James Williams 11-23-1833
Mercer, Elizabeth to John C. Robison 1-13-1852
Mercer, Mary M. to John H. McGee 8-18-1856 (8-19-1856)
Merick, Rhoda to Benjamin Brooks 2-3-1835
Meshow?, Selina to Irvin Kennedy 6-26-1834
Miller, Betsy J. to Charles Matthews 7-28-1856
Miller, Catharine to Thomas R. Smith 4-28-1853
Miller, Elizabeth to Hiram Clyne 3-13-1843
Miller, Mary E. to Jasper N. Smith 6-30-1855 (7-1-1855)
Miller, Mary to Leonidas Bills 5-18-1857
Miller, Mary to Nathaniel Stricklin 10-14-1840 (10-15-1840)
Miller, Sophia H. to Wm. W. Wiggins 11-16-1859
Miller, Unicy? to Raiford C. Patterson 10-29-1842 (11-2-1842)
Mills, Abby to John M. Pennington 12-28-1831 (12-29-1831)
Mills, Alice to Sandy Scott 2-5-1835 (2-6-1835)
Mills, Amanda L. to Jesse Crouse 11-5-1847 (11-7-1847)
Mills, Cyntha to James W. Chaddick 3-20-1837 (3-30-1837)
Mills, Frances to Henry M. Savage 1-21-1858 (1-22-1858)
Mills, Harrett to Newton C. Scott 7-7-1841 (7-8-1841)
Mills, Harriett to Joseph Crouse 6-22-1843
Mills, Jane to Hamilton Murley 2-4-1839 (2-7-1839)
Mills, Jane to John Rogers 12-10-1845
Mills, Louisa to Lytle B. Roberts 2-8-1844
Mills, Margarett Eveline to William C. Erven 2-6-1847 (2-7-1847)
Mills, Mary to James Hamilton 7-19-1845 (7-20-1845)
Millsap, Elizabeth to William Brimm 6-8-1836
Minter, Elizabeth E. to Adolphus G. Dennis 4-20-1849
Minter, Hester A. to Wheetly Dennies 6-18-1855 (6-24-1855)
Minter, Lydia Ann to B. A. Bangues 3-8-1844 (3-12-1844)
Minter, Mary A. to Benjamin F. Williams 3-22-1842
Minter, Rebecca W. to Josiah S. White 4-20-1849 (4-24-1849)
Minter, Sarah F. to E. R. Cage 1-20-1847 (1-21-1847)
Minter, Sarah Jane to Timothy T. House 9-12-1853
Minton, Martha J. to Joseph S. Raynard 12-10-1833 (12-17-1833)
Mitchael, Nancy to P. E. Greer 7-3-1854 (7-4-1854)
Mitchell, Ann to Able Stewart 12-26-1853
Mitchell, Betsy to Harris Wiggins 12-31-1827
Mitchell, C. M. to Jessee Jeter 12-2-1849
Mitchell, E. J. to John W. Wilkes 3-13-1858 (3-17-1859?)
Mitchell, Elizabeth Jane to Thomas S. Garrett 12-19-1848 (12-21-1848)
Mitchell, Hannah to Adam Smith 11-24-1834
Mitchell, Harriet to Samuel Simpson 12-11-1838 (12-12-1838)
Mitchell, June to Martin L. Hanis 12-16-1845
Mitchell, Louisa G. to William Kerr 7-8-1837 (7-13-1837)
Mitchell, Mary M. to Calvin Shofer 2-6-1854 (2-10-1854)
Mitchell, Mildred to Permanis Howard 1-1-1851
Mitchell, Nancy to William Murrell 10-19-1829
Moffitt, Dolly H. to Eli Smith 12-12-1831 (12-15-1831)
Moffitt, Mary to William Smith 10-29-1838 (10-30-1838)
Mohundro, Emily P. to Wm. C. May 7-24-1839] (7-28-1839)
Molloy?, Jane to George L. Campbell 7-24-1828 (7-29-1828)
Monom, Genevia to Clayton L. Bolling 7-1-1829 (7-2?-1829)
Montgomery, Cynthia to Joseph A. Stafford 12-24-1834 (12-25-1834)
Montgomery, Elizabeth to Pleasant Robinson 12-21-1835
Montgomery, Ellen R. to Robert L. Lightforte 7-23-1851 (7-24-1851)
Montgomery, Jane to William A. Allen 9-1-1826) (9-7-1826)
Montgomery, Mollie E. to W. J. Redd 1-19-1861 (1-24-1861)
Monton, Jane to Elija Overton 4-4-1846 (4-5-1846)
Moody, Mary Levinia to Leonard H. Millikin 7-5?-1841
Moon(Moor), Elizabeth to Henry Jackson 8-2-1832
Moon(Moore), Frances M. to W. P. Anderson 12-26-1849
Moon(Moore), Mary Ann Eliza to Jas. H. Palmer 11-23-1844 (12-24-1844)
Moon(Moore), Mary to Christopher Bullard 11-6-1844 (11-?-1844)
Moon(Moore), Sarah to John Hardcastle 6-26-1830
Moon(Moore?), Frances to Wm. C. Johnson 6-1-1846 (6-11-1846)
Moon(Moore?), Lucy to Wm. P. McKinnie 10-5-1846 (10-6-1846)
Moon(Moore?), Margaret C. to Robert C. Hardwick 2-28-1850 (2-7?-1850)
Mooney, Mary J. to Thomas W. Tate 12-3-1859
Moore, Adaline to Steven Box 11-25-1854 (11-30-1854)
Moore, Amanda to John S. Belotte 2-11-1853
Moore, Amy to Stephen Sanders 10-25-1853 (10-27-1853)
Moore, Ann L.(T?) to Joel Parker 3-18-1835
Moore, Charity to John H. Johnson 5-16-1860
Moore, Clara Ann to A. J. King 12-9-1854 (12-6?-1854)
Moore, Dacare to Aden Laughhon 6-21-1825
Moore, Frances D. to Robt. W. Benson 5-4-1859 (5-5-1859)
Moore, Harriett A. to David F. Ham 7-11-1840 (7-17-1840)
Moore, Lucina to Hamblin L. Williams 1-12-1832 (1-17-1832)
Moore, Lucinda to Archibald Breeding 11-15-1832
Moore, M. F. to M. H. Lake 12-20-1856 (12-23-1856)
Moore, Maria to William Ham 12-3-1850 (12-4-1850)
Moore, Martha M. to Overton Forbush 10-6-1834 (10-10-1834)
Moore, Mary E. to B. W. Sadler 12-26-1859 (12-29-1859)
Moore, Mary E. to William G. Moore 12-21-1853
Moore, Mary to Milton P. Cross 3-1-1841 (3-3-1841)
Moore, Sarah J. to Elihu Stout 5-11-1855 (5-13?-1855)
Moore, Sarah to Thomas R. Cordle 3-1-1855
Moore, Susan E. to Edward M. Myrick 6-24-1844
Moore, Susan S. to Willie Ham 5-1-1844 (5-2-1844)
Moore, Winneford C. to James W. Harvard(Howard?) 2-3-1842
Morgan, Mary Elizabeth to John B. Hendricks 10-20-1828 (10-25-1828)
Morphis, Amanda M. to James Crocker 6-20-1846 (6-21-1846)
Morphus, Eliza Jane to W. J. Brumley 8-27-1861 (8-29-1861)
Morril, Eliza A. to R. M. Crow 2-10-1862 (2-12-1862)
Morris, Clarisa to James Lea 9-8-1828 (9-9-1828)
Morris, Eliza to John S. Brotherton 6-13-1843 (6-15-1843)
Morris, Frances to Andrew J. Mills 8-27-1850 (8-29-1850)
Morris, Jane to Mayfield Bell 11-28-1855 (12-3-1855)
Morris, Levina to Charley Coor 6-20-1843 (6-22-1843)
Morris, Melinda to Charles Freeman 8-28-1843 (8-29-1843)
Morris, Minnie to E. Jouvenat 1-15-1862
Morris, Octavia to Isaac Shinault 12-18-1860 (12-19-1860)
Morrison, Ann M. to John Bartlett 8-19-1833 (8-20-1833)
Morrow, Ann to Thomas Polk(Pack) 12-18-1833
Morrow, Mary E. to John C. Barnett(Bennett) 2-21-1832 (2-23-1832)
Moss, Martha Ann to Patrick H. Birdsong 12-20-1852 (12-21-1852)
Moss, Mary J. to P. O. Hamer 1-18-1854
Moss, Melvina to Henry H. Hardy 10-21-1846
Moss, Nancy to Matthew Wilhite 9-5-1833
Mulby, Ann to Edward Bruhl 10-29-1859 (11-1-1859)
Muldan, Rody E. to Andrew Gossett 12-26-1831
Mullens, Frances E. to George C. Millsted 5-3-1849
Mullikin, Emeline to John J. Fleet 1-9-1847
Mullikin, Susan to William Maddox 12-11-1849
Mullins, Elizabeth to James L. Russell 8-10-1829 (8-11-1829)
Mullins, Martha Ann to James C. Wise 7-4-1846

Mullins, Sarah to Willis Horn 7-7-1856 (7-13-1856)
Mullins, Susan to Abner Null 12-21-1846 (12-24-1846)
Murdaugh, Elizabeth to Robert Cozby 8-5-1835
Murdaugh, Martha J. to William L. Knott 1-19-1858
Murdaugh, Mary to James A. Barham 11-2-1853 (11-3-1853)
Murdough, Rachael to Sydney S. Knott 1-10-1861
Murley, Mary to Jeremiah Hooper 12-18-1846 (12-20-1846)
Murphy, Elizabeth C. to Oney S. Harvey 12-29-1847 (12-30-1847)
Murphy, Elizabeth W. to J. F. Hull 3-2-1843
Murphy, Elizabeth to H. C. Griggs 9-9-1854 (9-13-1854)
Murphy, Jane to James S. Marsh 1-12-1846 (1-25-1846)
Murphy, Margaret to Bryant Cannon 10-10-1843 (10-12-1843)
Murphy, Margret to James M. Harvey 4-14-1845
Murphy, Martha M. to Vachel W. Pullum 11-11-1848 (11-16-1848)
Murphy, Mary to John Roark 2-14-1843 (2-15-1843)
Murphy, Mary to Robert Ford 10-8-1836
Murphy, Nancy to Isaac P. Richie 7-29-1834 (7-30-1834)
Murphy, Nancy to James A. Edwards 5-30-1848 (6-1-1848)
Murphy, Polly Ann to Stephen S. Gayler 12-14-1839 (12-19-1839)
Murphy, Rachael to David W. Babb 1-27-1852 (1-29-1852)
Murphy, Rachel to Edward L. Peters 6-30-1840 (7-2-1840)
Murphy, Rhody to James McWilliams 5-25-1847 (5-27-1840
Murphy, Sarah to Jeremiah Lee 2-2-1841 (2-4-1841)
Murphy, Sarah to John C. Warren 9-10-1828 (9-11-1828)
Murray, Elizabeth to Wm. A. Kerr 3-1-1861
Murray, P. C. to Wm. F. Black 1-26-1858
Murray, Polly to J. D. Lane 8-6-1857 (8-20-1857)
Murray?, Aussale? N.? to Charles Boatman 2-16-1834
Murrell, Elizabeth to E. P. Skinner 11-18-1857 (11-19-1857)
Murrell, Mary Jane to Jesse C. Tucker 3-14-1850
Murrell, Sarah A. to William T. Fausett 12-24-1850
Murry, Adalin to James Coffey(Coffer?) 3-2-1840
Muse, Catharine to Obediah Cain 1-25-1847
Muse, Mary Jane D. to Jacob Hainline 12-26-1839 (1-16-1840)
Musgrave, Mehala to Joel Grantham 1-1-1829
Myers, Mary to John Cherry 4-1-1832 (4-5-1832)
Myrick, Jane to Hugh Harkins 2-3-1847
Myrick, Jane to R. L. Daniel 6-30-1860 (7-3-1860)
Myrick, Sarah J. to John C. Boyd 11-30-1859
Nabers, Malinda to Jerimiah Highfield 11-10-1851 (11-11-1851)
Nabers, Margaret to Efel D. Fortner 6-23-1838 (7-1-1838)
Nabers, Nancy to James Ward 6-12-1830 (6-13-1830)
Nabers, Sarah to Isaac J. Norton 7-11-1837
Nabors, L.? A. to Joseph E. Lake 12-29-1845
Nabors, Martha A. to Calloway Caine 4-13-1841
Nail, Mary Ann to J. A. Hamilton 9-16-1837 (9-19-1837)
Nail, Rebecca to John Pruett 2-7-1831 (2-9-1831)
Nailor, Margaret E. to William Rush 12-2-1850 (12-12-1850)
Nailor, Rhoda Jane to Eliazer Burkhead 1-1-1856 (1-3-1856)
Napier, Laura V. to John W. Gould 10-17-1853
Napier, Martha C. to Wilson N. Peacock 2-17-1846 (2-18-1846)
Napier, Mary W. to John D. Perryman 6-3-1843 (6-4-1843)
Nappier, Ellen D. to Christopher G. Joy 12-22-1842
Nappier, Louisa E. to John R. Craddock 6-5-1845
Naylor, Bethinia B. to Joberry King 10-26-1852 (10-27-1852)
Neal, E. O. to A. P. Gillam 1-19-1858
Nealy, Eleanor E. to Nathan Johnson 5-23-1861 (6-2-1861)
Neece, Edmonia T. to W. McReaves(Reaves?) 4-7-1859 (4-9-1859)
Neece, Malinda to James P. Means 8-7-1848 (8-8-1848)
Needham, Patsy to William Needham 4-17-1832 (4-19-1832)
Needham, Rebecca to Saml. Couch 2-10-1842
Needham, Susan to William R. Alexander 4-30-1830
Neelly, Eighty Eveline to A. M. Callahan 3-1-1826 (3-7-1826)
Neelly, Louisa to Carter C. Collier 3-4-1824
Neely, Adelia to James G. Bell 4-26-1831
Neely, Harriet to John A. Jarratt 5-7-1857
Neely, Louisa to A. A. Coleman 7-6-1859
Neely, Margaret S. to Nathan Johnson 11-30-1854
Neely, Margaret to Elihu C. Allison 9-11-1829 (9-17-1829)
Neely, Mary Bell to James H. Unthank 7-24-1855
Neely, Mary C. to William W. Atwood 6-9-1829 (6-10-1829)
Neely, Nancy G. to Russell J. Crawford 11-5-1827
Neely, Nancy to James Pool 1-1-1830
Neely?, Sarah A. J. to Wm. C. Belieu 4-15-1846 (4-16-1846)
Neighbors, A. A. to W. F. Stewart 2-9-1856
Neill, Elizabeth to George M. Brogden 10-18-1850 (10-20-1850)
Nelson, Justianna to R. H. Mitchell 9-22-1861
Nelson, S. J. to W. S. Hall 12-19-1861
Nelson, Sarah L. to Jacob Allbright 10-1-1827
Nelson, Sarah W. to Jacob H. Butler 12-23-1858
Nesbit, Selina? to Jehu? Murphy 12-10-1829
New, Harriet to James Bates 3-7-1836
New, Sally Ann to Lindsey Lea 3-12-1828
New?, Mary Ann to Stephen Hightower 12-19-1836
Newland, Eliza W. to Wm. C. Adams 5-4-1846 (5-5-1846)
Newland, M. J. to H. B. Birdsong 12-27-1845 (12-31-1845)
Newman, Amanda to David W. Eaton 10-9-1855
Newman, Gila Ann to William Pipkin 1-17-1855 (1-21-1855)
Newman, Nancy J. to James Benson 10-2-1858 (10-7-1858)
Newsom, Elizabeth A. to Thomas B. Ramsey 10-10-1854
Newton, Henrietta to Needham Pipkins 12-8-1834
Newton, Susannah to Benjamin Hamblin 12-18-1831 (12-23-1831)
Nicholls, Elizabeth to Thomas Richardson 10-30-1841 (10-31-1841)
Nichols, Elizabeth to Jonathan Burleson 2-4-1833 (2-7-1833)
Nichols, Lucinda to Thomas D. Cody 8-3-1831
Nichols, Nancy to Samuel Pettigrew 7-17-1826 (7-18-1826)
Nicholson, Mary to Nathaniel Nicholson 9-8-1827 (9-12-1827)
Nixon, Altetha E. to Robert Morriss 6-21-1841 (6-29-1841)
Nixon, America to A. D. Lunsford 5-23-1839
Nixon, Cornelia to JSames F. Ellis 5-12-1827
Nixon, Margaret to Joel Foster 9-22-1829
Nixon, Mary C. to Thomas Lunsford 10-19-1847 (12-24-1847)
Noland, Pernecy to Zeddack Mulikin 2-23-1839 (2-28?-1839)
Norman, Delila to George Vaughan 1-15-1842 (1-16-1842)
Norman, Sarah B. to Robert L. Wood 3-2-1835
Norment, Elizabeth to R. A. Marsh 2-5-1844 (2-6-1844)
Norment, Mary A. to Robert Elgin 3-19-1827 (3-21-1827)
Norris, Clarissa to John M. Thompson 12-23-1847 (12-26-1847)
Norris, Ellen to Isaac Smith 12-5-1835
Norris, Emily to Robert Thompson 6-17-1835 (6-26-1835)
Norris, Hannah to Elijah Bailey 1-12-1837
Norris, Margaret to James Kinnard 11-10-1841
Norris, Matilda to Martin Shell 2-24-1834
Norris, Sarah Jane to Hinton J. Pipkin 5-23-1840 (5-28-1840)
Norris, Sarah to Levi Smith 1-22-1839 (1-25-1839)
North, Mary W. to James Bates 5-8-1848 (5-9-1848)
Northcross, Rachel to John Henry Taylor 12-27-1851 (1-1-1852)
Norton, Ann J. to Lemuel M. Crisp 1-1-1857
Norton, Jane to John Causeby 3-3-1825
Norton, M. A. to W. H. Hewett 5-17-1858 (5-20-1858)
Norton, Martha A. to J. A. Jones 8-24-1858
Norton, Polly Ann to Solomon Doile 12-27-1847 (12-28-1847)
Norton, Rachel to Benjamin M. Hillhouse 12-20-1833
Norwood, Lucinda to Robert Read 5-29-1827
Nuckolls, Emily to John Bradford 7-19-1849
Nuckolls, Jane to James Mullhall 12-28-1843
Nuckolls, Lucretia to N. B. Dorris 12-28-1857
Nuckolls, Narcissa C. to James M. Bradford 2-25-1860 (2-26-1860)
Nuckolls, Olvizara? to Strong Crowley 6-24-1839
Null, Jane to Elijah G. Duncan 1-5-1829
Nunnally, Mary to John Adams 12-24-1833
Nunnelly, Harriett to John L. Casey 11-23-1836 (11-24-1836)
Nunnelly, Jane to John C. Armstrong 10-18-1837 (?-19-?)
Nutall, Celestia A. to J.E. Spencer 9-21-1859
Nutt?, Mary Ann to Mathew Joyner 7-3-1837 (7-4-1837)
O'Brien, Leonora S. to D. B. Gally 6-11-1861
O'Brien, Susan L. to J. S. Moore 10-25-1859
Oakes, Minerva to Robert S. Lyons 1-17-1842
Oates, Elisa to W. G. Bradford 8-6-1848
Odum, Arrena to John Henson 10-21-1848 (10-22-1848)
Ogin(Agin), Susan to John Lewis 8-25-1856
Ornsby, Elisza to David Bell 8-21-1826 (8-23-1826)
Orr, Mary W. to John H. Moore 11-30-1840 (12-1-1840)
Orrell?, Martha C. to Green B. Johnson 8-26-1857
Osment, Rachael to Jesse King 9-28-1859
Oswald, Catharine to John H. Robley 12-16-1858
Overall, Elizabeth to Gary Gay 5-9-1831 (5-10-1831)
Overton, Abigale to J. F. Roach 10-23-1854 (10-26-1854)
Overton, Agness to Jacob T. Pirtle 10-4-1852 (10-9-1852)
Overton, Amanda to Abram Lewis 12-17-1849 (1-20-1849)

Overton, Amelia to William C. Smith 7-17-1851
Overton, Arkansas to Philip P. Phelps 9-23-1848 (9-28-1848)
Overton, Sarah Ellen to Daniel R. Chambliss 10-8-1849 (10-9-1849)
Owen, Elizabeth to Eli Harris 12-13-1832
Owen, Elizabeth to Jefferson Warren 12-21-1831 (1-5-1832)
Owen, J. F. to James P. Bagby 12-8-1855 (12-12-1855)
Owen, Jane to Walker B. Wilson 6-8-1838 (6-11-1838)
Owen, Margaret to Thomas Boyle 11-23-1847 (11-25-1847)
Owen, Mary to Jno. C. F. Hill 12-8-1837
Owens, Mary to Jacob Lowery 4-26-1830 (4-27-1830)
Ozburn?, Violett O. to John Cozby 11-30-1846 (12-1-1846)
Ozment, Elizabeth S. to Alexander McCarley 12-28-1848
Ozment, Sarah to James P. Hollaway 4-20-1854 (4-24-1854)
PSankey, Emily S. to John Warren 1-29-1855 (1-30-1855)
Pace, Elizabeth to Jefferson R. Bickers 12-22-1853
Pace, Martha to James L. Glenn 6-18-1861 (6-23-1861)
Pace, Nancy Jane to James W. Harrell 8-20-1855 (8-21-1855)
Pain, Marinda to John Kelly 2-22-1834
Palmer?, Mary Ann to West Harriss 11-25-1846 (11-26-1846)
Pankey, Caroline to Jesse A. Thrasher 8-12-1858
Pankey, Caroline to W. G. Brown 12-11-1850
Pankey, Eliza C. to Elija Graham 2-27-1850 (2-28-1850)
Pankey, Eliza to James Little 8-11-1852 (8-12-1852)
Pankey, Jane to Jehu H. Armstrong 1-13-1844 (1-17-1844)
Pankey, M. J. to F. Lambeth 8-16-1856 (8-17-1856)
Pankey, Margaret to J. N. B. Hobson 2-13-1860
Pankey, Martha to Ruffin Brown 7-22-1851 (7-24-1851)
Pankey, Mary M. to John Cox 8-11-1852 (8-12-1852)
Pankey, Nancy to James Yarbrough 3-10-1852 (3-11-1852)
Pankey, Rebecca Ann to Washington D. Cheshier 8-31-1846 (9-1-1846)
Pankey, Rebecca to James E. Smith 11-6-1848 (11-8-1848)
Panky, May Ann Elizabeth to Enoch Sain 3-10-1847 (3-12-1847)
Pannell, Eliza to Geo. Steele 5-16-1860
Park, Jane to Alexander L. Hughes 4-2-1851 (4-3-1851)
Park, Jane to Henry T. Chisum 10-26-1829
Park, Martha to J. May 12-26-1860 (12-27-1860)
Park, Sarah M. to James H. Jewell 1-5-1850 (1-6-1850)
Parker, Catharine W. to Wm. C. Ervin 5-19-1841
Parker, Elizabeth I. to Lafayette Weaver 9-11-1852
Parker, Frances to Wm. James Brown 11-13-1860 (11-15-1860)
Parker, Joanna to Joseph B. Terry 11-26-1856
Parker, Lettrice to Edward L. Peters 1-27-1827 (2-1-1827)
Parker, Mary Ann to Allen Cox 10-15-1858 (10-3?-1858)
Parker, Mary to Philip N. Smith 4-28-1842
Parker, Mary to Thomas G. Graham 2-8-1838
Parker, Massa to George W. Taylor 9-10-1828 (9-12-1828)
Parker, Nancy to Jacob Finley 11-14-1826
Parker, Obedience to Richard Finley 11-24-1836
Parker, Olivia C. to James Fish
Parker, Rebeccah to Amos C. Reynolds 1-16-1838
Parker, Rosusey Fine to Matthew Crowly 12-16-1843 (12-17-1843)
Parker, Sarah Jane to Aquilla Mullican 5-17-1853
Parker, Sarah to Gillum Harris 9-2-1834
Parker, Willie Ann to W. F. Ross 1-21-1861 (1-23-1861)
Parkes, Jane to Eli Cox 10-1-1832 (10-?-1832)
Parks, Eliza to Amos Foster 9-30-1826 (10-3?-1826)
Parks, Jane to William P. Johnson 11-24-1857 (11-26-1857)
Parks, Mary Ann to John F. Moore 9-13-1855 (9-15-1855)
Parks, Mary C. to P. D. Job 3-12-1858 (3-16-1858)
Parmer, Christian to W. H. Monroe 2-28-1850
Parmer, Margaret to Cullen Benson 2-7-1839
Parr, Rebecca to Hamilton Savage 2-17-1857 (2-18-1857)
Parris, Alpha Jane to Andrew Thomas King 3-7-1852 (3-9-1852)
Parris, Susan V. to William Gibson 2-28-1861 (3-7-1861)
Parrish, Parthena to William Cates 11-18-1839
Partridge, Jane to Ickabad Flowers 12-21-1833
Partridge, Nancy(Ann) to Bailey Mayfield 8-1-1833 (8-7-1833)
Pascal, Racheal to NiNicholass Fortune 4-30-1834
Pate, Edny to Cullin Benson 7-1-1835
Pate, Elizabeth to James R. Benson 11-30-1836
Pate, Sythia to John E. M. Mayfield 11-10-1836
Paterson, Juliann to Mathew G. Bagg 10-7-1854 (10-9-1854)
Patrick, Olive P. to William Ramsey 1-16-1830 (1-17-1830)
Patridge, Martha to Calvin Jackson 3-23-1852
Patridge, Susan to Joseph Hendly 2-24-1839
Patterson, Cathanne to John Hooper 2-10-1858
Patterson, Celia A. to William H. Highfill 9-11-1852 (9-19-1852)
Patterson, Charlotte to John sr. Henson 3-28-1859 (3-29-1859)
Patterson, Malvina E. to F. M. Hooper 1-21-1861 (1-22-1861)
Patton, Mary Jane to Jerimiah W. Robertson 2-11-1854 (2-19-1854)
Payne, Nancy C. to Wm. E. M. Graham 8-16-1843
Pearson, Nancy to Wm. Thomas 12-20-1831 (12-22-1831)
Peck, Elizabeth to Thomas Raines 10-29-1851 (10-30-1851)
Peeler, Joycy to Joseph Webb 9-20-1854
Pegran, Martha T. to Munford Wilson 6-8-1835
Pendleton, Abbey to Lycurgus Scott 1-29-1838 (1-30-1838)
Perkins, Mary T. to James Fentress 8-24-1859
Perkins, Nikolas Ann to George A. Brinkley 3-26-1844
Perry, Catharine T. to John W. Lee 3-5-1855 (3-7-1855)
Perry, E. W. to Chamberlin H. Anderson 2-7-1845 (2-9-1845)
Perry, Eliza Jane to Reubin S. Scott 5-20-1850 (5-23-1850)
Perry, Elizabeth to Richard B. B. Randolph 1-4-1842
Perry, Elizabeth to Richard B. B. Randolph 5-6-1844 (5-30-1844)
Perry, Jackey Ann to Elias Moore 2-4-1850 (2-5-1850)
Perry, Kezirah to Elijah W. Graves 7-7-1845
Perry, Prudence N. to William S. Perry 1-19-1848 (1-20-1848)
Peters, Ann Maria to Alfred N. Clayton 9-10-1846 (10-16-1846)
Petigrue, Virginia W. to Jonathan B. Griffin 12-30-1852
Pew, Catherine Manerva to John Pew 11-21-1850
Phelps, Arkansas to P. M. Rainer 8-7-1858 (8-8-1858)
Philips, Jane to James Jarnigan 10-21-1851
Philips, Margaret to John M. Johnson 8-27-1849 (8-29-1849)
Philips, Sarah Ann to A. F. Mitchell 12-18-1844 (12-19-1844)
Phillips, Hannah M. to Wm. H. Gaddy 1-29-1861
Phillips, Julia A. F. to W. B. Savage 9-22-1860 (9-23-1860)
Phillips, Mary E. to Geo. M. Carricker 9-16-1857
Phillips, Phetama to James P. Gray 1-31-1843 (2-7-1843)
Phillips, Polly to John Henson 12-19-1856
Phillips, Sarah to H. L. Bray 10-13-1859
Philpot, Mary to James Thompson 6-1-1833 (6-4-1833)
Philpott, Emily to James A. Heaslet 5-3-1827
Philpott, Mary to John Blackwell 11-2-1829
Pickens, Leeann E. to James B. Key 5-14-1856
Pickens, Martha to Abraham Lawrence 2-17-1837
Pickett, M. A. to James Lockhart 2-7-1859 (6-20-1859)
Pickins, Mary to William McClain 12-4-1839 (12-5-1839)
Piles, Hester to Samuel Deason 11-1-1834
Piles, Maria Jane to Stephen L. Pipkins 2-20-1861
Piles, Sally to Jesse Pipkin 1-4-1828 (1-6-1828)
Piles, Sarah to Augustus Thebold 11-14-1860 (11-15-1860)
Pingleton, Elizabeth to Neil Smith 5-20-1861 (5-26-1861)
Pipkin, Ann Eliza to Robert Brown 11-23-1857
Pipkin, Mary A. H. to Allen M. Thompson 9-17-1855 (9-18-1855)
Pipkin, Minerva M. to James M. Piles 4-3-1861 (4-4-1861)
Pipkins, Kissiah H. to John H. Brown 12-28-1853 (12-29-1853)
Pipkins, Talitha to Wm. Henson 6-2-1856
Pirtle, Elizabeth to Richard Lamb 1-7-1828 (1-8-1828)
Pirtle, Malinda to Joseph D. Hackney 11-15-1852
Pirtle, Martha to Wiley A. Carrington 4-30-1859 (5-2-1859)
Pirtle, Mary Ann to Isaac B. Hubbard 1-3-1849
Pirtle, Mary Ann to Thomas L. Carter 9-10-1859
Pirtle, Mary Ann to William Black 2-6-1854 (2-12-1854)
Pirtle, Mary to Thomas Smith 8-6-1827 (8-7-1827)
Pirtle, Nancy to Danl. W. Brown 7-30-1859
Pirtle, Rebecca to Benjamin A. Harriss 12-27-1837 (12-28-1837)
Pitman, Mary Ann to Samuel Park 1-29-1848 (1-31-1848)
Plant, Sarah to Moses McCarty 8-31-1831
Pled;ge, Sarah E. to D. R. Carter 11-26-1855 (11-27-1855)
Pledge, Mary E. to Jas. M. Peers 3-28-1855 (4-2-1855)
Pledge, Melora S. to Robert A. Burrow 7-25-1852 (9-8-1852)
Poiner, Cordelia L. to Green? L. Irwin 12-18-1844
Poiner, Mary S. to Henry Holly 9-10-1838 (9-11-1838)
Polk, Ann to John C. McNeill 5-10-1859 (6-15-1859)
Polk, Benigna to William H. Woods 7-12-1834
Polk, Clarissa to Andrew Taylor 6-7-1824 (6-11-1824)
Polk, Eliza to William jr. Nuckolls 9-5-1850
Polk, Elizabeth to Alfred Neal 9-16-1829 (10-3-1829)
Polk, Eugenia to Alexander G. Neilson 7-18-1827
Polk, Lucy N. to William N. Lennard 4-18-1827

Polk, Mary to Jacob Garrett 9-12-1829 (10-3-1829)
Polk, Mary to Nathaniel Rodgers 2-23-1843
Polk, Mary to Wardlaw Howard 12-29-1834
Pool, Elizabeth to Isaac Glass 9-11-1848 (9-14-1848)
Pool, Sarah to Washington Read 11-28-1828 (11-30-1828)
Pool, Tebitha D. to John Vantresse 12-25-1840
Poole, Elizabeth to Samuel Washington 3-22-1830
Pope, K. C. to Benj. F. Tucker 10-13-1857 (9?-18-1857)
Porch, Mary A. to L. L. Wright 5-18-1859 (5-22-1859)
Porter, Eliza to Cullen Strickland 6-6-1849 (6-7-1849)
Porter, Elizabeth to Lemuel Powell 3-25-1851 (3-27-1851)
Portice, Mary F. to James E. Akin 12-25-1847 (12-30-1847)
Portis, Equilla to Eli Chapman 3-1-1850 (3-3-1850)
Poston, Mary P. to James A. Paine 7-11-1856
Poston, Sophronia E. to J. C. Folts 12-23-1844
Potts, Susan to James Peek 5-1-1835
Powell, Alice to Wm. H. Ammons(Powell?) 7-28-1847 (7-29-1847)
Powell, Amanda to John R. Crawford 1-12-1850 (1-24-1850)
Powell, Leusi to James H. Brint 3-16-1850 (3-19-1850)
Powell, Maria J. to Eleazar Gaugh 8-2-1856 (8-3-1856)
Powell, Mary Ann E. to D. F. Gadd 12-9-1857
Poyner, Elizabeth to David B. Pipkins 4-15-1848 (4-16-1848)
Poyner, Frances to Johns Brantly 6-20-1840 (6-27-1840)
Poyner, Jula Ann to Buckhanan James 12-20-1845 (12-23-1845)
Preston, Amanda to Henry Hurst 1-11-1850
Prewett, A. M. to J. L. Jenkins 12-24-1860
Prewett, Mary E. to John K. Gordon 1-1-1861
Prewett, Mary F. to J.C. Stinson 9-26-1860 (10-24-1860)
Prewett, Sabella to B. A. Clifft 2-19-1859 (2-22-1859)
Prewett, Susan to James M. Fleet 6-14-1843
Prewitt, E. J. to H. H. Hursh 1-23-1862 (1-28-1862)
Prewitt, Eliza Jane to Thomas Williamson 11-16-1850 (11-28-1850)
Prewitt, Elizabeth to Hardeman Bishop 11-20-1855 (11-22-1855)
Prewitt, Elizabeth to John P. Taggart 4-3-1848 (4-4-1848)
Prewitt, Mariah W. to Milton W. Prewitt 8-9-1847 (8-12-1847)
Prewitt, Nancy E. to William R. Tagart 7-10-1852 (7-13-1852)
Prewitt, Sarah A. to L. Tanner 4-9-1856 (4-23-1856)
Prewitt, Sarah to J. H. Johnson 1-4-1849
Price, Darthula V. to Geo. N. Morrow 3-23-1856 (4-1-1856)
Price, Elizabeth A. to Edmund F. Duke 5-18-1849 (5-20-1849)
Price, Elizabeth to A. G. Hornesby 2-29-1860 (3-1-1860)
Price, Elizabeth to Henry Brewer 10-31-1839 (11-1-1839)
Price, Louisa to J. C. Bostian 10-5-1859 (10-6-1859)
Price, Lucille W. to Orris Harris 8-30-1858
Price, Malissa to Thomas W.(M?) Wallace 2-24-1840 (2-25-1840)
Price, Mary S. to John Hudson 9-4-1845
Price, Susannah to Jackson Brazeal 4-10-1836 (4-12-1836)
Priest, Susan to John B. Pirtle 5-6-1850 (5-8-1850)
Priest?, E. A. to James Pirtle 5-5-1847
Pryor, Martha E. to James H. Alexander 9-14-1837
Puckett, F. G. to H. B. Toombes 2-21-1857 (3-1-1857)
Puckett, Mary M. to John J. Shinault 9-19-1861 (9-21-1861)
Pugh, Amanda E. to W. T. McLeary 9-14-1854 (10-3-1854)
Pugh, Martha to Edward Dixon 7-21-1841 (7-22-1841)
Pugh, Neety Jane to John A. Pipkin 1-16-1848
Pugh, Racheal to Worley Linvell 3-23-1829
Pugh, Sarah to Edward Dickson 11-30-1842 (12-1-1842)
Pulla(Pully), Martha to Samuel W. Ridge 7-17-1829
Pullam, Alsa to Persan Ussery 2-7-1840
Pullam, Ann to Leonard Malone 8-18-1849 (9-1-1849)
Pulliam, Jane to Geo. W. Beasley 9-29-1859
Pulliam, Rosanna to John T. Middleton 6-14-1858
Pullum, Caroline to John W. Shinault 1-13-1840 (1-14-1840)
Pully, Betsy to Samuel Shipman 11-21-1828 (11-23-1828)
Pully, Susanah to Benjamin Newhouse 8-10-1829 (8-13-1829)
Punch, Elizabeth J. to A. D. S. Foster 4-26-1856 (4-27-1856)
Punch, Elizabeth to W. W. Taylor 4-6-1848
Purnell, A. E. to W. H. Loud(Land) 12-14-1858 (12-16-1858)
Purtle(Pirtle?), Louisa Jane to John G. Chisum 6-3-1839 (6-6-1839)
Ragan, Jemima to Lott Breeding 11-21-1833
Ragan, Leah? to Enoch King 3-14-1837 (3-15-1837)
Ragan, Lucindia to Isaac Shinault 12-16-1833 (12-17-1833)
Ragan, Martha to Samuel Webster 2-6-1827
Ragan, Mary C. to James R. Bland 10-26-1860 (10-27-1860)
Rainer, Catharine to Edward Coodey 5-28-1829
Rainer, Louisa W. to Geo. E. McDaniel 4-24-1861 (4-25-1861)
Rainer, Mary Matilda to Albert G. Parrott 10-4-1849 (10-18-1849)
Rainer, Susan Ann to Henry Wellions 3-13-1843 (3-13?-1843)
Rainey, Eliza Ann to Josiah H. D. Thompson 10-8-1855 (10-16-1855)
Rainey, Nancy to Daniel Guthrie 1-17-1848 (1-18-1848)
Rainey, Rebecca to Levin Savage 8-4-1829
Rainey, Susan W. to Saml. Irvin 10-2-1837 (10-12-1837)
Rainy, Sarah C. to H. G. Adams 3-1-1858
Ramage, Margaret to James Y. Rook 2-27-1828
Ramsey, Elizabeth E. to Rosell Needham 10-26-1836
Ramsey, Mahuldy to William T. Land 7-25-1827 (7-26-1827)
Ramsey, Margaret to James W. Fields 6-18-1838
Ramsey, Sarah to Philip I.? Kearney 1-6-1829
Ramsy, Catharine L. to D. J. Newbern 11-18-1850 (11-19-1850)
Ramsy, Hanah to John Murchison 8-3-1829 (8-9-1829)
Randolph, Elizabeth to Theopulus Shaw 6-5-1850 (6-6-1850)
Rankin, Eliza H. to Calvin Williams 2-13-1835
Rankin, Elizabeth to Garner D. Campbell 11-11-1850 (11-14-1850)
Rankin, Emily F. to Hendley Stone 9-7-1843 (9-14-1843)
Rankin, Mary Ann C. to Thurene E. Reynolds 12-14-1840
Rankin, Mary to John M. Park 12-16-1848 (12-21-1848)
Rankin, Nancy (Jane) to Sample A. Fortner 1-9-1858 (2-11-1858)
Ratliff, Jnnu? to John P. Johnson 5-7-1845 (5-14-1845)
Rawlings, Emily to William Todd 11-27-1832
Ray, Anne to John G. Parker 7-25-1850
Ray, Elizabeth to John Stricklin 1-27-1857
Ray, Elizabeth to Saml. S. Caldwell 1-1-1856 (1-3-1856)
Ray, Ellen E. to Pitser M. Crawford 2-6-1860 (2-9-1860)
Ray, Fannie W. to Thomas L. Harris 10-19-1859 (10-26-1859)
Ray, Martha to John T. Parker 10-29-1856 (10-30-1856)
Ray, Mary A. to W. W. B. Hicks 12-30-1857
Ray, Mary to Jasper Hizer 2-23-1857 (2-26-1857)
Ray, Ruth to Joseph L. Rosson 2-24-1851
Rayner, Mary to John Williams 9-8-1827 (9-13-1827)
Raynor, Kesiah to Benedict Yeary 11-1-1827 (11-2-1827)
Read, Nancy to Berry Johnson 6-10-1834 (6-12-1834)
Read, Rhoda to Hiram Seaton 12-10-1840
Reagan, Ciely to Moses Foren 4-27-1824 (4-29-1824)
Reagan, Cynthia to William Baker 5-8-1828 (5-11-1828)
Reagan, Elizabeth to Mathew L. Punch 10-11-1838 (10-12-1838)
Reagan, Jane to Edwin Crawford 2-24-1824 (2-26-1824)
Reagan, Martha B. to John Price 8-1-1853 (8-15-1853)
Reagan, Martha J to lHiram G. Hinson 9-28-1846 (9-30-1846)
Reagan, Mary to Richard Hatley 1-5-1825 (1-9-1825)
Reagan, Nancy C. to John D. Smith 12-1-1854 (12-3-1854)
Reagan, Sarah J. to James B. Young 11-4-1858
Reasens?, C. A. to E. L. Johnson 7-15-1846
Reason, Mary to John Powell 7-19-1847 (7-27-1847)
Reaves, Eliza C. to Anderson Faris 7-29-1840 (7-30?-1840)
Reaves, Elizabeth C. to John McKinnie 3-8-1841 (3-11-1841)
Reaves, Sophronia A. to B. B. Rutherford 9-3-1861
Redd, Mary Jane to William W. Farley 4-17-1851 (4-20-1851)
Reece, Mary E. to Wm. P. Stricklin 12-6-1851 (12-11-1851)
Reecks?, P. to F. Elks 3-22-1860
Reed, Hannah Adeline to Stephen H. Russell(Russell) 9-8-1827
Reed, Lucindia to Thos. Williams 10-12-1830
Reed, Margaret to Matthew Black 1-30-1828 (2-3-1828)
Reed, Peggy to John Turner 7-8-1833 (7-9-1833)
Reed, Permelia to Wm. R. Anderson 9-21-1839
Reedon, Mahala to Samuel Reedon 1-9-1862
Reeves, Mary to R. D. Jones 2-28-1856 (3-5-1856)
Rennick, Racheal to John D. Carroll 1-28-1828
Renolds, Jane E. to Archibald Craft 11-19-1838
Reprogle, Rebecca to John W. Yopp 8-6-1855
Reynolds, Amanda M. to John B. Cox 5-23-1843 (5-25-1843)
Reynolds, Elizabeth to Nathaniel Scott 11-15-1835 (11-19-1835)
Reynolds, Margrett M. to Daniel Sinclair 3-22-1847 (3-25-1847)
Reynolds, Mary Ann E. to James G. Bucke 12-26-1854 (12-31-1854)
Reynolds, Mary L. to James H. Saterfield 7-19-1836 (7-20-1836)
Reynolds, Nancy to Thomas Floyd 2-29-1840 (3-4-1840)
Reynolds, Polly to James Glidell 9-23-1856
Reynolds, Rebecca to Thomas W. Walker 3-29-1858
Reynolds, Sarah M. to Andrew Lidy 8-1-1831 (8-2-1831)
Rhodes, Charlotte to William Sasser 1-15-1842 (1-16-1842)
Rhodes, Emily to Madison Nelms 9-14-1853 (9-15-1853)

Rhodes, Emily to Robert Gentry 9-29-1851 (9-30-1851)
Rhodes, Eviline to Chas. A. Coor 8-10-1854 (8-11-1854)
Rhodes, Narcissa to Thomas E. Toller 9-6-1845 (9-14-1845)
Rhodes, Rhoda M. to N. T. Bansfield(Bunsfield) 12-7-1858 (12-9-1858)
Richardson, Celia to J. B. Wallace 12-8-1856
Richardson, Frances to Walton H. Vaughn 9-10-1832 (9-15-1832)
Richardson, Lucinda to Oliver C. May 4-4-1836 (4-5-1836)
Richardson, Lucy J. to Jno. C. Anderson 10-3-1859
Richardson, Mary F. to Joseph O.(C.) Stephens 6-21-1858 (6-23-1858)
Richardson, Nancy to William Garner 6-2-1835
Richardson, Prudence to William Williamson 9-8-1856 (9-10-1856)
Richardson, Tamer to John H. Tims 7-31-1861 (8-1-1861)
Richardson, Wincey C. to Wm. C. C. Comer 11-14-1860 (11-15-1860)
Ricks, Mary A. to William Oswell 5-22-1845
Ricks, Olivia to Danl. M. Guin 9-13-1832
Riddle, Elizabeth A. to William M. Griggs 1-31-1849 (2-1-1849)
Riddle, Elizabeth Ann to Nathan W. Tuttle 2-2-1826
Riddle, Elleanor G. to E.A. Randolph 10-3-1854
Riddle, Jennet to Talafaro B. Chaffin 12-27-1831 (12-29-1831)
Riddle, Mary E. to Daniel B. Sain 1-13-1838 (1-14(16)-1838)
Riddle, Nancy to John C. Whitaker 1-14-1833 (1-15-1833)
Riggins, Louisa Jane to Joseph H. Scarbrough 9-21-1856
Riggs, Louisa J. to Elijah F. Warren 8-12-1854 (8-17-1854)
Riggs, M. J. to James M. Goad 7-22-1856 (7-23-1856)
Riggs, Mary Ann to William N. Moore 10-16-1850 (10-22-1850)
Riggs, Mary to Edward Roach 11-10-1830
Riley, Amanda E. to Elbert Welty 7-3-1861 (7-4-1861)
Riley, June to Henry G. Rainy 6-23-1846 (6-25-1846)
Rine, Maria to William Lunsford 1-12-1837 (1-22-1837)
Riplogle, Dosha to James Ferrell 6-21-1851 (7-24-1851)
Riprogle, Mary to Richard Rogers 10-19-1858
Ritchie, Louisa S. to Robert S. Dongan 2-28-1839
Ritchie, Mary to Wm. F. McClain 4-8-1835
Rivers, Emeline C. to William B. Grove 12-22-1831 (12-23-1831)
Rivers, Sarah Jane to Robert W. Shelton 1-24-1829
Roach, Elizabeth E. to Isaac Woodell 4-9-1859
Roach, Elizabeth to Reubin Leathers 7-28-1852
Road, Rebecca to William Cruse 8-2-1833 (8-7-1833)
Roark, Amanda to Elisha Haulton 6-25-1850 (6-28-1850)
Roark, Rebecca F. to Thomas D. Hudson 2-9-1854 (2-21-1854)
Roark, Sarah to Geo. G. Burkhead 12-30-1847
Robb, Mary Ann to James B. Harris 4-22-1835
Roberts, Alethea to James Oliver 11-5-1850
Roberts, Altamyra to Thomas Waller 8-9-1842 (8-11-1842)
Roberts, Clarissa to Thomas Pebles 10-5-1850
Roberts, Eliza Jane to Samuel jr. Vails 3-28-1844
Roberts, Eliza to Henry P. Thomas 4-10-1841 (4-15-1841)
Roberts, Elizabeth C. to Stephen B. Jones 9-9-1839
Roberts, Elizabeth to Harvy M. Gossett 9-15-1841
Roberts, Elizabeth to Magnis Tate 11-12-1848
Roberts, Letty to Jesse Carley 8-17-1849 (8-19-1849)
Roberts, Martha A. to Jas. M. Phillips 6-4-1859 (6-5-1859)
Roberts, Permilia to John Swindle 7-26-1836
Roberts, Sarah C. to Thomas Jenkins 12-6-1841 (12-15-1841)
Robertson, Amanda to George Langster 3-9-1856 (4-9-1856)
Robertson, Catherine to William Champion 11-25-1826
Robertson, Emily E. to Aquilla H. Carouth 5-23-1850
Robertson, Frances E. to James H. Gurley 7-29-1848 (8-1-1848)
Robertson, Frances I? to W. W. McCarley 3-12-1859 (3-15-1859)
Robertson, Frances to Benjamin Sutton 2-10-1845 (2-13-1845)
Robertson, Frances to Curtis Moore 2-10-1845 (2-13-1845)
Robertson, Lucinda to James Jordon 1-20-1846
Robertson, M. E. to John T. Hicks 12-28-1859
Robertson, Martha Adeline to Addison H. Douglass 2-2-1842
Robertson, Minerva to Lafayette Tanner 4-7-1854 (4-13-1854)
Robertson, Neomi to William Jones 4-19-1838 (4-26-1838)
Robertson, Sarah Eliza to Andrew Jackson Gamble 1-6-1852 (1-7-1852)
Robinson, Cleopatra to Harvy S. Clark 9-16-1854 (10-19-1854)
Robinson, Elizabeth to H. O. Easum(Eastham?) 3-29-1848
Robinson, Elly Jane to John C. Hardin 1-2-1858
Robinson, Georgeanna to J. W. Elmore 11-27-1850 (11-28-1850)
Robinson, Loty to Overton Pyles 2-19-1833 (2-?-1833)
Robinson, Lucy Jane to William W. Pirtle 5-14-1850 (5-16-1850)
Robinson, Mary E. to Ezekiel Z. Alexander 7-20-1846 (7-24-1846)
Robinson, Nancy Ann to Abner B. Mercer 4-12-1850 (4-16-1850)
Robinson, Nancy to William R. Rogers 5-7-1828
Robinson, R. A. to David S. Moore 11-22-1854 (11-23-1854)
Robinson, Rebecca L. to Joseph A. Mercer 2-20-1860 (2-23-1860)
Robinson, Sarah to John Chisum 12-29-1834
Robinson, Sarah to Pryor L. Vernon 9-27-1852
Robinson, Sarah to William Legate 4-7-1827
Robson, Caroline to James Litteral 10-27-1843
Robson, Crotia Ann to Neel Barter? 6-4-1829
Rodgers, Mary to Wm. Y. Mills 8-16-1841 (8-17-1841)
Rogers, Ann to William B. Foster 5-1-1835 (5-14-1835)
Rogers, Bethuenia P. to Wm. M. Justice 12-25-1861 (1-1-1862)
Rogers, Betsy(Elizabeth) to Scion Grantham 9-29-1838 (10-3-1838)
Rogers, Celia A. to J. H. Thorpe 8-6-1860
Rogers, Eliza to W. B. Foster 5-1-1851
Rogers, Elizabeth H. to Isaac N. McCommon 6-19-1838
Rogers, Elizabeth J. to Jacob M. Webb 11-23-1843
Rogers, Elizabeth M. to William Cheak 1-30-1846
Rogers, Elizabeth to James T. Hodges 12-26-1848 (1-4-1849)
Rogers, Elizabeth to Thomas Davis 10-14-1826 (11-20-1826)
Rogers, Frances to Mansil Webb 1-25-1853 (1-27-1853)
Rogers, Harriett W. to Peter H. Burnett 8-13-1828 (8-20-1828)
Rogers, Jane S. to Jacob Loudermilk 10-23-1838
Rogers, Jane to Archibald Gibson 11-13-1844
Rogers, Martha A. to Jas. W. Bonds 9-5-1857
Rogers, Mary Ann to Jarman Hudson 12-17-1842 (12-20-1842)
Rogers, Mary E. to J. B. Harriss 10-12-1857 (11-8-1857)
Rogers, Mary E. to Jesse T. Ammons 10-28-1848 (10-29-1848)
Rogers, Mary to Elhennan McGraw 10-31-1844
Rogers, Nancy to Thomas Ferrill 10-7-1853
Rogers, Nancy to William H. Wells 6-18-1827
Rogers, Oney to Samuel Ray 11-27-1833 (11-29-1833)
Rogers, Peggy to Thomas B. Dyke 1-26-1838 (1-8?-1838)
Rogers, Polly(Mary) to Robert Thompson 11-24-1834
Rogers, Rebecca to Belfield S. Shearin 11-24-1854
Rogers, S. E. W. to T. B. McKey 9-18-1861 (9?-29-1861)
Rogers, Sally to Joseph Cox 12-19-1837 (12-21-1837)
Rogers, Sarah Ann to Calvin J. Holley 10-9-1830 (10-10-1830)
Rogers, Sarah C. to Joseph J. Henson 2-22-1851 (3-5-1851)
Rogers, Sarah M. to Glenn O. Burnett 1-4-1830 (2-1-1830)
Rogers, Sarah to J. W. Rose 12-17-1856 (12-18-1856)
Rogers, Sarah to Thomas S. Wells 8-18-1830
Rogers, Susannah to John Terry 1-15-1838 (1-16-1838)
Rollan, Harriet R. to Westley Rhodes 12-27-1855
Rolong, Margaret G. to James J. Rankin 1-2-1856
Ron?, Edny to Robert Box 7-31-1830 (8-10-1830)
Rook, Amy to Paul May 1-2-1827 (1-4-1827)
Rook, Elinder to Van S. Bell 7-2-1833 (7-10-1833)
Rook, Pamillia Ann to Thomas Parker 8-12-1846 (8-16-1846)
Rook, Polly to Abram Cox 10-24-1830 (11-3-1830)
Rook, Tempe to Hezekiah Highfield 9-17-1829
Rose, Elizabeth C. M. to C. C. McDaniel 5-18-1859 (5-19-1859)
Rose, Ellen to Thomas Adkins 5-13-1846 (5-14-1846)
Rose, Jerutia to William W. Thompson 8-12-1837 (8-17-1837)
Rose, Mary M. to B. F. Bullington 3-31-1855 (4-?-1855)
Rose, Mary to Lamuel Britt 7-22-1839 (7-25-1839)
Rose, Nancy A. J. to Bryant Davis 12-24-1855 (12-26-1855)
Rose, Nancy Ann to James H. Rhodes 5-23-1844 (6-2-1844)
Rose, Sally M. to T. G. Thompson 11-1-1841 (11-6-1841)
Rose, Sarah K. to W. W. Castor 1-21-1861 (1-24-1861)
Rose, Sarah to John M. Porter 2-15-1848
Rose, Susannah to William Porter 5-19-1841 (5-20-1841)
Roshel?, Ann Elizabeth to Thomas Moore 10-31-1859 (11-1-1859)
Ross, Cynthia C. to Charles Grimmet 8-27-1860 (8-28-1860)
Ross, Margrett K. to Thomas Hickman 3-9-1847 (4-8-1847)
Ross, Mary J. to Daniel Henson 10-19-1860
Ross, Mary Matilda to Enoch Eskue? 7-29-1841
Ross, Mary to Joshua Hudson 1-12-1842 (1-19-1842)
Rosser(Roper), Mary P. to Nathan Roberts 10-20-1831
Rossin?, Debby to Littleberry Spain 9-30-1850
Rosson, Eliza A. to A. J. Carson 3-4-1856 (3-6-1856)
Rosson, Elizabeth to John Null 3-22-1845 (3-23-1845)
Rosson, Margret to Thomas Higgs 12-30-1845
Rosson, Mary to Allen Ayres 8-21-1830 (8-22-1830)

Rosson, Phoebe N. to John J. Teadford 2-14-1850 (2-19-1850)
Rosson, Susan Caroline to Moses Ray 11-17-1836
Rosson, Susan to Thomas L. Duncan 6-6-1854 (12-5-1854)
Rouch, _____ to Rufus Perkins 2-10-1860
Roundtree, Elizabeth A. to James Howell 7-10-1833 (7-14-1833)
Route, Mary H. to J. M. Boswell 2-7-1857 (2-8-1857)
Rucker, Cinthia W. to WilliamH. Counsel 1-10-1832
Rucker, Mary E. D. to James W.(M?) Spight 12-31-1840
Rucker, Olivia to Cyrus Davis 4-8-1844 (4-9-1844)
Ruddle, Elizabeth to Charles R. Gordon 4-11-1855 (4-12-1855)
Ruddle, Margaret M. to Henry W. Duncan 1-2-1849 (1-3-1849)
Ruddle, Sarah M. to William Needham 9-10-1836
Rudolph, Mary to John A. Carithers 8-22-1831
Ruff, Julia to Newnham Reynolds 3-9-1859
Ruffin, Basina to James D. Ruffin 7-8-1834 (7-17-1834)
Ruffin, Eliza A. to Henry L. Pettus 9-25-1851
Ruffin, Lucy Ann to Charles W. Hunt 9-2-1834
Ruffin, Maria A. to Edwin H. Price 4-27-1836 (4-29-1836)
Ruffin, Mary L. to Obediah Gravett 12-22-1856 (12-24-1856)
Russell, Ann Eliza to Hamilton Black 3-29-1854 (3-30-1854)
Russey, Mary J. to John E. G. Davis 8-13-1840
Rutherford, Casandra to George Gray 1-10-1833
Rutherford, Louisa A. C. to George I. Walden 12-29-1830 (1-2-1831)
Rutherford, Lucinda to Washington Hudson 8-19-1836 (9-16-1836)
Rutherford, Nancy C. to William B. Ragan 9-3-1847 (9-5-1847)
Rutherford, Sarah to William A. Shilling 3-2-1836 (3-10-1836)
Sacer(Sasser), Emily to Solomon Granthan 9-8-1838 (9-9-1838)
Sadler, S. A. to B. R. Herndon 11-24-1849
Sadler, Sarah Ann to James Campbell 12-22-1859
Sain, Elizabeth A. to Alpha Bailey 1-9-1855 (1-11-1855)
Sain, Hester to Cornelius McDaniel 12-9-1848 (12-14-1848)
Sain, Nancy to Eliphalet Brown 1-6-1834 (1-9-1834)
Sammons, Ann to Thomas Kenney 4-11-1840
Sammons, Martha to Martin Moore 3-6-1841 (3-11-1841)
Sanders, Abedian to Edward Ozwell(Oswald) 10-15-1856
Sanders, Elizabeth to Jno. H. McGraw 8-12-1845
Sanders, Martha to Alexander Hale 7-22-1831 (7-?-1831)
Sanders, Mary Ann to John Bolin 8-31-1840
Sanders, Nancy to Jonathan J. Young 8-17-1843
Sanders, Rachel to Needham Raiford 8-13-1841
Sassems, Nancy to George M. Kirk 8-9-1826 (8-10-1826)
Sasser, Betsy A. to Ransom Stephens 11-26-1849 (12-3-1849)
Sasser, Elizabeth to John Wamble 1-5-1852 (1-8-1852)
Sasser, Mary Z. to Hillery H. Stanly 2-2-1847
Saul, Elizabeth to Berry Futrell 7-25-1853 (7-28-1853)
Sauls, Amanda to John C. Russell 1-13-1857 (1-14-1857)
Saunders(Launders?), Martha to John Goodwin 3-22-1828
Saunders, Tabita to George B. Thompson 3-10-1831 (3-11-1831)
Savage, Amanda to John Bohanon 11-18-1852
Savage, Cynthia Ann to John C. Tims 9-23-1830
Savage, Elizabeth to John Turner 12-20-1860
Savage, Elizabeth to Wm. S. Liggett 12-18-1841 (12-26-1841)
Savage, Jane to James Casey 8-4-1829
Savage, Mary E. to James B. Hale 10-18-1851 (10-30-1851)
Savage, Mary to Peter Hunnel 1-21-1836
Savage, Nancy to Moses B. Faris 10-26-1842 (10-28-1842)
Savage, Polly Ann to John Carley 9-26-1840 (9-27-1840)
Savage, Sarah Jane to Jesse King 7-5-1841 (7-6-1841)
Savage, Satira to W. D. Hankins 6-1-1861 (6-2-1861)
Scoggins, Juda E. to John R. Harty 8-16-1855
Scoggins, Nancy E. to Thomas J. Mitchell 12-16-1858 (12-17-1858)
Scoot, Harret? to John Y. McGuire 10-13-1845 (10-14-1845)
Scott, Amanda L. to Noah Damon? 11-14-1849 (11-15-1849)
Scott, Ann to Adam Lockhart 5-25-1861 (5-26-1861)
Scott, C. R. to T. J. McMillen 9-10-1859 (10-10-1859)
Scott, Carrie to Thomas C. Park 12-5-1857 (12-8-1857)
Scott, Eighty to James Farris 5-15-1848
Scott, Elizabeth to Will Lockhart 12-23-1837
Scott, Hannah to Samuel E. Hays 2-6-1835 *
Scott, Hannah to Samuel E. Hays 2-6-1836 (2-11-1836)
Scott, Liney(Siney) to John Freeman 4-4-1831 (4-14-1831)
Scott, Mary E. to Wm. G. Parker 6-14-1861
Scott, Mary to John Waller 10-11-1849
Scott, Ophelia Ann to Samuel Tozier 7-18-1861
Scott, Rebecca H. to Samuel White 6-28-1842 (6-29-1842)
Scott, Rebecca to Samuel P. Ingram 11-6-1841 (11-12-1841)
Scott, Seragh Jane to H. H. Falls 10-27-1852 (10-28-1852)
Scripson?, Abigal to John McPherson 2-8-1834
Seate(Scott?), Elizabeth to George Pervis 6-29-1838
Seaton, Ally M. to Joseph Burleson 10-8-1827 (11-1-1827)
Seaton, Elizabeth V. to David Williams 9-26-1834
Seaton, Minerva Jane to Aaron Burleson 8-21-1838 (8-23-1838)
Seaton, Sarah G. to A. G. Barrett 4-13-1832 (4-16-1832)
Sebastian, Martha Ann to Kimbro Hornsby 4-6-1833
Sebastin, Hetta Eliza to Headly Polk 6-3-1845
Sellers, Elizabeth Ann to Thos. K. Brown 2-3-1847 (2-4-1847)
Sellers, Kerah H. to Thomas A. Thompson 7-29-1834 (7-31-1834)
Sellers, Kezier? to William McKey 10-18-1847 (10-19-1847)
Sellers, Polly to Anson Brown 12-30-1835 (12-31-1835)
Sellers?, Mariah to James Alford 3-31-1847 (4-1-1847)
Sexton, Eliza C. to Eli Rainer 1-18-1854 (1-19-1854)
Sexton, Elizabeth to Jessee T. Goff 4-11-1848
Sexton, Jerusha A. to Saml. J. Doyle 1-7-1860 (1-10-1860)
Sexton, M. A. to J. W. Hood 11-17-1860 (11-18-1860)
Shackleford, Harriett to Alexander Crawford 4-8-1828
Sharp, Catharine Lavina to Reese McCommon 3-24-1848 (3-28-1848)
Sharp, Elizabeth to John Smithey 1-9-1825
Sharpe, Eliana M. to W. H. Rowsey 1-23-1851
Shaw, Agness E. to William Coward 6-7-1845 (6-12-1845)
Shaw, Cordelia A. to F. M. Burford 10-22-1849 (10-25-1849)
Shaw, Lavanda to D. M. Edmundson 9-15-1832 (9-18-1832)
Shearin, Lucy W. to John W. Justice 12-23-1858
Shearon, Arabella to Albert Sharon 8-8-1851 (8-10-1851)
Sheckels?, Sarah Ann to Jos. John Carter 12-27-1842 (12-28-1842)
Sheets, Mary Ann to Edward J. W. Peters 3-11-1854 (3-12-1854)
Sheets, Nancy A. to Calvin Bowles 5-30-1854 (6-1-1854)
Sheets, Sarah to T. Bray 1-15-1857
Shelby, Louisa to George W. White 7-11-1836
Shelby, Malinda to Alfred Kelly 2-16-1835
Shelly, Martha C. to Riley Gatlin 4-26-1835 (4-29-1835)
Shelton, Eliza J. to John B. Morphis 11-26-1855 (11-28-1855)
Shelton, Lethe to Manin Tackett 5-17-1858 (5-18-1858)
Shephard, Mary A. to Jno. L. T. Sneed 8-26-1848 (8-27-1848)
Shepherd, Elizabeth A. to Thos Turner 3-4-1843
Shepherd, Elizabeth B. to William Roark 12-27-1832
Sheppard, ElizabethS. to R. H. D. Ewell 11-2-1843
Shepperd, Mary Ann to Milton J. Hamer 11-7-1838 (11-8-1838)
Sherly], Sarah to Daniel Olds 9-11-1824
Sherron, Temperance A. to Willie Clift 11-30-1854
Shickles, Nancy to Levi Mullekin 12-29-1846
Shinault, Hannah to Henry Webster 12-6-1827
Shinault, Mary E. to R. M. Lax 12-26-1854 (12-28-1854)
Shinault, Mary to Lennard Malam 12-28-1839 (12-29-1839)
Shinault, Rosanna to Erasmus R. Cothran 1-10-1838 (1-11-1838)
Shinault, Rosanna to Zachariah Davis 5-22-1824
Shinn, Martha Jane to John A. Baker 5-31-1848 (6-8-1848)
Shinn, Sarah to Minas Sparks 1-27-1851
Shipman, Belinda to William B. Garrison 12-2-1826 (12-7-1826)
Shipman, Elizabeth to Uriah Costello 11-15-1826 (11-16-1826)
Shipman, Menerva to John Harley 1-5-1829 (1-8-1829)
Shipman, Sarah to James Caborne 4-25-1826
Shopher, Nancy J. A. to Giles Scroggins 1-19-1858 (1-20-1858)
Shore, Frances A. to John E. Lester 12-2-1843 (12-3-1843)
Short, Ann to Edward Norton 9-27-1833
Short, Charlotte to Edward H. Stewart 10-25-1849 (11-17-1849)
Short, Delelah to Wm. B. Jones 4-25-1846 (4-30-1846)
Short, Elizabeth to Joseph Cloud 2-24-1836
Short, Lucinda to Benjamin Bumpass 3-30-1829 (4-5-1829)
Short, Sophia to William Norton 9-25-1832
Shull, Rachel to Andrew J. Moore 6-8-1836
Siler, Mary A. to Thomas Sommerville 4-26-1838
Sills, Frances R. to J. G. Dorris 2-14-1861
Simmons, Eliza J. to Jas. Edwards 12-18-1843
Simmons, Eliza to G. B. New 5-1-1830 (5-2-1830)
Simmons, Heisey H. to Stephen Sanders 1-8-1838
Simmons, Jane to W. D. Spivy 10-22-1857 (10-26-1857)
Simmons, Margaret A. to Thomas C. Thompson 1-1-1861 (1-3-1861)
Simmons, Mary Eliza to Alexander White 2-22-1847 (2-23-1847)
Simmons, Nancy to Elias Forte 10-13-1825 (10-15-1825)
Simmons, Percilla to Jesse Harriss 9-20-1856 (10-1[7]-1856)

Simms, Martha E. to Wm. Gatewood 8-1-1858
Simms, Sarah to Ellison Childress 7-13-1829
Simpkin, Sarah Ann to John Foster 5-5-1830 (5-6-1830)
Simpson, Amanda C. to George W. Sutton 10-26-1853 (11-12-1853)
Simpson, C. E. to David Sanders 9-30-1858
Simpson, Catharine to John S. Hunt 1-16-1849 (1-17-1849)
Simpson, F. J. to Job Stricklin 10-2-1861 (10-3-1861)
Simpson, Frances to Marshall Seddens 11-24-1828
Simpson, Harriet to William Cole 8-31-1858
Simpson, Jane to Needham Ingram 12-18-1830 (12-23-1830)
Simpson, Nancy I. to W. D. Ward 12-22-1853
Simpson, Susan to S. C. Knight 2-20-1855 (2-21-1855)
Sims, Bashiba to Shelton Littrell 12-29-1849 (12-30-1849)
Sims, Catharine to Martin Holliday 8-8-1859 (8-9-1859)
Singleton, Sarah to Joseph McCoy 1-28-1832 (1-29-1832)
Skinner, Louisa to Archabald Campbell 12-24-1847 (12-30-1847)
Slaughter, Polly to James Alsup 10-24-1829
Sloan, Helen to Wm. C. Priest 7-2-1860 (7-4-1860)
Sloan, Temperance to Jesse Wolfe 6-29-1850 (6-30-1850)
Smalley, Mary to Hardin Joyce 4-16-1838 (4-19-1838?)
Smally, Jane Elizabeth to J. C. Tilton 2-2-1848 (2-3-1848)
Smart, Sarah to J. M. Arnett 12-18-1858 (12-22-1858)
Smith, A. J. to G. F. Smith 1-17-1843
Smith, Agness W. to D. S. Boxley 11-23-1835
Smith, Ajesty to Calvin Norris 4-18-1839
Smith, Amelia to Wm. J. Sturdivant 9-4-1855 (9-5-1855)
Smith, Ann B. to John B. Lacy 12-15-1853 (12-16-1853)
Smith, Ann Jane to Hamilton McClanahan 11-5-1829
Smith, Betsy P. to James H. Tisdale 1-16-1832 (1-17-1832)
Smith, Christianna G. to John Dawson 12-19-1838 (12-20-1838)
Smith, Dephy to Charles Adams 1-1-1838 (1-6?-1838)
Smith, E. P. to Sidney Smith 6-11-1831
Smith, Elisabeth to James V. Haskins 11-30-1857 (12-10-1857)
Smith, Elizabeth to Jeremiah Hollady 6-5-1847 (6-13-1847)
Smith, Elizabeth to Lemuel Poyner 11-14-1840 (11-15-1840)
Smith, Elizabeth to Thomas Young 9-10-1849
Smith, Ellen to John Hudson 11-27-1830 (12-2-1831)
Smith, Frances J. to Willie Coor 5-2-1836 (5-5-1836)
Smith, Lavicy to Will W. Rhodes 4-4-1839 (4-10-1839)
Smith, Lucinda to Ira Beliles 6-6-1835
Smith, M. E. to John F. Newsom 8-6-1860
Smith, M. J. to Phillip J. Neely 12-19-1859 (12-22-1859)
Smith, Martha A. F. to Walter M. Murphy 1-10-1844 (1-11-1844)
Smith, Martha C. to Solomon C. Sparks 3-23-1841
Smith, Martha J. to W. A. Finch 11-12-1849 (11-14-1849)
Smith, Martha J. to W. B. Morrow 7-17-1855 (7-19-1855)
Smith, Martha J. to W. S. Bell 2-22-1859
Smith, Mary Ann to West W. Wiggins 6-1-1839 (6-5-1839)
Smith, Mary C. to Geo. Wilson 2-2-1846 (2-5-1846)
Smith, Mary F. to Samuel A. Hogue 3-22-1851 (3-27-1851)
Smith, Mary James to Samuel Duncan 12-27-1855
Smith, Mary L. to George A. Woodson 8-4-1851
Smith, Mary Louisa to Alexander McDaniel 2-8-1835 (2-12-1835)
Smith, Nancy Eliz. Ellen to Alfred Moore 1-23-1849 (1-30-1849)
Smith, Nancy S. to James K. Hill 5-12-1840 (5-13-1840)
Smith, Pamelia Jane to Charles Dennis 4-17-1854 (4-18-1854)
Smith, Polly to Benjamin Rook 12-16-1829 (12-17-1829)
Smith, Sally to Willoughby Rogers 1-4-1837
Smith, Sarah A. to Thomas G. Hill 2-7-1848 (2-8-1848)
Smith, Virginia to Albert Kimbrough 5-1-1843
Smithwick, Sarah C. to Tilmon Murphy 10-6-1845
Sneed, Elizabeth to Benjamin Bell 12-29-1860 (12-31-1860)
Snidy?(Sniedy?), Aggy to Hugh Wilson 6-5-1828
Somers, Ellen to R. J. McKissick 10-6-1858 (10-7-1858)
Somers, Martha to W. B. Foster 8-31-1860 (9-2-1860)
Spalding, Racheal to Jeramiah Needham 10-23-1827
Sparks, E. A. to D. S. Birkhead 8-17-1861 (8-19-1861)
Sparks, Susan to Wm. Patterson 10-7-1857
Spears, Miss Sarah to George Davis 1-12-1852 (1-14-1852)
Sperling, Sarah to Jesse Henson 3-7-1827 (3-14-1827)
Springfield, Charity to James F. Ingram 6-29-1850 (6-30-1850)
Springfield, Elizabeth to J. B. Carrington 6-21-1861 (6-22-1861)
Springfield, Siddy J. to E. S. Duncan 9-5-1859 (9-6-1859)
Spurlin, Penny to William Fellow 6-3-1831 (6-12-1831)
Spurling, Frances to Randle Hamilton 12-11-1833
Spurling, Mary to Bird Bazel 6-22-1827 (6-24-1827)
Stabough, Jane to Josiah Brook 5-20-1830 (5-25-1830)
Stafford, Sarah Ann to James Robertson 5-31-1838
Stamps?, Theay to John Brumbelow 8-28-1834
Standback, Rebecca to Clement Belotte 7-23-1855 (8-16-1855)
Standly, Polly to Mastin Prewitt 2-26-1838 (2-27-1838)
Starky, Nancy to Hugh Middleton 2-29-1828
Staten?, Sally A. to George Washington 1-13-1843
Statler, Fannie to Robert E. Smith 1-27-1858
Steagall, Martha to Robt. B. McMahan 5-13-1846 (5-17-1846)
Steel, Mary V. to B. F. C. Brooks 3-8-1858
Steel, Mary to David B. Carnes 10-7-1828 (10-9-1828)
Steel, Ruthy to Thomas Hamilton 11-29-1828 (12-4-1828)
Steele, Elizabeth to Theodore Lackie 12-27-1836 (12-28-1836)
Steele, Prudence E. to Robert W. Carnes 11-10-1842
Stephens, Bethena to William H. Maxwell 8-25-1825
Stephens, Elizabeth to Asa Bishop 5-23-1850
Stephens, Fanny M. to J. J. Neely 5-11-1848
Stephens, Martha to Saml. Nelms 6-12-1838 (6-26-1838)
Stephens, Mary E. to Edmund Cooper 10-22-1844
Stephenson, Eliza Jane to William Hodges 12-13-1841
Stephenson, Emily to Payton Parker 6-17-1844
Stephenson, Martha R. to Benj. J. Edwards 10-28-1854 (10-29-1854)
Stephenson, Mary Elizabeth to Amos A. Edwards 8-5-1850 (8-6-1850)
Stephenson, Matilda L. to Joshua D. Wright 1-10-1844
Stephenson, Sarah Ann to Calvin Philly 12-25-1838
Stevens, Pheriby to M. C. Young 9-28-1853 (9-29-1853)
Stevens, Sarah Ann to Pitser Miller 12-19-1834 (12-21-1834)
Stevens, Susan E. to William B. Thompson 11-7-1849 (11-8-1849)
Stevenson, Nancy Issabella to Jerimiah Burton 12-10-1850 (12-13-1850)
Steward, M. H. to J. L. Vaughan 12-15-1856 (12-17-1856)
Steward, Mrs. Hulda to Wesley Laster 1-2-1854
Steward, N. S. to W. R. Mills 11-1-1859 (11-3-1859)
Steward, Sarah T. to Thos. J. Farris 12-23-1856 (12-25-1856)
Steward, Sarah to Alsy Morphis 2-13-1835
Stewart, Elizabeth C. to Zachariah Lockett 2-2-1846
Stewart, Marilda to John L. Casey 8-8-1844
Stewart, Mary Ann to Robert N. Parks 1-31-1842 (2-2-1842)
Stewart, Nancy to James Hanna 4-9-1842
Stewart, Sarah A. to Isaac Futrell 2-4-1839 (2-5-1839)
Stewart, Susan E. to Wm. N. Fortune 5-15-1861
Still?, Cynthia to William Wilson 11-17-1829 (11-25-1829)
Stinson, Eliza J. to Albert? S. Norman 10-29-1845 (10-30-1845)
Stinson, Mary J. to Thomas Medlock 7-30-1838
Stinson, Mary to Miles Philley 6-4-1838
Stinson, Sarah E. to Claiborn Smith 2-7-1843
Stockton, Eliza to William Cole 6-17-1835
Stockton, M. O. to A. D. Keith 9-14-1854
Stockton, Pheby to Calvin Campbell 11-3-1848 (11-9-1848)
Stone, Elizabeth S. to James M. Rogers 2-26-1838 (3-13-1838)
Stone, Elizabeth to Anderson Dale 1-9-1830
Stone, Jane to Saml. Snellgroves 2-16-1856 (2-17-1856)
Stone, Jane to William Newland 2-1-1845 (2-6-1845)
Stone, Martha to E. M. Pannell 5-16-1860
Stone, Mary A. to Horrace C. Knolton 8-15-1848 (8-17-1848)
Stone, Mary Ann to J. R. Doyle 1-18-1860 (1-20-1860)
Stout, Mary to John P. Rose 8-12-1854 (8-13-1854)
Strickland, Malisa E. to Samuel W. Montgomery 1-7-1848 (1-9-1848)
Strickland, Mary to Benjamin Rogers 4-23-1851
Stricklin, A. C. to C. W. McCommon 10-6-1860 (10-11-1860)
Stricklin, Melissa A. to O. H. P. Johnson 7-7-1857 (7-8-1857)
Strothers, Hannah to John Clifton 12-23-1841 (12-30-1841)
Stuart, Frances A. to William H. Adkins 2-12-1842 (2-17-1842)
Suggett?, Mary E. to Daniel I. Wells 11-24-1836
Suggs, Julian to Benj. F. Haltom 12-15-1855 (12-19-1855)
Suggs, Nancy to William J. Blair 2-6-1856 (2-7-1856)
Sulivan, Jane to John Harris 7-10-1854 (7-18-1854)
Sullenger, Sarah to John Bass 4-15-1826 (4-20-1826)
Sullivan, Louisa to Jas. W. McAnaly 7-21-1857 (7-22-1857)
Sullivan, Mary Ann to John McDonald 7-8-1852
Suttles, Mary to Jackson Wilkerson 3-28-1859
Sweeton, Mahala to Michael Griffin 4-19-1860
Sweeton, Malinda to John R. Clark 4-13-1832 (4-15-1832)
Sweeton, Nancy to P. N. Estes 10-3-1861

Sweeton, Permelia Jane to Jackson Bohanon 8-4-1841
Sweeton, Synthia to Ellis Harlin(Hardin?) 8-14-1826 (8-15-1826)
Swindle, Emily Adaline to Josiah D. Miller 9-14-1853 (9-15-1853)
Swindle, Martha to John T. Jones 4-13-1836
Swindle, Sarah Ann to Andrew J. Meador 12-25-1860
Sylvester, Martha Ann Minerva to William Holford 12-22-1840 (12-24-1840)
Taber, Lucinda to James Plank 10-9-1833
Tackett, Mary Ann to James Crawford 2-20-1861 (2-21-1861)
Taggart, Elizabeth to Benjamin Owens 11-3-1830
Taggart, Mary Jane to Robert Pirtle 3-13-1830 (3-17-1830)
Tally, Lety to Cokely P. Williams 2-17-1831
Tannehill, Mary J. to J. L. Morphys 6-27-1855 (7-5-1855)
Tarver, Mary W. to Linsey P. Rucker 11-15-1836
Tate, Catharine to Joshua Hazlewood 5-27-1826 (6-7?-1826)
Tate, Mary Ann to William Hazlewood 5-29-1827
Tate, W. L. to J. W. Mullen 8-2-1854 (8-3-1854)
Taylaor, Sarah F. to Thomas F. Short 11-2-1853
Taylo, Nancy E. to Christopher Robertson 11-1-1854 (11-2-1854)
Taylor, Delina to John Rosson 12-7-1853 (12-8-1853)
Taylor, Eliza Ann to Robert Webb 8-26-1854 (8-26-1854)
Taylor, Elizabeth G. to Henry R. Bevils 12-22-1832
Taylor, Elizabeth to James Wiley 2-8-1836
Taylor, Elizabeth to John Wesley Sanders 3-25-1841
Taylor, Emily to Ewing Willoughby 1-13-1836
Taylor, Julia Ann M. to Tinsley Chowning 5-11-1839 (6-12-1839)
Taylor, Lucy to Elijah Overton 2-19-1838
Taylor, Lydia to John Scoggins 3-20-1837 (3-22-1837)
Taylor, Martha L. to J. W. C. Smith 1-19-1861
Taylor, Mary Ann to Edward Philpott 4-25-1829
Taylor, Mary Ann to William C. Jernigan 8-16-1849 (8-19-1849)
Taylor, Mary Jane to Ashly G. Willoughby 7-3-1841 (7-5-1841)
Taylor, Mary to Samuel Hannis 4-10-1824 (4-11-1824)
Taylor, Nancy Ann to Terry Yeats 2-18-1837 (2-20-1837)
Taylor, Nancy J. to William T. Sills 8-16-1856 (8-17-1856)
Taylor, Nancy to Charles Holland 8-24-1832
Taylor, Rachel B. to John S. McKaughan 1-21-1848 (1-23-1848)
Taylor, Sarah Frances to F. G. Cossitt 8-29-1861 (8-30-1861)
Taylor, Susan Jane to John N. Whaley 1-17-1842 (1-20-1842)
Teague, Catharine to James M. Walton 11-24-1847 (11-25-1847)
Teague, Dorothy H. to John Ellison 2-20-1843 (2-21-1843)
Teague, Elizabeth to John J. Walton 12-27-1838
Teague, Mary A. to Jas. C. Love 12-24-1855
Teague, Oregon N. to Wm. S. McLemore 12-21-1861 (12-24-1861)
Teague, Rhoda to Isaiah Flin 12-31-1828
Teague, Sarah to Lusnford Whitaker 7-8-1835
Tedford, Matilda to Andrew J. Carson 2-28-1854
Tedford, Militha to Thomas J. Tipler 1-22-1842 (2-3-1842)
Tedford, Polly to Willie Davis 8-14-1830 (8-16-1830)
Tedford, Sophronia O. to A. C. Nelms 11-20-1843 (11-22-1843)
Terry, Eleanor to James G. Jenkins 8-9-1830
Terry, Elizabeth to Vincent Cooksey 9-28-1842 (9-29-1842)
Terry, Elizabeth to William Henley 10-6-1853 (10-7-1853)
Terry, Nancy A. to John C. Williams 10-5-1849
Terry, Susan? to Hiram Ammon 11-1-1832
Thomas, Elisa to John Isom 9-3-1828
Thomas, Elizabeth A. to Silas M. Josslyn 9-10-1833 (9-19-1833)
Thomas, Elizabeth S. to Aaron Freeman 1-18-1853
Thomas, Elizabeth to E. D. Hammonds 9-24-1859
Thomas, Joysy W. to John Joslyn 11-15-1833 (11-21-1833)
Thomas, Lucinda to Thomas D. Hammons 12-19-1837
Thomas, Martha A. to J. F. Roach 6-7-1858
Thomas, Mary to Will Parker 5-7-1836
Thomas, Molly to William G. Teague 10-14-1831
Thomas, Nancy E. to J. W. Snow 9-28-1859 (9-29-1859)
Thomas, Nancy to Benjamin Alsup 12-25-1833
Thomas, Tobitha to William Langston 6-18-1825 (6-19-1825)
Thompson, America A. to Isham N. Smith 10-29-1838
Thompson, E. V. to John W. Luttrell 1-20-1857 (1-22-1857)
Thompson, Eliza Ann to Thos. B. Willoughby 6-15-1854 (6-29-1854)
Thompson, Elizabeth to Charles Burrus 3-16-1835 (3-19-1835)
Thompson, Elizabeth to Randolph Mayfield 11-6-1843
Thompson, Frances E. to John A. Garner 6-29-1852
Thompson, Harriet to Benj. F. L. Clarke 2-13-1847
Thompson, Holly S. to Milton C. Young 1-2-1854 (2-1-1854)
Thompson, Jane to William Myrick 5-24-1842 (5-31-1842)
Thompson, Julia Ann to Washington G. Robb 12-11-1833 (12-12-1833)
Thompson, Lucy T. to John J. Dowdy 11-10-1853
Thompson, Margaret to John L. Grove 1-2-1860 (1-24-1860)
Thompson, Margarett to George H. Hall 9-13-1834
Thompson, Mary A. to Nathan Holloway 9-24-1861
Thompson, Mary A. to Wyatt Hickman 2-16-1838 (2-20-1838)
Thompson, Mary Ann to Thomas Hines 11-17-1846 (11-19-1846)
Thompson, Mary E. to James V. Fortune 8-4-1856 (8-7-1856)
Thompson, Nancy A. to H.K. Frederick 9-22-1860 (9-23-1860)
Thompson, Priscilla to James L. Gossett 3-29-1829
Thompson, Rebecca to William Horton 12-24-1834 (12-26-1834)
Thompson, Sarah Ann E. to Tho. McCarter 3-4-1857 (3-5-1857)
Thompson, Sarah to Jno. W. McKizzick 12-14-1850
Thompson, Sarah to John Rose 7-15-1835 (7-23-1835)
Thompson, Sarilla to John C. Harris 10-17-1827 (10-18-1827)
Thomson, Elizabeth D. to Geo. W. McCommon 2-9-1853 (2-10-1853)
Thornton, Henrietta to Wm. R. McGlothlin 1-6-1862
Thornton, Sarah to Henry Looton(Tuoton?) 3-19-1858 (3-21-1858)
Thrailkill, Nancy to John W. Boney 2-12-1842 (2-13-1842)
Thrailkill, Nancy to Perry Brown 4-18-1848 (4-20-1848)
Thrasher, Rachel M. C. to Martin Hensly 1-22-1846 (1-23-1846)
Thrift, Mary Ann to David Humphrey 11-21-1842
Thurman, Elizabeth to James S. Alestock 7-26-1837 *
Thurmond, Amelia L.(S?) to Jessee D. Franklin 1-25-1849 (1-30-1849)
Thurmond, Caroline M. to R. H. Carroll 3-21-1836 (3-24-1836)
Thurmond, M. E. to C. M. Franklin 10-22-1859 (10-27-1859)
Thurmond, Sarah to Daniel Hunt 3-21-1833 (3-26-1833)
Tiger?, Catherine to Atheriah Gayler 12-3-1834
Tillman, Caroline to Wm. Cannon 6-11-1861 (6-13-1861)
Tillman, Elizabeth to John Calvin Brown 1-3-1852 (1-11-1852)
Tilmon, Nancy Ann to Bryant Foster 12-2-1841
Tilmon, Nancy C. to Henry Bizzell 4-20-1857
Timms, Mary Ann to Timothy Glidwell 8-18-1853
Tims, Ann to Peter A. Collins 1-18-1842
Tims, Lydia to Joel Hammers 8-31-1846 (9-3-1846)
Tims, Sarah E. to James N. Jackson 2-15-1848
Tipler, Elizabeth to David Reaves 12-28-1840 (12-31-1840)
Tipler, Mary Jane to Nathan M. Burnes 7-31-1846 (8-4-1846)
Tisdale, Arpy? to Wm. H. Crews 2-7-1855 (2-8-1855)
Tisdale, Elizabeth A. F. to Isaac T. Crews 11-5-1853 (11-7-1853)
Tisdale, Elizabeth to David Lofland 4-7-1824
Tisdale, Mary Jane to John Crews 12-31-1849 (1-10-1850)
Tisdale, Matilda to Andrew Jackson 12-27-1845 (9?-30-1845)
Todd, Margaret J. to Gastin Hailey 12-14-1859 (12-15-1859)
Toller, Clarissa A. to Josiah Ammons 3-8-1842 (3-16-1842)
Toone, Elizabeth R. to James W. Price 4-28-1852 (4-29-1852)
Toone, Mary A. to David Thron 6-8-1857
Toone, Nannie to Luke Carrington 12-10-1858 (1-11-1859)
Toone, Rebecca J. to Robert J. Pirtle 12-20-1848 (12-21-1848)
Toone, Sarah E. to Isaac W. Pirtle 11-12-1844 (11-14-1844)
Toons, Eliza A. to Robert R. Black 5-10-1855
Townsend, Jane to Rubin A. Embrey 3-7-1835
Townsend, Mary Ann to John A. Jones 8-5-1840 (8-9-1840)
Townsend, Mary E. to Charles J. Allen 6-23-1835
Townsend, Polly to John C. Manuell 12-18-1827
Traylor, Margaret A. to Peter A. Avant 2-19-1855 (2-21-1855)
Treese, Ann to W. L. Glenn 7-26-1859 (7-28-1859)
Treese, Issabella to Thomas Kerr 10-17-1854 (10-18-1854)
Trezevant, Rachael to M. C. Young 5-8-1861 (5-9-1861)
Truett(Pruett), Elizabeth to John Reed 3-18-1828
Tuberville, Mira to Alexander Stewart 5-12-1827 (5-15-1827)
Tucker, Ann Jane to Bird Wolverton 10-27-1835
Tucker, Lucinda to George Kenny 1-11-1834 (1-13-1834)
Tudor, Celia to Harmon Cocke 12-28-1829 (12-31-1829)
Tull(Taber?), Elizabeth Martin to Robt. Kyle 12-16-1835
Tune, Mary to Joseph A. Swindle 3-15-1837 (3-16-1837)
Tuning?(Luning?), Julia Ann to Wyatte Harlon 9-19-1850
Turner, Edy to William J. Hill 2-27-1843
Turner, Elizabeth J. to John C. Robinson 12-23-1848 (12-26-1848)
Turner, Elizabeth W. to James Y. McGuire 8-11-1845 (8-12-1845)
Turner, Elizabeth to Isaac R. Harris 6-18-1850
Turner, Frances to Samuel R. Brooks 10-13-1852
Turner, Lucretia to Cicero Beaty 2-25-1861

Turner, Mary A. to Ollen Boyte 12-12-1848 (12-21-1848)
Turner, Mary Ann to Lodwick(Ridwick) Moore 10-18-1848 (10-19-1848)
Tuttle, Rebecca to Eli Murphy 7-4-1826 (7-5-1826)
Tyler, Julia C. to Silvester Bailey 3-28-1833
Upton, Mary Ann to Josiah Teague 10-19-1852 (10-20-1852)
Usery, Mary Elizabeth to Washington Bryant 4-30-1854
Usher, Ann to John jr. Lax 2-26-1849 (2-27-1849)
Usher, Eliza J. to Darius Robinson 1-17-1843
Usher, Nancy C. to Cannon Smith 12-22-1848 (12-20?-1848)
Usher, Rebecca A. to Geo. L. Whitmore 11-10-1845 (11-12-1845)
Usher, Sarah to Thomas H. Hancock 2-9-1848 (2-10-1848)
Ussery, Elizabeth to J. M> Reeves 12-17-1860 (12-19-1860)
Ussery, Martha A. to Wm. T. Lee 11-16-1860
Ussery, Matilda F. to John H. Webster 7-15-1861 (7-18-1861)
Ussery, Sarah J. to Wm. A. Cardwell 1-12-1857
Vaden, Martha Jane to A. T. Robertson 10-27-1845 (11-2-1845)
Vails, Amanda M. to Wm. F. Roberts 12-12-1839
Vails, Arrena to Gabriel Dillard 12-26-1837
Vails, Elizabeth to Robert Campbell 2-27-1847
Vails, Louisa to Wm. H. Owens 12-29-1842 (12-30-1842)
Vails, Lucinda to Will Carvan 1-1-1853 (1-2-1853)
Vails, Mary Ann to Jackson Bohanan 7-23-1848
Vandegrift, Edna F. to Jessee Scott 10-30-1861 (10-31-1861)
Vandergrifft, Martha Ann to John Scott 7-25-1861 (7-15?-1861)
Vandygriff, Mary E. to Carrol Climer 1-22-1853 (1-30-1853)
Vantrice, Catharine to James Read 11-24-1828 (11-27-1828)
Vaugan, Nancy I. to John Welch 12-27-1852 (12-28-1852)
Vaughan, Nancy R. to Hiram Scott 4-8-1831
Vaughn, Jane M. to Joseph F. Cloud 1-22-1832
Vaughn, Martha to Wm. Marrs 5-9-1846 (5-10-1846)
Vaught, Elizabeth to Josiah Thornton 8-27-1833 (9-3-1833)
Vaught, Mary to James Mitchell 9-12-1835
Vaught, Sarah to Samuel Harvey 8-1-1844 (8-20-1844)
Vernon, Ellen A. to James A. Sumners 2-23-1852 (2-24-1852)
Vernon, Hellen E. to Edward Robinson 2-9-1850 (2-19-1850)
Vernon, Julia to Garland Anderson 10-17-1854
Vernon, Nancy to James Robinson 3-26-1860
Vickers, Jane to James S. Glass 4-29-1843 (5-4-1843)
Vincent, Amelia to James Wilson 5-21-1832
Vincent, Elizabeth to Redman Anderson 7-30-1832 (8-3-1832)
Vincent, Mary to Nathaniel Ragan 2-9-1842 (2-10-1842)
Vincent, Sarah K. to Willis V. Taylor 1-14-1840
Vinson, Elizabeth R. to Jos. Harriman 9-17-1859 (9-18-1859)
Vinson, Martha A. B. to William Crawford 11-3-1853
Vinson, Martha to James B. Mills 1-24-1856 (1-26-1856)
Vinson, Nancy to Charles J. Burnett 2-24-1841 (2-26-1841)
Wafford, L. C. to John A. McCommon 8-5-1857 (8-6-1857)
Walden, Maria to Calvin Musgrave 7-21-1830 (7-29-1830)
Walden, Mary to Washington Adams 2-18-1832
Waldrop, Louisa J. to Hiram C. May 7-19-1858 (7-27-1858)
Waldrup, Isbele to James Cooksey 6-15-1832
Walker, Eliza Jane to Killis McDonald Smith 6-13-1853 (6-14-1853)
Walker, Margaret E. to Harvey P. Smith 10-6-1842
Walker, Martha A. to Alexander Campbell 9-6-1856 (9-7-1856)
Walker, Nancy M. to John N. Chambliss 6-4-1852 (6-6-1852)
Wallace, M. E. to J. A. Hogue 1-3-1861 (1-4-1861)
Waller, Catharine to S.(L) B. Roberts 10-4-1850
Waller, Sarah to Erwin Estes 9-9-1861
Walls, Harriet A. to Jack Thomas Champion 3-10-1849 (3-13-1849)
Walpole, Mary(Nancy) to Thomas J. Bryant 12-29-1856 (1-1-1857)
Ward, Elizabeth J. to Ashly R. Crawford 2-26-1848 (3-2-1848)
Ward, Margaret Jane to A. F. McGehee 11-27-1854 (11-28-1854)
Ward, Martha Ann to Wm. F. Crawford 5-10-1845 (5-22-1845)
Ward, Polly to George Welch 1-6-1844 (1-7-1844)
Ward, Priscilla to Moses H. Williams 5-27-1838 (5-30-1838)
Warford, Martha to Wm. Neal 1-25-1858
Warford, Ruan J. to Russell P. Crawford 5-7-1858 (5-11-1858)
Warr, Angerona to James F. Humphrey 8-16-1852
Warr, Louisa T. to George W. Minter 2-13-1849 (2-14-1849)
Warren, Ailsy to Isaac M. Hubbard 6-1-1849 (6-3-1849)
Warren, Ailsy to John J. Tedford 12-5-1859 (12-15-1859)
Warren, Elizabeth to Jno. L. Wood 1-3-1848 (1-4-1848)
Warren, Sally to Thomas Beard 7-10-1830
Warren, Susanah to J. T. Wood 6-6-1851 (6-7-1851)
Warren, Zilpha to William Greenly 10-12-1834 (10-15-1834)
Washburn, Percilla to John H. Cain 10-18-1829
Washington, Emily P. to G. W. Baldwin 4-30-1849 (5-2-1849)
Watkins, Hattie A. to C. W. Fackler 1-15-1859
Watson, Elizabeth to J. M. C. Robertson 8-1-1832 (8-2-1832)
Watson, Frances to James R. Westbrook 8-31-1853
Waxter, Emily to Cornelius Bulger 6-20-1861 (6-21-1861)
Weatherford, Ada to J. H. Osborne 11-7-1833
Weaver, Delila to Frederick Shofer 11-4-1825 (11-6-1825)
Weaver, Peggy to Joseph Rummage 12-29-1825
Weaver?, Nancy to Alfred Robinson 7-23-1831
Webb, Eliza Jane to John Oliver 11-26-1853
Webb, Elizabeth to William Smith 9-24-1846
Webb, Frances A. to Daniel Justice 2-16-1856 (2-17-1856)
Webb, Harriet E. to James L. Heckon? 12-20-1858
Webb, Mary Ann to William C. Mashburn 11-30-1849 (12-5-1849)
Webb, Mary Jane to D. C. Parker 11-27-1860 (11-28-1860)
Webb, May to John Clifton 9-28-1858 (10-7-1858)
Webb, Nancy C. to Harbert H. Edwards 11-10-1853 (11-13-1853)
Webb, Nancy M. to Needham J. Powell 11-24-1849 (11-27-1849)
Webb, Sarah to Hyram Barnett 2-10-1832 (2-14-1832)
Webster, Emeline to T. H. Russell 8-1-1836 (8-23-1836)
Webster, Emiline to James F. Gates 12-15-1846
Webster, Jane C. to Jesse B. Shearin 2-16-1857 (2-18-1857)
Webster, Lucinda to Charles Reagan 6-16-1827
Webster, Sarah R. to Jno. P. Wheeler 7-29-1849
Webster, Tempe to Josiah Taylor 2-27-1832 (3-1-1832)
Weedin, Melisa Ann to L. B. King 6-18-1844
Weir, Margaret E. to William Scoggins 4-5-1859 (4-6-1859)
Welch, Elizabeth to John W. Marrs 12-17-1842 (12-18-1842)
Welch, Martha to Stephen Scoggins 2-6-1837 (2-7-1837)
Welch, Nancy to Stephen Herriman 1-25-1851 (1-26-1851)
Welch, Polly to Jessee Reagan 12-20-1838
Wellins, Polly to Joel Rainer 9-27-1837
Wellman, Ruthey to Alvin Warren 12-24-1834 (12-28-1834)
Wells(Wills?), Minerva to Gary Gay 1-29-1850 (1-31-1850)
Wells, Elizabeth to Jno. Adams 1-4-1838 (1-5-1838)
Wells, Martha M. to Jas. (Jos.) H. McCommon 3-9-1858 (3-10-1858)
Wells, Sarah M. to John Kenney 5-21-1857
Wells, Susan to James H. Jones 1-1-1850
West, Ann M. to James Roper 5-25-1848
West, Jane to Andrew S. Gatlin 10-22-1836
West, Mary E. to WilliamH. Fewell 2-8-1844 (2-9-1844)
Westbrook, Mary Jane to James M. Savage 7-21-1858 (7-24-1858)
Westbrook, Nancy to Joseph Casey 7-16-1850 (7-21-1850)
Westbrook, Pearcy to William Monroe 11-8-1852
Whitaker, Amanda to John A. Bowers 1-24-1831
Whitaker, America to Jackville R. Easter 6-27-1833 (6-30-1833)
Whitaker, Dorthey E. to Albert A. Hall 11-6-1826 (11-14-1826)
Whitaker, Martha to William R. Jacobs 12-17-1849 (12-20-1849)
Whitby, Lucinda to James McKee 11-17-1848 (11-24-1848)
White, Ann to S. F. McNutt 1-5-1848 (1-11-1848)
White, Catharine(Elisabeth) to Ira Atkinson 7-11-1859
White, Elizabeth E. to Samuel Crowley 4-23-1851 (4-24-1851)
White, Elizabeth to James B. Irvin 12-14-1835 (12-15-1835)
White, Elizabeth to Valentine Walker 3-14-1853 (3-15-1853)
White, Frances to William Irion 1-7-1851 (1-16-1851)
White, Hester Ann to James Cruise 3-2-1844 (3-6-1844)
White, Jane to J. M. Montgomery 11-3-1834 (11-4-1834)
White, Margaret Jane G. to George S. Scarbrough 11-10-1840 (11-12-1840)
White, Martha Jane to King W. Ward 4-15-1851 (5-1-1851)
White, Martha M. to Jesse S. Burford 5-9-1842
White, Mary Jane to Harrison G. Folts 6-7-1841
White, Mary Jane to Phillip R. Jones 9-22-1841 (10-5-1841)
White, Mary W. to Jeremiah Holliday 8-28-1827 (8-31-1827)
White, N. A. C. to William B. Hardison 3-18-1851 (3-19-1851)
Whitehorn, Jane to V. A. Davis 3-14-1837
Whitehorn, Sarah Emily to Thomas Sanders 4-18-1842 (4-22-1842)
Whitess, Martha to Stephen Wilson 9-11-1837
Whitfield, Mary to S. E. Rosson 9-22-1837
Whitford, Sarah Jane to James M. Marsh 12-20-1859
Whitford, Sarah to George W. Tate 8-13-1836
Whitley, Jane to James Nicholson 1-5-1837
Whitlock, Catherine to Alexander Spine 4-29-1830

Whitmon, Amandy P. to Hamilton Mask 12-13-1847 (12-14-1847)
Whitmore, Eliza B. to James T. Pugh 8-21-1835 (8-27-1835)
Whitmore, Martha V. to Houston Mitchell 11-30-1853
Wiggins, Jane to William Philips 8-23-1856
Wilbanks, Martha A. to William Jones 12-28-1860 (1-1-1861)
Wilbanks, Mary A. to J. S. Wilbanks 5-11-1860 (5-20-1860)
Wiley, Elizabeth J. to Wm. C. Duncan 7-17-1861 (7-18-1861)
Wilie, Matildy to William G. Bradford 1-24-1829
Wilkerson, Eliza to Lemon Gay 1-2-1834
Wilkerson, Mrs. S. B. to C. W. Henry 11-28-1851 (12-10-1851)
Wilkerson, Susanna to Almeron Dickerson 5-24-1829
Wilkes, A. E. J. to Perry C. Wilkes 11-12-1856 (11-13-1856)
Wilkes, Elizabeth A. to Daniel A. Ross 10-14-1860 (10-15-1860)
Wilkes, Elizabeth A. to John House 10-15-1860
Wilkes, Elizabeth to Hardy Saunders 7-6-1836 (8-7-1836)
Wilkes, Henrietta C. to H. A. Sammons 11-11-1859 (11-7?-1859)
Wilkes, Juliann to Ezekiel Owens 10-11-1847 (10-12-1847)
Wilkes, Martha F. to Wilie Sammons 10-4-1850 (10-10-1850)
Wilkes, Mary M. to John H. Sammons 10-16-1854 (10-26-1854)
Wilkeson, Mary to John Brown 3-15-1836
Wilkins, Mary Ann to D. L. Dalton 8-23-1849 (8-28-1849)
Wilkins, Rebecca to John G. Johnson 2-23-1852 (2-24-1852)
Wilkinson, Clarissa F. to B. H. Cooper 1-3-1861 (1-7-1861)
Wilkinson, Elisa Virginia to James B. Edwards 10-29-1827 (10-30-1827)
Wilkinson, Elizabeth to L. W. Foster 12-28-1852
Wilkinson, Joycy Ann to Matthew D. Garrett 3-6-1843
Wilkinson, Mary to W. L. Bailey 1-4-1832 (1-5-1831?)
Wilkinson, Nancy A. to J. C. McKean 11-3-1830
Wilkinson, Parilee to Lewis Moore 12-20-1853 (12-21-1853)
Wilkison, Adaline to R. L. Short 10-15-1849 (11-25-1849)
Wilks, Eliza to Archibald B. House 11-21-1840
Wilks, Naoma T. to J. W. Sammons 12-3-1858 (12-9-1858)
Wilks, Narcissa Jane to William Hamilton 7-27-1835
Willey, Mary to William H. Tisdale 3-21-1825 (3-24-1825)
Willheight, Ann to William Holley 4-20-1833
Williams, Ann to Ezekiel P. McNeal 1-22-1835
Williams, Catharine to Hal Boyd 1-13-1859 (1-17-1859)
Williams, Cyntha A. to James B. Crawford 6-7-1852
Williams, Elena to Masias J. Moore 9-9-1834 (9-10-1834)
Williams, Eliza Anne to Asbury Warren 7-23-1847 (8-4?-1847)
Williams, Elizabeth Ann to Wm. C. Pew 10-8-1838 (10-14-1838)
Williams, Elizabeth to Harrison Clark 1-30-1841 (2-14-1841)
Williams, Elizabeth to Levin B. Moone 12-13-1828 (12-18-1828)
Williams, Elizabeth to Yimri? Richardson 5-26-1848 (5-22?-1848)
Williams, Frances A. to Richard H. McCord 1-11-1854 (1-12-1854)
Williams, Hannah E. to William H. Crofford 5-19-1845 (5-20-1845)
Williams, Louisa to Charles Burns 1-10-1861
Williams, Malinda to John Guffey 12-28-1835
Williams, Malinda to John Jones 1-12-1837
Williams, Margaret to James A. K. M. Everett 11-13-1860
Williams, Margarett E. to John F. Ford 10-13-1828
Williams, Martha A. to John R. Westbrook 9-3-1850
Williams, Mary to Amos Boyd 2-6-1861 (2-8-1861)
Williams, Mary to G. R. Schrimsher 6-2-1858 (6-6-1858)
Williams, Mary to Harmon Bishop 10-9-1834
Williams, Mary to Wm. Smith 4-1-1844
Williams, Nancy to John Bird 8-16-1859
Williams, Narcissa to George B. Peters 5-9-1839
Williams, Rebecca J. to William N. Belotte 10-31-1854 (11-2-1854)
Williams, Rispha to William Martindale 5-19-1830 (5-21-1830)
Williams, Sally Ann to William Hardy 2-1-1847 (2-4-1847)
Williams, Sarah A. to Daniel E. Warren 4-6-1853
Williams, Sarah E. to William James 3-13-1843
Williams, Sarah Jane to A. G. Lambeth 3-11-1850 (3-21-1850)
Williams, Sarah to Henderson Conlee 12-30-1835
Williams, Silphia to Fleming Haile(Hails?) 5-25-1829 (5-1?-1829?)
Williams, Temperance H. to Calvin M. Hervey 12-14-1841
Williams, Zarina to Beverly R. McKinnie 3-24-1839 (3-28-1839)
Williamson, Mahaly to Billam? Field 12-4-1830
Willie, Elizabeth to James J. Barnett 3-22-1834 (3-27-1834)
Willouby, Evelina to Elihue G. Graham 8-24-1850 (8-25-1850)
Willoughby, C. A. M. to D. T. Smith 10-4-1857
Willoughby, Elizabeth J. to Silas M. W. Marsh 11-8-1842
Willoughby, Elizabeth L. to Joshua J. Yarbrough 3-9-1859 (3-10-1859)
Willoughby, Jackey Ann to M. G. Scott 9-10-1857
Willoughby, Mamena? to Andrew H. Burkhead 11-28-1844
Willoughby, Margaret to Thomas Harris 12-3-1835
Willoughby, Martha to Thomas Walker 3-1-1841
Willoughby, Nancy to Thomas O. Burkett(Burkhead) 2-7-1839 (2-8-1839)
Wiloughby, Amanda to Hamilton Savage 9-3-1849 (9-6-1849)
Wilson, Amelia C. to Samuel Ray 12-19-1860 (12-10?-1861?)
Wilson, Caroline to Eli Ayres 10-13-1829 (10-15-1829)
Wilson, Charlotte to Nelson Huddleston 10-8-1849 (10-10-1849)
Wilson, Delila to Philip Deaton 3-2-1836 (3-6-1836)
Wilson, Elizabeth W. to Ruebin W. Oliver 2-3-1836
Wilson, Elizabeth to John Bennett 9-13-1848
Wilson, Jane to Haywood Smith 6-24-1861 (6-25-1861)
Wilson, Lavinia J. to William Y. Newbern 3-16-1840
Wilson, Livinia Jane to Robert A. Franklin 6-29-1842
Wilson, Lucy B. to M. H. Smith 3-7-1859 (3-9-1859)
Wilson, Martha to Thomas L. Ross 2-1-1849 (2-4-1849)
Wilson, Mary to Benjamin F. Bibb 2-21-1851
Wilson, Mary to James Lyer? 1-18-1836
Wilson, Mary to Solomon Waggener(Wagner) 4-14-1834
Wilson, Mary to William Porter 12-7-1856
Wilson, May C. to Jesse B. Franklin 11-10-1845
Wilson, Minerva to Serel Evans 8-31-1833 (?-19-183-)
Wilson, Mrs. Elizabeth to Geo. W. Whitfield 9-7-1850 (9-10-1850)
Wilson, Nancy M. to Greenberry Dyal? 6-13-1836
Wilson, Nancy to John A. Ross 2-3-1843 (2-4-1843)
Wilson, Sarah E. to James H. Robinson 1-24-1848 (1-25-1848)
Wilson, Sarah to Henry Hatch 9-21-1858 (9-23-1858)
Wilson, Sarah to James Thomas 11-22-1852 (11-23-1852)
Wilson, Sarah to William Lee 10-26-1860 (10-28-1860)
Wire(Wise?), Jane to Larkin T. Smyth 11-2-1825
Wisdom, Martha M. to Robert K. Bradshaw 11-5-1850
Wlkinson, Melissa P. to James Vaughan 11-9-1860 (11-11-1860)
Wolverton, Elizabeth to Allen Hanks 1-23-1833 (1-24-1833)
Wolverton, Mary to George A. Shelton 10-27-1835
Womack, Mary to Enoch King 6-12-1841
Womack, Rebecca to James L. Cozby 2-21-1839 (2-25-1839)
Wood, A. E. to Montezuma Jones 10-11-1849
Wood, Amy C. to W. R. Crawford 12-20-1859 (12-21-1859)
Wood, Angeline to John T. Brown 12-18-1841 (12-19-1841)
Wood, Caroline to Benjamin Williams 1-13-1847 (1-14-1847)
Wood, Jane M. to Paul T. Jones 2-26-1849 (3-1-1849)
Wood, Laura H. to Robt. H. Shepperd 12-29-1858 (12-30-1858)
Wood, Lucy C. to Wilson T. Bills 12-2-1857
Wood, Maria C. to Thomas A. Parran 11-2-1848
Wood, Martha to Joshua Estes 3-25-1843 (3-26-1843)
Wood, Mary M. to Napoleon Hill 7-7-1858 (7-8-1858)
Wood, Mary to Elijah Comer 10-25-1837
Wood, Rhoda to Major Estes 10-23-1845
Wood, Sarah B. to George W. Wilkerson 10-20-1843
Woodard, Eliza to John H. Brough 1-16-1836
Wooden, Mary J. to Benj. R. Belote 12-28-1856
Woodfin, Mary T. to Thomas A. Osborn 2-17-1853
Woods, Margaret Ann to Joseph S. McAnulty 11-17-1842 (11-18-1842)
Woods, Mary to Walter Shinault 6-19-1849 (6-27-1849)
Woodson, Isabella to John A. Gatlin 9-17-1854
Woodward, Elizabeth to Elisha Robertson 5-24-1860
Woolberton, Mary A. to Saml. W. Rogers 9-29-1860
Wooley, Eliz. Ann to David B. Cheairs 11-30-1841 (12-1-1841)
Worrell, Margaret to James M. Martin 9-16-1854 (9-21-1854)
Wright, Clemintine to H. L. Lassiter 2-28-1857 (3-5-1857)
Wright, Elizabeth to Hiram Piles 12-30-1833 (1-3?-1834)
Wright, Elizabeth to John Crews 10-31-1832 (11-1-1832)
Wright, Precilla to Thomas Burris 3-5-1825 (3-6-1825)
Wright, Sarah to Vance Huffman 3-26-1857 (3-27-1857)
Wright, Winney to John Cooper 8-28-1833
Wycoff, Lydia to Daniel Muntz 1-7-1825
Yancey, Martha to Burrell Wise 12-27-1831 (12-25?-1831)
Yarbrough, Arlesa to Samuel H. Justice 3-16-1853 (3-17-1853)
Yarbrough, Elizabeth J. to Edward Willoughby 6-15-1854 (6-22-1854)
Yarbrough, Elizabeth M. to David H. Pipkin 9-28-1853 (9-29-1853)
Yarbrough, Elizabeth to Joel S. Raines 8-27-1832
Yarbrough, Jane to George R. Rains 1-5-1836

Yarbrough, Lissa to Jesse Scroggins 3-6-1835 (3-11-1835)
Yarbrough, Meranda to Marcellas Knott 3-17-1860
Yarbrough, Parella to Regis Jarvis 1-5-1836
Yarbroy?, Betsy to Jarvis Sweeton 2-2-1836
Yeary, Anny to John Campbell 7-10-1828 (4-6-1829)
Yeary?, Cassandria to Leroy Montgomery 1-30-1827
Yewing(Ewing), Melinda to Robert Jones 4-2-1827 (4-5-1827)
Yokum, Mary C. to G. W. Yopp 12-2-1859
Yopp, Martha Jane to Dugan Park 10-26-1858 (11-3-1858)
Yopp, Mary C. to Saml. B. Rogers 2-4-1861 (2-7-1861)
Young, Ann A. to David T. Butler 6-18-1852 (6-23-1852)
Young, Elisabeth to Lemuel Jones 8-6-1846
Young, Elizabeth to A. J. Dunn 10-7-1853 (10-9-1853)
Young, Elizabeth to Eli Cox 4-19-1847 (4-20-1840
Young, Nancy P. to W. F. Dorris 12-4-1851
Young, Rhoda to John C. Stockton 8-3-1826
Young, Sarah A. C. to James Scoggins 6-30-1855 (7-4-1855)
Young, Sarah Ann to Jones K. Orr 5-15-1835 (5-21-1835)
Young, Susan to William Henry Evens 2-11-1851 (2-13-1851)
Youngblood, Jula Ann to Stanhope? McCommons 12-29-1846 (12-31-1846)
Zamples, Ruth to Sterling Burrow 2-6-1834
_____, _____ to Needham K. Simpson 12-20-1853
_____, Elizabeth A. to Thos. Whitlock 7-28-1832

www.ingramcontent.com/pod-product-compliance
Lightning Source LLC
LaVergne TN
LVHW061256100826
845148LV00008B/1147

* 9 7 8 1 5 9 6 4 1 0 5 0 3 *